C000164170

Echoes of a Voice

OTHER BOOKS BY JAMES W. SIRE

Papers on Literature: Models and Methods

Jeremiah, Meet the 20th Century

The Universe Next Door

Scripture Twisting

Beginning with God

How to Read Slowly

The Discipleship of the Mind

Jesus the Reason

Chris Chrisman Goes to College

Why Should Anyone Believe Anything at All?

Habits of the Mind

Václav Havel: Intellectual Conscience of International Politics

Naming the Elephant: Worldview as a Concept

Learning to Pray Through the Psalms

Why Good Arguments Often Fail

A Little Primer on Humble Apologetics

Praying the Psalms of Jesus

Deepest Differences: A Christian-Atheist Dialog, with Carl Peraino

Rim of the Sandhills: Why I Am Still a Christian (eBook)

Apologetics Beyond Reason: Why Seeing Really Is Believing

Echoes of a Voice

We Are Not Alone

JAMES W. SIRE

CASCADE *Books* · Eugene, Oregon

ECHOES OF A VOICE
We Are Not Alone

Copyright © 2014 James W. Sire. All rights reserved. Except for brief quotations in critical publications or reviews, no part of this book may be reproduced in any manner without prior written permission from the publisher. Write: Permissions, Wipf and Stock Publishers, 199 W. 8th Ave., Suite 3, Eugene, OR 97401.

Cascade Books
An Imprint of Wipf and Stock Publishers
199 W. 8th Ave., Suite 3
Eugene, OR 97401

www.wipfandstock.com

ISBN 13: 978-1-62564-415-2

Cataloging-in-Publication data:

Sire, James W.

Echoes of a voice : we are not alone / James W. Sire.

xvi + 244 p. ; 23 cm. Includes bibliographical references and index.

ISBN 13: 978-1-62564-415-2

1. Apologetics. 2. Faith and reason. 3. Christianity and other religions. I. Title.

BT1103 S58 2014

Manufactured in the U.S.A.

All Scripture quotations are from the New Revised Standard Version Bible, copyright © 1989, Division of Christian Education of the National Council of the Churches of Christ in the United States of America. Used by permission. All rights reserved.

To Marjorie

—a beautiful signal of transcendence—

Lord, how can man preach thy eternal word?
                He is a brittle crazy glass;
        Yet in thy temple thou dost him afford
        This glorious and transcendent place,
            To be a window, through thy grace.

—GEORGE HERBERT, "THE WINDOWS"

Contents

Preface

One summer a young boy, living in a little house on a prairie, rides his pony to fetch the cows for milking. Three thunderheads rise higher and higher above the western horizon. As they approach, the air turns electric, a cool breeze shivers his spine, his little horse lifts its head. Where he is there are no cattle; they are grazing just over the rise in a nearby ravine. He is alone in the vast reaches of ranchland. Suddenly he wonders and thinks and realizes he is being pursued by the Father, the Son, and the Holy Ghost. He continues his search for the cows, finds them, and returns to the ranch house with a memory he will never forget.

This boy had grasped what struck Stephen Daedalus, James Joyce's stand-in for himself in his novel *A Portrait of the Artist as a Man*. Stephen's musings are triggered by a list of words he had written on the flyleaf of his geography text. Beginning with his name and specific geographical location, he added his county, country, and continent, ending with "The Universe." Then he pondered.

> What was after the universe? Nothing. But was there any-
> thing around the universe to show where it stopped before
> the nothing place began? . . . It was very big to think about
> everything and everywhere. Only God could do that. . . .
> God was God's name just as his name was Stephen.[1]

On and on he ponders, moving from names to things, from colors to politics, becoming lost in endless pondering. The young boy may have done something similar. He doubts it; Stephen is more sensitive and more philosophical than that small boy. It took him longer to do such pondering. I know because I was that small boy on the prairie.

---

1. Joyce, *Portrait*, 16.

This book deals with experiences like those above—emotional, intellectual, highly charged, usually sudden, unannounced, often odd, some weird, others glorious. Do these experiences mean anything? Are we puzzling over questions we can't answer no matter how long we try? Is that puzzling itself meaningful? If so, is that meaning significant? Are these experiences actually *signals* that there is something more than to human life—*our* human life, *my* life—perhaps something transcendent?

This book meditates on the facts or experiences that lie behind such statements as:

> We step and do not step into the same river (Heraclitus).

> Whereof we *cannot* speak, thereof we must be silent
> (Ludwig Wittgenstein).

> I think; therefore I am (René Descartes).

Even the most awesome statement of all that ever is or was or ever could be:

> I Am Who I Am (Jahweh).

Nonetheless, this book does not pretend to be brilliant (Augustine), eloquent (Pascal), expansive (Calvin). And, though I draw on all of them, I hope it is not arrogant (Dawkins), wrong-headed (Emerson), cryptic (Bashô), phantasmal (MacLaine) or, most importantly, obscure (Wallace Stevens).

Let me be more specific: This book is about what Peter Berger calls *signals of transcendence*. Others name these experiences *spots of time* (William Wordsworth), *oceanic feeling, cosmic consciousness* (R. M. Bucke), *altered states of consciousness* (psychologists), *holes torn in life* (Os Guinness), *windows through which the mind looks out upon a more extensive and inclusive world* (William James).

I prefer the label *echoes of a voice* given these experiences by N. T. Wright. *Echoes of a voice* emphasizes not only the signal but the personhood of the signaler, the Creator who stands behind, before, below, beyond all creation, the Father, Son, and Holy Ghost, the awesome God of the Universe, who is, after and before all, both the greatest mystery and the greatest revelation, the transcendent who transcends and the immanent who is eternally present, both the only Other who made us like himself and the *Totaliter Aliter*, the Totally Other who is like nothing else, for he is, in the final analysis, *Being* himself, all there really *is*.

Here we approach the limits of language and should probably stick with Wittgenstein: *Whereof we cannot speak, thereof we must be silent.* But we must also recognize that what comes in silence may be more "telling" than that which comes in many words. In other *words*, we must be sensitive to the *echoes of the only Voice* that counts, the voice that *signals,* often in silence, both who he is and who we are.

The book ends with a discussion of the need for an apologetic that includes a wide range of biblical revelation—not just religious experience, but historical and scientific evidence and rational arguments involving both a positive case and a negative refutation of objections. It envisions such an apologetic as a stage on which plays a variety of dramatic scenes that, when enacted with zest and care, give a highly credible witness to the truth of the Christian faith. But this is to leap past the voice that speaks directly from the arena of the divine. So do listen and hearken to the voice that speaks directly to us throughout both time and space.

Note: As the present book is published, so is my *Apologetics Beyond Reason* (InterVarsity Press, 2014). The two books are both similar and different. The present book—*Echoes of a Voice*—focuses on *signals of transcendence*, delving deeply into their nature, their varying power to lead to God and the many alternative explanations that can be given for such amazing religious experiences. *Apologetics Beyond Reason* examines the wide variety of good evidence and good arguments for Christian faith in everything, especially literature. Readers of both books will find similar, sometimes identical, commentary on two of Hopkins's poems ("God's Grandeur" and "I wake and feel the fell of dark") and Virginia Woolf's novel *The Years*. The duplicated commentary is necessary to the arguments of both books. Cascade Books and InterVarsity Press have both granted permission for this dual publication.

Acknowledgments

This has been a book long in coming to be. Normal thanks go to my acquiring editor, Rodney Clapp, and the staff of Cascade Books, all of whom proved helpful in the production of the book.

Most of the ideas feeding into this book come from others. One is Os Guinness who turned me on to Peter Berger, another Rudolf Otto who popped up somehow, another Gerard Manley Hopkins, chief among Christian poets. Then, too, there's Wendell Berry, who first emerged when a friend recommended his take on the environment. I also owe Annie Dillard, the Tinker Creek pilgrim; Václav Havel, the dissident intellectual; Gary Snyder and William Wordsworth. Forsooth!—Every poet cited and those peeking in from behind the curtain. Abundant thanks to them.

But extraordinary thanks go to my wife Marjorie.

Marjorie, you put up with my erratic and frenetic writerly habits— the ignoring of calls to lunch or dinner, phone calls, and knocks on the door. You calmly kept peace with my the bursts of frustration as pages of my work magically disappeared off my desk only to be found later exactly where I left them and also when with my cries of anguish as my computer suddenly swallowed forever the work of hours.

Marjorie, you with your stellar typesetting skills, stuck with me, often suffering with your multiple pains, as we struggled as never before to produce a final manuscript ready for printing.

Marjorie, I picture you now, across the desk from me as we doubled-proofed the manuscript and double-checked the quoted sources, and you waited for me to tweak more than the multiple misspellings and inept phrasings. You are my beautiful, first and final, *signal of transcendence*. How many thanks are there for you!

Thank you, however, is not enough for the Voice that prompts the echoes—Jesus the Christ, the Incarnate, Transcendent and Immanent Reality. For you—Ten thousand thanks in ten thousand places.

James W. Sire
February 2014

Permissions

"The Avowal" By Denise Levertov, from OBLIQUE PRAYERS, copyright © 1984 by Denise Levertov. Reprinted by permission of New Directions Publishing Corp.

"No Matter, Never Mind" By Gary Snyder from TURTLE ISLAND, copyright © 1974 by Gary Snyder. Reprinted by permission of New Directions Publishing Corp.

Copyright © 1998 by Wendell Berry from *A Timbered Choir*. Used by permission of Counterpoint.

Copyright © 2012 by Wendell Berry from *New Collected Poems*. Used by permission of Counterpoint.

Copyright © 1999 by Gary Snyder from *The Gary Snyder Reader*. Used by permission of Counterpoint.

Counterpoint © 1983 by Gary Snyder from *Axe Handles*. Used by permission of Counterpoint.

"Of Mere Being" from THE COLLECTED POEMS OF WALLACE STEVENS by Wallace Stevens, copyright © 1954 by Wallace Stevens and renewed 1982 by Holly Stevens. Used by permission of Alfred A. Knopf, an imprint of Knopf Doubleday Publishing Group, a division of Random House LLC. All rights reserved. Any third party use of this material, outside of this publication, is prohibited. Interested parties must apply directly to Random House LLC for permission.

1

Signals, Signals, and More Signals

Introduction and Definition

> What hours, what memories!
> The vestiges they leave behind are enough
> to fill us with belief and enthusiasm,
> as if they were visits of the Holy Ghost.
>
> —HENRI FRÉDÉRIC AMIEL[1]

Sudden ecstatic experiences strike our conscious minds. They come without being called, they come when not expected, they come from who knows where. Almost all of us have them, some of them so profound that they change our lives; others so deep that their memory stays with us from here to eternity; others so frequent we learn to live with them as constant companions. Still others are quickly dismissed because they are not striking enough to be ecstatic nor recognized as anything but quirks of the mind. In this case it never dawns on us that these odd experiences might be signals of genuine *transcendence*. Maybe this best describes the experience of the pure naturalist who never sees anything that doesn't have a material explanation.

We will not argue the case for *transcendence* here. We will rather take these experiences as potential clues to the reality beyond the natural,

1. Quoted by James, *Varieties*, 303.

1

though some of them may indeed be nothing more than the malfunctioning of our mind. And we will begin this study of *signals of transcendence* modestly by first understanding what just a plain, ordinary *signal* is, at least as we will be using the concept in this book.

Signals

A *signal* can be any action, event, thing, image, sound, taste, touch, smell, word, metaphor, or idea that sparks curiosity beyond its own identity. In other words a *signal* is anything that calls out to anyone who is struck by what they perceive and wants (becomes curious) to know more about it, more about how it fits into the context in which it occurs, in short, what it is in relation to what it is surrounded by.

If, for example, I suddenly look up from my computer screen and see my bookcase, it reminds me of where I am. I am no longer lost in the thoughts I am transferring to black letters on a white background. I am no longer paying attention solely to my writing, but I am also taking in my setting, my location in the world that surrounds me. At this point my world is not just the world of words but the world of my den. If I then begin to be aware of constant low, mumbled words in the background, I know that the TV is on in the living room. A *signal*, then, is whatever I am seeing and hearing, everything from my computer to other objects in the den, everything from my sensation of keyboard touch to the constant parade of my inner thoughts, some of which are being captured in an English language text. Every impression is indeed a signal of more than itself. All are signals of my being conscious of my inner and outer world. In short, everything I perceive is signaling something more than itself, but, in the present example, there is not much that strikes me as special. For years, this is just how writing has been for me and how I think it will be for some time (who knows how much?) to come.

Of course, the number and kinds of *signals* increase as soon as my environment becomes larger and richer, when, for example, I step outside the room, see and talk with my wife, or notice that my grandson has come without my noticing. I begin to realize how his coming makes my world more complex. If I leave my house, get in the car, and drive through busy streets to the Dairy Queen, the signals multiply dangerously, but they still signal nothing out of the ordinary.

Suddenly a police siren stirs my emotion. But even the blaring siren that *signals* that I should pull to the side of the street is not out of the ordinary. It may have caused a sudden shiver up my spine, but it has not taken me out of this world. Cops are always after some errant driver. Nothing for me to be concerned with. If, however, I see that the police are rushing past me to an accident that has happened just ahead, or if I see a body bleeding on the pavement, I see something that takes me a long way from both the reasonably quiet world of my den and the busy world of suburban driving. I am now in two places—the normally normal world and the world of human tragedy, the world of ordinary life and the world of, perhaps, sudden death. I don't know yet if death has occurred or is occurring just ahead of me. But the events have signaled more than what I see and know. They have launched in me a reminder that my world and my life, even life itself, is tenuous; that, when I am driving or riding in a car, pain is potentially inches away and so is death.

Here, then, the siren, the accident and the whole context I am in are *signals of transcendence.* They take my mind to issues that are highly relevant to my own survival, to the meaning of my life, to the realization that those I love, those I live with, could be gone in a flash. Indeed, death itself is one of the most powerful *signals* that there may be something somewhere in the totality of reality that is not just ordinary (purely physical) material. The consciousness of death may easily trigger thoughts of God, not experiences of God himself, but experiences that raise the issues of who he is, or if he is, or even if God is a he or a she or an it. And is God there for the accident victims and for *me*?

With these two illustrations we begin, first, with ordinary this-worldly *signals*, *signals* that trigger a thought or image or intuition that remains in the ordinary world. My impressions in my den take me no further than the material world, albeit a world of ideas as well as of physical things. The same is true of those perceptions I have when I am driving. The siren, however, acts not only as a *signal* that suburban policemen do what suburban policemen do (mostly handle the failure of drivers to keep the law), but the blinking lights and the ensuing events *signal* something more—the possible *presence* of pain, suffering, dismemberment, and death. They place me solidly in a world that extends beyond the physical. They are *signals of transcendence.* Still, for precision and clarity, in fact, we can identify at least four levels of these *signals.*[2]

---

2. William James also identifies four levels of religious experience, but his levels

Level—1: Signals Per Se

Let me begin at the bottom level and repeat what I said above:

> *A Level 1 signal, a signal as such, is any action, event, thing, image, sound, taste, touch, smell, word, metaphor or idea that sparks curiosity beyond its own identity.*

Examples are endless. Every identifiable thing in the universe can be a *signal* of not only its own identity but of its place in the ordinary world of human thought and experience. A leaf *signals* the existence of a tree, an acorn of an oak, a headache of a disposition I don't like and would like to be rid of. There is nothing mysterious about a *signal* per se. We live and move and have our being in a world of *signals*. Sometimes, of course, there is so much more to these "eureka" moments, as David Lyle Jeffrey and Gregory Maillet call them. Poet Richard Wilbur, for example, sees in a sudden helter-skelter flight of birds "the cross-purposes" by which the "world is dreamt," thus evoking a truly *transcendent* insight. But here I leap three levels ahead in this discourse.[3] We should first consider the next level.

Level 2

As soon as we move away from the material world to matters of distinctly human significance, that is, matters that involve more than the mere fact of a *signal's* own existence and its place in the seemingly neutral (to human interest) material world, we begin to experience glimmers of *transcendence*.

> *A Level 2 signal of transcendence is anything that when what it signals is properly understood turns out to require (or seem to require) a non-material foundation.*

---

are stages in the subjective depth of experience rather than of metaphysical transcendence. Moreover, he writes from what he takes to be a neutral or scientific standpoint, that is, one that is uncommitted to the accuracy of any particular metaphysical conclusion that those who have these experiences might have. Readers should avail themselves of Williams's massive evidence and conclusions, but should notice as well the incoherence of his explanation of their epistemological authority (ibid., 292–328). See my analysis in chapter 10 below.

3. Jeffrey and Maillet, *Christianity and Literature*, 132.

This definition is intentionally a reflection of Peter Berger's definition: "By signals of transcendence I mean phenomena that are to be found within the domain of our 'natural' reality but that appear to point beyond that reality."[4] We will look in more detail at Berger's own examples. Here we need to note only three of the four he mentions. First is the apparent *order* in daily life, one demonstration of which is the calming love of a mother for her child terrified in the night. Against all prospect that the child's life along with her own will ever end, she says, "There, there. It's all right. Everything is all right." That can only be true if there is more to reality than material.

> Every parent (or, at any rate, every parent who loves his child) takes upon himself the representation of a universe that is ultimately in order and ultimately trustworthy. This representation can be justified only within a religious (strictly speaking a supernatural) frame of reference.[5]

Second is *play*. Play takes place in a Secondary World with its own rules, its own order; time is suspended; eternity is assumed. Third is *hope*. From birth to death we live in hope of a future, one that is challenged by suffering and death but not conquered, for we project our lives out into eternity and see beyond for a satisfaction of our longings.

Another example of a Level 2 *signal* is humankind's universal moral sense, the sense that there is often a difference between that which is and that which should be. Unless there is some standard outside our human sense of right and wrong by which we can know that our sense is really correct, morality becomes relative to each person or society's sense of right and wrong. If there are no absolutes outside our own judgment as either ourselves as individuals or our society (no matter how large), there is no foundation for thinking that our sense of right and wrong participates in anything other than the historical moment in which decisions are made and their effect is registered among us. The very existence of the moral sense itself is as present in Stalin as in Mother Teresa, in a serial killer as in those who sacrifice their own life to save another's. Such a sense cannot be moral if it can sense utter opposites to be good. In other words, the existence of the moral sense is a *signal* that there is an *ought*, something other than, and *transcendent* over, what *is*. We will look again at this *signal* when we examine how atheists (those who do not believe a

4. Berger, *Rumor*, 53.
5. Ibid., 57.

transcendent of any kind exists) deal with what some of them take to be the fact of morality.

On a more intellectual note, the question, Why is there something rather than nothing? puzzled philosopher Gottfried Wilhelm Leibniz (1646–1716). Every thing or event or idea in the universe is caused by something prior. That is, every thing that exists must have a sufficient cause. Even an infinite string of natural causes can't cause itself. It must be caused by something beyond the chain of causes. What is that? Leibniz concluded that "[O]ne Being dominating the universe not only rules the world but he creates and fashions it, is superior to the world, and, so to speak, extra mundane, and by this very fact is the ultimate reason of things."[6] In other words the very existence of finite, contingent being (matter and energy or whatever else might constitute physical reality) *signals* the existence of an infinite *Cause* or *Being* as its cause. *Being* itself needs no cause because it contains within itself the reason for its own being. It is the eternal.[7]

A child's version of this puzzle begins with the question, "Mommy, where did I come from?" A complete answer to this question will have to deal somehow with an infinite *transcendent*. Most mothers, in the Western world at least, will perhaps say, "God made you." Then, if the mother is pious, she may add, "Isn't God good to do that?"[8]

A complex, let alone complete, theistic theology does not flow from these simple experiences or even from the conclusions of sophisticated philosophy. Rather, we get merely the distinct impression that there is more than machinery to the universe. Somewhere *behind* it or *beyond* it, there simply must be some meaning or purpose, something that explains why the things we experience are as they are—from the ordinary sticks and stones that break our bones, to our bones themselves, and on to the glorious dome of the sky. The starry sky on a cloudless, moonless night viewed from a glen deep in the woods, or better, the aurora borealis on a summer midnight in northern Minnesota, or, while one is hiking, the sudden appearance of a Swiss valley with chalets dotting

6. Leibniz, "Of the Origin of Things," 100.

7. Leibniz's argument for the existence of God has been challenged. But so has every other philosophic or theological argument. The point is to notice that this sophisticated argument for the existence of God begins with a potential *signal*—a wonderment, a puzzle—that triggers a mental process that leads to the conclusion that this material world can only be explained by the existence of a *transcendent*.

8. Sire, *Rim*, chapter 3.

the mountainside and a village at it base, like a set of perfectly carved and painted toys placed with intent on a brilliant green backdrop: In all these, beauty and design, complexity and unity, intensity and significance come together to say, "Here is something that is beyond the sum of its parts. Here is more than matter. Here is mind; here is *transcendence*." At this point little personality shines through, little of moral goodness, but lots of aesthetic grandeur. "The world is charged with the glory" of WHAT? Perhaps not Yahweh or Christ or Allah or Krishna. Perhaps just *transcendent* Glory itself. Perhaps the inherent Glory of the universe, a universe that is announcing to us its own *self-transcendence* or perhaps itself enjoying its own immense beauty.[9]

Those with a deep and prior understanding of a religious tradition may well conclude that much, much more than mere matter is present or being signaled. The experience is not so much of a personal God as of an awesome, magnificent nature that is more than nature, that is, perhaps, itself spirit manifest in matter. The deistic and panentheistic God of some scientists, especially physicists, goes no further than this. Neither do some of the experiences of William Wordsworth, Wallace Stevens, Loren Eiseley, and Annie Dillard, though, as we shall see, some of their experiences go much further.

Level 3

With Level 3 the personally transcendent comes into play.

> At Level 3 the signal points more explicitly to something other than the obviously material—some "presence" from beyond ordinary reality but manifest within it, something "personal" that seems to be there (or here) just behind the surface of what we are directly experiencing, often something with which one feels at peace or even at one, or, perhaps, as dangerous or threatening.

William James cites numerous experiences that suggest that the subject of the experience is not just living in an ordinary world of people and things but is profoundly connected to this reality in a way unaccounted

---

9. Of course, how an impersonal "thing," the universe, can enjoy "itself" is a question worth contemplating. Enjoy? Does that not imply a "personal" being "who," not "what," enjoys? Language itself and the ways we use it are also *signals of transcendence*.

for by any or all of his five senses. Here is one of James's accounts. It comes from Henri Frédéric Amiel's *Journal*:[10]

> One day, in youth, at sunrise, sitting in the ruins of the castle of Faucigny; and again in the mountains, under the noonday sun, above Levey, lying at the foot of a tree and visited by three butterflies; once more at night upon the shingly shore of the Northern Ocean, my back upon the sand and my vision ranging through the milky way;—such grand and spacious, immortal, cosmogonic reveries, when one to reaches the stars, when one owns the infinite! Moments divine, ecstatic hours; in which our thought flies from world to world, pierces the great enigma, breathes with a respiration broad, tranquil, and deep as the respiration of the ocean, serene and limitless as the blue firmament; . . . instants of irresistible intuition in which one feels one's self great as the universe, and calm as a god. . . . What hours, what memories! The vestiges they leave behind are enough to fill us with belief and enthusiasm, as if they were visits of the Holy Ghost.[11]

The Jewish scholar-poet-philosopher Martin Buber identified this manifestation of personal transcendence as a *Thou* that addresses us as a *Thou*. We always have, as he says, an *I-It* relationship with material things, but we can also have *I-Thou* relationships not only with other people but with fundamental reality. We must not think of this reality as an *It*. Rather when we are truly human, fundamental reality addresses us as *Thou* and we respond to that reality as *Thou*.[12]

William Paley's well-known and much more intellectual argument for the existence of a designer God is also a *signal*, at least for those who *see* either the necessity or the high probability of Paley's conclusion. In brief the argument goes like this. If I find a watch in the forest, it is highly likely that, rather than appearing there as a product of the forest doing what forests do or as having no cause for its appearance at all, the watch has had an intelligent designer as its maker. This by analogy is extended to the universe itself. Given the apparent vastness of the universe and the complexity and seemingly purpose-driven nature of living matter, it

10. Amiel (1821–1881), according to Wikipedia, "was a Swiss philosopher, poet, and critic . . . descended from a Huguenot family," whose private journal (*Journal Intime*) was published after his death.

11. James, *Varieties*, 203.

12. Buber in *I and Thou* is famous for elaborating on this relationship in highly poetic as well as philosophic and theological language.

is more likely that the universe and the biosphere in particular has had its origin in the intentions of an intelligent designer with many of the characteristics of the traditional theistic notion of a personal, omniscient, omnipresent, omnipotent God. The universe itself suggests this.[13] As the psalmist says, "The heavens are telling the glory of God; and the firmament proclaims his handiwork" (Ps 19:1).

When the *Thou* of Martin Buber or the sense of the Holy Spirit of Amiel are understood to have more and deeper personal characteristics than mere mind or intelligence, the *signals* are approaching *Level 4*.

Level 4

Level 4 takes us deeper and more fully into the personal and holy character of the divine.

> *At Level 4 comes direct experience of the profound depths of Thou, the Person who is Ultimate Being and should be described in terms of the holy, the numinous, and the mysterium tremendum.*

I wish I could describe this level without the special language employed by the German theologian Rudolf Otto. But his somewhat arcane terminology has been found useful by many subsequent philosophers, theologians, and spiritual writers who comment in depth on the nature of religious experience, especially in its deepest and most personal form.

The holy: For Christian theologians, the *holy* is the utter separateness, perfect righteousness, and exhaustive intelligence of God.

The idea of the holy lies deeper than "pure reason": [It lies in] the *fundus animae*, the "bottom" or "ground of the soul" (*Seelengrund*). The ideas of the numinous and the feelings that correspond to them are (quite as much as the rational ideas and feelings) absolutely "pure," and the criteria that Kant suggests for the "pure" concept and the "pure" feeling of respect are most precisely applicable to them.[14]

---

13. Wiker and Witt, *Meaningful World*, chart a wide range of meaningful elements in the world. So too does Karl W. Giberson as he focuses on the cosmos, physics and the fine-tuning of the universe, in *Wonder*, 95, where he writes: "If we find the world filled with wonders that move us spiritually or point beyond themselves or inspire us in ways not captured by our ordinary nets, we need not simply shrug our shoulders about what that might be. I think we can reasonably embrace the idea that there must be a transcendent reality in which these experiences are grounded."

14. Otto, *Idea*, 129.

The numinous: Otto wants to be clear that the idea of the *holy* in-cludes more than righteousness, more than morality. We need, he says, "to invent a special term to stand for 'the holy' *minus* its moral factor or 'moment,' and . . . minus its 'rational' aspect altogether."[15] The *numinous* is that word, coined from the Latin *numen* in the same way *omen* gives us the word *ominous.*[16] It denotes the transcendent itself, that which is the Totally Other but which manifests itself (or himself) as a powerful Presence.

But how much further can we go in properly understanding the numinous? Not much, for it turns out that "this mental state is perfectly *sui generis* [utterly unique] and irreducible to any other; and therefore, like every absolutely primary and elementary datum, while it admits of being discussed, it cannot be strictly defined."[17] The term *numinous* is like the terms *substance, meaning, being,* and a host of other terms; in the final analysis we can only define them in terms of themselves.[18] We either immediately grasp what they signify or we don't understand them. The *numinous* cannot be taught; it can only be evoked or awakened.

Moreover, Otto says:

> The numinous . . . issues from the deepest foundation of cog-nitive apprehension that the soul possesses, and, though it of course comes into being in and amid the sensory data and em-pirical material of the natural world and cannot anticipate or dispense with those, yet it does not arise *out of* them, but only *by their means.*[19]

15. Ibid., 20.

16. Ibid., 21.

17. Ibid.

18. Otto is working within the framework of post-Kantian thought. The *numinous* is a Kantian-like category; we can't think without these terms but we can't, strictly speaking, define them. As he writes, "The rational ideas of absoluteness, completion, necessity, and substantiality, and no less so those of the good as an objective value, objectively binding and valid, are not to be 'evolved' from any sort of sense-perception. . . . Rather, seeking to account for the ideas in question, we are referred away from all sense-experience back to an original and underivable capacity of the mind implanted in the 'pure reason' independently of all perception" (ibid., 129). And again, "Now this is the criterion of all *a priori* knowledge, namely, that, so soon as an assertion has been clearly expressed and understood, knowledge of its truth comes into the mind with the certitude of first-hand insight" (ibid., 154).

19. Ibid., 130.

Indeed, the *numinous* makes us conscious that we are not our own; we are creatures. The *numinous* evokes "the emotion of a creature, submerged and overwhelmed by its own nothingness in contrast to that which is supreme above all creatures. . . . The numinous is thus felt as objective and outside the self."[20] There is no way that the *numinous* can be taught; it must rather be "'awakened' from the spirit. . . . induced, incited, and aroused."[21] There are many ways in which this arousal can be sparked. Otto, however, suggests that one way is direct:

> If a man does not *feel* what the numinous is, when he reads the sixth chapter of Isaiah, then no "preaching, singing, telling," in Luther's phrase, can avail him. . . . He who "in the spirit" reads the written word lives in the numinous, though he may have neither notion of it nor name for it, nay, though he may be unable to analyse [*sic*] any feeling of his own and so make explicit to himself the nature of that numinous strand running through the religious experience.[22]

The *numinous* may also be sparked through the arousal of the fearful or the horrible: "The hard, stern, and somewhat grim pictures of the Madonna in ancient Byzantine art attract the worship of many Catholics more than the tender charm of the Madonnas of Raphael."[23] There are the experiences of grandeur and sublimity in nature, art, and architecture, especially the Gothic. Then too, darkness in art, silence in music, emptiness and empty distances may also open one to the *numinous*.[24] The witness of what can only be thought of as a miracle will do so as well.

Otto identifies many instances of the *numinous* in the Old and New Testaments and in the works of Luther. We will examine some of the biblical examples in chapter 2.[25] The *mysterium tremendum* in Otto's analysis provides a more detailed exegesis of the *numinous*.

The mysterium tremendum: First Otto gives a general description:

> The feeling of it [the *mysterium tremendum*] may at times come sweeping like a gentle tide, pervading the mind with a tranquil

---

20. Ibid., 24–25.

21. Ibid., 75.

22. Ibid., 75–76.

23. Ibid., 77.

24. The holy in Bach is in the silences, illustrated by his Mass in B Minor, esp. the "Incarnatus" more than in the "Sanctus," says Otto, *ibid.*, 85.

25. Ibid., 120.

mood of deepest worship. It may pass over into a more set and lasting attitude of the soul, continuing, as it were, thrillingly vibrant and resonant, until at last it dies away and the soul resumes its "profane," non-religious mood of everyday experience. It may burst in sudden eruption up from the depths of the soul with spasms and convulsions, or lead to the strangest excitements, to intoxicated frenzy, to transport, and to ecstasy. It has its wild and demonic forms and can sink to an almost grisly horror and shuddering. It has its crude, barbaric antecedents and early manifestations, and again it may be developed into something beautiful and pure and glorious. It may become hushed, trembling, and speechless humility of the creature in the presence of—whom or what? In the presence of that which is a *mystery* inexpressible and above all creatures.[26]

When he describes the *mysterium* part of the pair of terms, he emphasizes the positive, yet dark obscurity of what is being experienced: "Conceptually *mysterium* denotes merely that which is hidden and esoteric, that which is beyond conception or understanding, extraordinary and unfamiliar . . . [W]hat is meant is something absolutely and intensely positive."[27]

The *mysterium* denotes the Wholly Other and triggers "blank wonder, an astonishment that strikes us dumb, amazement absolute."[28]

Elements of the *tremendum* include:

(1) Awefulness—tremor, fear, notably fear of God, dread. This began in primitive man with the uncanny, the weird, a shudder, a sense of the impending wrath of God;[29]

(2) Overpoweringness—"absolute unapproachability," majesty, a feeling of nothingness, of being dust and ashes, consciousness of createdness and creaturehood, annihilation of the self, or, as in mysticism, identification of "the personal self with the transcendent Reality"; "[T]here is the feeling of one's own submergence, of being but 'dust and ashes' and nothingness."[30]

26. Ibid., 26.
27. Ibid., 27.
28. Ibid., 40, 45–55.
29. Ibid., 27–33.
30. Ibid., 34–37.

(3) Energy or Urgency—"vitality, passion, emotional temper, will, force, movement, excitement, activity, impetus."[31]

The nature of the *numinous* as characterized by the *mysterium tremendum* may give us a clue to which *signals of transcendence* are most likely to point unambiguously to the existence of a specifically Christian notion of God. But we will return to this later.

Ontology and Epistemology

There are several ways to classify *signals of transcendence* as experienced by Christians. One way is to rank them as we have done above, Level 1 to Level 4. This categorizes by the depth (or height) of the *transcendence* they signal.

A second way is to divide them into (1) *ontological signals* that record a profound sense of the *presence* of *transcendence* and (2) *epistemological signals* that stimulate a curiosity that leads to learning more about the *transcendent* dimensions of reality.

Among the *signals* that we have already noted, those that are *ontological* include my experience of the three thunderheads (Preface) signaling the Trinity; astonishing scenes in nature signaling the presence of God as creator; Amiel's "cosmogenic reveries" pointing to the presence of the Holy Spirit; and, most notably, Otto's idea of the holy, his *numinous* and *mysterium tremendum*.

Those *signals* that are *epistemological* include Peter Berger's parent comforting a child, his notion of hope and sense of morality; Leibniz's case for the existence of God; William Paley's intellectual move from the universe as a clock or as behaving with evolutionary convergence to his conclusion that some *telos* (purpose) must be behind the existence of this universe (Paley).

The final effect of both types of *signals* is, of course, the same. They point to an *ontological* end—the first directly, the second by way of human reason that concludes in a deep sense that an intellectual argument could and does lead to this conclusion.

31. Ibid., 37.

Form and Content

A third classification looks at the forms in which the deeply private experiences of *transcendence* are made public. Do we learn about them (a) through our personal experience (b) by relatively straightforward narrative prose or (c) by carefully crafted poetry?

Which form they embody will have an effect on how we evaluate their power to be *signals* for us as well as for those who have had the experiences. As we examine these experiences in the pages to follow, we would do well to remember the differences in the form of their transmission.

We turn now to those *signals of transcendence* that have been highly significant in the tradition of Jewish and Christian experience. For Christians these *signals* should form the base evidence for the relevance and meaning of any other claim to the significance of any other experience bidding to be treated as a *signal* of the Presence of God. Chapter 10 will expand on this notion. Suffice it now to look more closely at some highly significant examples.

2

Holy, Holy, Holy

Signals in the Bible

Holy, holy, holy is the LORD of hosts;
the whole earth is full of his glory.

—ISAIAH 6:3

Rudolf Otto sets the highest standard for a *signal of transcendence*. In its fullest form it puts one in immediate touch with the *numinous*. It shivers our timbers with its *mysterium tremendum*—the deep experience of the Presence of the Holy God. We exist for that moment in the holy of holies, a place reserved for only the ancient Hebrew chief priest, and that, only once a year.

In this chapter we will look at the way the Hebrew and Christian Scriptures spoke of God's Presence and the sense of that Presence. We begin with the biblical text that Rudolf Otto considered the primary illustration of what we have called a Level 4, (1), (a) signal.

Isaiah 6: Isaiah in the Temple

That story in Isaiah is double-barreled. It is both the story of a Level 4 signal and a *signal* itself. Do we always respond to the story as such a *signal*? No, but we fail to do so because of the condition of our own soul, perhaps from the terrible state of spiritual blindness.

In the temple the Seraphs proclaimed what should be the most obvious fact of our ordinary world. The whole earth, everything created, is full of the glory of God. How could we miss it! In the final analysis everything proclaims God's glory—his holy magnificence. But day after day and year after year, even Sunday after Sunday we miss it, or misconstrue it. Even when we sense a bit of it, we turn away and ignore it. Perhaps we sense that being in the presence of the glory of God will only frighten us and only make us feel our own insignificance. Maybe God's glory will make demands on us or lead us into living a purer life, thus missing the pleasures of this life. We fail to know or even to learn what life in the Spirit really is—revealing the glory of God by what we say and do, and by what we are. Those are the barriers that cloud our perception. Let's see if in reading it now we get at least a twinge of its power to refocus attention.

> In the year king Uzziah died, I saw the Lord sitting on a throne, high and lofty; and the hem of his robe filled the temple. Seraphs were in attendance above him; each had six wings: with two they covered their faces, and with two they covered their feet, and with two they flew.
> And one called to another and said:
>
> "Holy, holy, holy is the LORD of hosts;
> the whole earth is full of his glory."
>
> The pivots on the thresholds shook at the voices of those who called, and the house filled with smoke. And I said: "Woe is me! I am lost, for I am a man of unclean lips, and I live among a people of unclean lips; yet my eyes have seen the King, the LORD of hosts!"
> Then one of the seraphs flew to me, holding a live coal that had been taken from the altar with a pair of tongs. The seraph touched my mouth with it and said: "Now that this has touched your lips, your guilt has departed and your sin is blotted out." Then I heard the voice of the Lord saying, "Whom shall I send, and who will go for us?" And I said, "Here am I; send me!" And he said, "Go and say to this people:
> Keep listening, but do not comprehend;
> keep looking, but do not understand.'
> Make the mind of this people dull,
> and stop their ears,
> and shut their eyes,
> so that they may not look with their eyes,
> and listen with their ears,

and comprehend with their minds,
>and turn and be healed."
Then I said, "How long, O Lord?" And he said:
Until cities lie waste
>without inhabitant,
and houses without people,
>and the land is utterly desolate;
Until the LORD sends everyone far away;
>and vast is the emptiness in the midst of the land.
Even if a tenth part remain in it,
>it will be burnt again,
like a terebinth or an oak
>whose stump remains standing
>when it is felled.
The holy seed is its stump. (Isa 6:1–13)

I am writing this present paragraph after a fresh reading of this passage of Scripture. I have, of course, read or heard it read many times before. Still, being reminded of its status as Otto's chief illustration from Scripture has made me more sensitive to the *numinous*. For me, that sensation came more from what God told Isaiah to say than from the temple scene itself. Yes, the scene is awesome. Yes, the Seraphs are glorious and humble in their adoration. Yes, I can envision the Lord seated on his throne, but I do so more from paintings of this scene than from the words. After all, the second commandment cautions us not to reduce God to a visual image. I also see the resplendent brightness of the glory-filled temple.

But above all, I hear with my mind's ear God's message to Isaiah's Hebrew nation. And what is it? It is not a bit of wisdom as from a sage. It is a command—or appears to be—for God's people to keep listening to his voice but not to understand. The Lord here reveals himself more as the *deus absconditus,* the hidden God who, while he wants to be recognized as God, does not want to be understood. This seems strange indeed to me, for God has been to his people a very wordy God. The "word of the Lord" seems always to be coming to the prophets both before and after the time of Isaiah. There is indeed judgment in both the tone and the content, for the words given to Isaiah come only after Isaiah has offered himself to God and has been forgiven his sin through the application of the hot coal from the altar.

God's own words, his very message, is ominous—an omen, a *signal,* of his infinite character, his utter holiness. It sparks the *mysterium tremendum* to which Otto refers. Isaiah has been penetrated by the *numinous* Presence of the Holy One—an experience utterly *sui generis*; there is nothing to which it can compare.

How long is Isaiah to proclaim this word of God? That too is frightening, for it looks like it is to be for a very long time. And it will be, for Jerusalem will be laid waste in a few centuries, and the people of God will be exiled in Babylon for seventy years. And many more years will pass till God's Word comes as Jesus Christ, a shoot out of the root of Jesse. Then Jesus will explain the people's lack of understanding of his parables by reference to God's word to Isaiah (Mark 4:12; John 39–40). And the disciples will now participate in the *numinous* as they try to understand Jesus' explanation by citing what must have struck them as the odd words of God to Isaiah's generation. Would they in the presence of this new prophet be able to do better than God's people down through the ages?

But there is for us something more ominous. When we stand in the presence of God's word to Isaiah and his community, are we also those who listen and do not understand? Is there for us, as Otto expected, a sense of the *numinous* when we read Isaiah? Does Scripture not at least sometimes chill us to the bone?

> If a man does not *feel* what the numinous is, when he reads the sixth chapter of Isaiah, then no "preaching, singing, telling," in Luther's phrase, can avail him. . . . He who "in the spirit" reads the written word lives in the numinous, though he may have no name for it, nay, though he may be unable to analyse [sic] any feeling of his own and so make explicit to himself the nature of that numinous strand running through the religious experience.[1]

Isaiah 6 puts us on notice.

Exodus 3: Moses in the Wilderness

No less *numinous* is God's appearance to Moses in the burning bush. Again, as in Isaiah 6, the account of the *numinous* sparks the sense of the *numinous* in the reader, though one suspects to a much less intensity than in Moses. Here again is that account in full. A summary does not trigger the same response. Read it aloud.

---

1. Otto, *Idea*, 75–76.

Moses was keeping the flock of his father-in-law Jethro, the priest of Midian; he led his flock beyond the wilderness, and came to Horeb, the mountain of God. There the angel of the Lord appeared to him in a flame of fire out of a bush; he looked, and the bush was blazing, yet it was not consumed. Then Moses said, "I must turn aside and look at this great sight, and see why the bush is not burned up." When the LORD saw that he had turned aside to see, God called to him out of the bush, "Moses, Moses!" And he said, "Here I am." Then he said, "Come no closer! Remove the sandals from your feet, for the place on which you are standing is holy ground." He said further, "I am the God of your father, the God of Abraham, the God of Isaac, and the God of Jacob." And Moses hid his face, for he was afraid to look at God.

Then the LORD said, "I have observed the misery of my people who are in Egypt; I have heard their cry on account of their taskmasters. Indeed, I know their sufferings, and I have come down to deliver them from the Egyptians, and to bring them up out of that land to a good and broad land, a land flowing with milk and honey, to country of the Canaanites, the Hittites, and the Jebusites. The cry of the Israelites has now come to me; I have also seen how the Egyptians oppress them. So come, I will send you to Pharaoh to bring my people, the Israelites, out of Egypt." But Moses said to God, "Who am I that I should go to Pharaoh, and bring the Israelites out of Egypt?" He said, "I will be with you; and this shall be the sign for you that it is I who sent you: when you have brought the people out of Egypt, you shall worship God on this mountain."

But Moses said to God, "If I come to the Israelites and say to them, 'The God of your ancestors has sent me to you,' and they ask me "What is his name?" what shall I say to them?" God said to Moses, "I AM WHO I AM." He said further, "Thus you shall say to the Israelites, 'I AM has sent me to you.'" God also said to Moses, "Thus you shall say to the Israelites, 'The LORD, the God of your ancestors, the God of Abraham, the God of Isaac, and the God of Jacob, has sent me to you':

This is my name forever,
and this my title for all generations." (Exod 3:1–15)

God then continues to speak to Moses and to lay out more details about how he will be with Moses and make his task possible.

Notice how both Moses' and Isaiah's encounters with God are set in time and space. Isaiah is in the temple during the reign of king Uzziah;

Moses is in the desert living a normal life after fleeing Pharaoh's judgment for slaying an Egyptian. He is now herding his father-in-law's sheep. In Scripture *signals of transcendence* and the further encounters with the *transcendent* are not lifted out of history; they are an intimate part of history. *Signals* sound in the normal world; they alert us—usually suddenly and without previous warning—but they take us beyond ourselves and engage us with the invisible world.

Signals alert us not to the oddness of the invisible world but to its normality. If the whole earth is filled with God's glory, then the curtain between the visible and the invisible is much thinner and permeable than we modern folk imagine. But we will treat this idea in more detail later.

Moses suddenly sees a bush that is burning but is not consumed. He is curious and turns aside to see just what is happening. There he hears the voice of God. The *signal* of the burning bush leads to the *present reality* of God. Moses doesn't just hear an "echo of a voice"; he hears *the Voice itself.* Sign has led to reality. And reality reveals itself in the Personal voice of God and in a propositional revelation.

Far more substantial revelation is given here to Moses than was given to Isaiah. Isaiah learns what to say as a prophet to Israel. It is a revelation from God about Israel more than about God himself. But here Moses learns what many theologians believe is the most profound statement of the Jewish (and Christian) conception of God. God's revelation here not only sets hearts afire but minds as well. The minds of rabbis, theologians, and philosophers have been kept busy for thousands of years, and the depths have not yet been plumbed.

God first identifies himself as Israel's God, rather than any of the gods of Egypt or the Middle East. But that only means that the people of Israel have not been wrong to think of him as God. Second, God declares himself not as one god among many, not even as the chief god. He is God in such a way that all other gods are not really gods at all. God is I AM— He Who Is. He is Being Himself—Personal and ultimate. He speaks. He reveals. He is foundational to all reality. He is what it is to *Be* and who it is who creates. He is Holy—Holiness itself—and where he appears is a holy place. Moses' response is to acknowledge that holiness. Israel, he says, is "my people." He hears their groaning. He will respond. He will rescue.

Only in Jesus does God come closer to anyone other than he does here to Moses and, as we will see, on the mountain after Moses has led the Hebrews out of Egypt. *Signals of transcendence* are fine, but they are only signals. Reality is the end to which they point, and God is the reality.

For us, the narrative of Moses and the burning bush is only a signal, but when we set our hearts and minds on this story, it may well lead us to God, first in silence, then in worship, in prayer, in thanksgiving, in joy, and even, at times, in ecstatic experience as we are lifted into what seems best to be described as a taste of the Presence of God himself. As Augustine confessed,

> Far away in the region of unlikeness, You cried to me . . . "I AM WHO I AM." I heard it as one hears a word in my heart, and no possibility of doubt remained to it; I could more easily have doubted that I was alive than that the truth exists, truth that is seen and understood from through the things that are made.[2]

Moses on the Mountain: Enigma without Variation

The life of Moses, in fact, the whole history of Israel, is filled with *signals of transcendence*. In a sense, every biblical story from Adam and Eve on is a *sign* that points to the reality of God. After all, "the whole earth is filled with his Glory." So we should expect to see many, if not all, of the events of the history of Israel and the church to sparkle with *signals*. And they do. In fact there are so many that picking a few examples is difficult. Much, as movie editors say, will be left on the cutting room floor. It is clear, however, that the ones I am choosing stand out.

The account of Moses and the Hebrew journey from Egypt to the holy land is rich in *signals*, but the one I have selected is, for me, the most revealing and the most puzzling. The text below comes from the story of Moses' second reception of the Ten Commandments. Moses has already received these and many more commandments; he has also received instructions from God for the construction of the ark of the covenant and the tabernacle (Exod 20–33). Moses then asks God for further assurance of his presence and instruction about the role he is to play in God's plans. We pick up the story here:

> The LORD said to Moses, "I will do the very thing that you have asked; for you have found favor in my sight, and I know you by

2. Augustine *Confessions, vii,* 16 (173), as quoted in Waltke and Houston, *Psalms,* 116.

name." Moses said, "Show me your glory, I pray." And he said, "I will make all my goodness pass before you, and will proclaim before you the name, 'The LORD'; and I will be gracious to whom I will be gracious; and will show mercy on whom I will show mercy. But," he said, "you cannot see my face; for no one shall see me and live." And the LORD continued, "See, there is a place by me where you shall stand on the rock; and while my glory passes by I will put you in a cleft of the rock, and I will cover you with my hand until I have passed by; then I will take away my hand, and you shall see my back; but my face shall not be seen." (Exod 33:17–23)

The Lord then asked Moses to cut two more stone tablets and take them to the top of Mount Sinai, and not to let anyone go with him or let sheep graze on the mountain. Moses did that.

The Lord descended in a cloud and stood with him there and proclaimed the name, "The LORD." The LORD passed before him, and proclaimed,

"The LORD, the LORD,
a God merciful and gracious,
slow to anger,
and abounding in steadfast love and faithfulness,
keeping steadfast love for the thousandth generation,
forgiving iniquity and transgression and sin,
yet my no means clearing the guilty,
but visiting the iniquity of the parents
upon the children
and the children's children,
to the third and the fourth generation." (Exod 34:5–7)

The story is not over, of course. Moses bows his head, asks God to continue to go with him and the people; God then covenants with the people to lead them forth into the promised land. When Moses returned from the mountain his face shone so brightly that he had to wear a veil when he was with the people.

Again we have both a signal and a reality. Moses was in the presence of *Being* (I AM) himself, the Alpha and Omega, the beginning and the end, the God, we might say, of both time and time out of mind. The event and its narration is a revelation of (1) God's "thereness" to Moses, (2) God's "hereness" to all his creation and (3) God's holiness, his separateness and righteousness, from even his most blessed prophet, (4) God's character of mercy, graciousness, love, faithfulness, and willingness to forgive, and (5) God's character of judgment and commitment to retain the effects of sin to all mankind. This reality meets Moses as God passes by showing Moses only his back side.

The enigma of God's character as both loving and just is manifest throughout the remainder of the Hebrew Scriptures and is only resolved when in Jesus Christ justice and peace kiss (Ps 85:10). When God in Jesus Christ bears the burden of human sin, redeeming his people, returning them to an intimate relationship with himself, he has undone the enigma, untangled the dilemma, resolved the paradox—in short, saved us from the wrath of God by substituting himself for us.

To the people of Israel, God's presence was a distant reality as they saw the shining face of Moses and realized he had walked with God, the shining face being a *sign* of the enlightening and transforming power of God. Today we listen to the story. We see and hear the *signal*, and in silence, in worship, in prayer, in obedience and disobedience, we sense of distance from God and our guilt before his holiness. Then, as we receive God's forgiveness through Jesus Christ, we sometimes sense in awe the very presence of God.

Throughout the Hebrew Scriptures *signals of transcendence* abound. On the one hand, some of the events stand out as blaring sirens. We have just examined three of these. There are many, many more: Noah and the Ark, the call of Abraham from Ur to Palestine, the salvation of Lot, Jacob wrestling with God, Joseph and his prosperous but problematic exile in Egypt, the exodus of the Hebrews from Egypt, Gideon and his fleece, Samson and his extraordinary strength, David and Goliath, the life and ministry of Jeremiah, the strange visions and behavior of Ezekiel, Daniel in the lion's den and in his vision of one like a son of man. And many, many more. Cast your mind over the Hebrew Scriptures; recall the fascinating stories of Ruth and Esther, Joshua and Rahab, David and Bathsheba, Jonah and the whale, and on and on. And then turn to the New Testament.

An Interlude: How Do Signals Work?

This morning, as I wrote these words, I had an experience that I count as a *signal of transcendence*. It is the day after Easter 2009 (signals, remember, come in space and time). I have just read the lectionary texts for Easter and the day after.

Isaiah 25:6–9 is a mysterious passage in which Isaiah says that "that day" and on "this mountain" God will prepare a magnificent feast for all people. He will destroy the "shroud that is cast over all peoples"; he will "swallow up death forever" and "wipe away the tears from all faces"; and "the disgrace of his people he will take away from all the earth." God has spoken. This he will do.

What did this mean to Isaiah? What did it mean to ancient Israel? I am not sure. Isaiah is not a book that I have studied from end to end. But I imagine (not always a good thing to do) that this Mountain is literally Zion on which Jerusalem rises as the "city of God" and that Isaiah is envisioning, not necessarily some coming event in the near future, but the events at the end of time, the wiping away of all tears as seen in the Revelation of John 21:4.

For my devotions Easter morning I also read Isaiah 25:69; our pastor read the text in the worship service; I reread it this morning. Each time the masterful wording struck me—the poetry of the passage and the vision it inspired in me as I contemplated it. Surely this was a *signal* sounded for me, a *signal* of the glorious end toward which God is moving the world. Things are not falling apart, as W. B. Yeats would have it. No, the center is holding. There may be a "blood-dimmed tide," but no "rough beast" is "slouching toward Bethlehem to be born." The Messiah has come. He has died and been resurrected. The victory over death has been won. He is risen. He is risen indeed.

Confirming all this were the remainder of the lectionary texts for Easter and the day after. Psalm 118:1–2, 14–24, the vision of the rejected stone (the Messiah) that becomes the cornerstone of the temple; 1 Corinthians 15:1–11, the first known creed for the early church; Mark 16:1–8 and Matthew 28:1–10, the story of the first people to find the empty tomb. Then came a second *signal* as I read Rueben Job's words in my devotional guide: "At this very moment when I write this and at the very moment when you read these words, *you and I are in the presence of God.*"[3]

Really! Really? I thought. Yes, really. Of course, really. I and Rueben Job (note the me first) . . . We are in the presence of God. We are always in the presence of God. Christ is risen. He is risen indeed!

3. Shawchuck and Job, *A Guide to Prayer*, 171.

Why is it that we so constantly need to be reminded? Where is the studied, steady practice of the presence of God in our lives? No matter the answer. We know we need to be reminded and we rejoice when we are.

Now let me imitate Rueben Job: *You and I are in the presence of God*—I when I write, you when you read. These studies in the *signals of transcendence* are intended, to raise your consciousness, dear reader (as the nineteenth-century writers would call you), to stimulate you by every means to recognize God's presence in all of life.

> Holy, holy, holy is the LORD God of hosts;
> the whole earth is full of his glory. (Isa 6:3)

Brennan Manning's remark may stand as a gloss on what you have just read:

> Everything that is comes alive in Christ—who, as Chesterton reminded, is standing behind us. Everything—great, small, important, unimportant, distant, and near—has its place, its meaning, and its value. Through union with Him (as Augustine said, He is more intimate with us than we are with ourselves), nothing is wasted, nothing is missing. There is never a moment that does not carry eternal significance—no action that is sterile, no love that lacks fruition, and no prayer that is unheard.[4]

Here is another gloss by Flora Slossen Wuellner:

> "I am with you always." This is the eternal source of our daily life of prayer. This is no technique. We are in deep waters of the most intimate of all possible relationships that flow to us—forever fresh and new—from minute to minute. And, as all that lives, our relationship with the ultimate Person is organic, open-ended, unexpected, asymmetrical, and unfolding.[5]

Meanwhile, back to the Bible!

Jesus and the Really Real

When we come to the New Testament, we are overwhelmed with *signals* much as the people of his time were overwhelmed with reality, for here we see Jesus—the really real.

---

4. Manning, *Abba's Child*, as quoted in ibid., 174.
5. Wuellner, *Feed My Shepherds*, as quoted in ibid., 176.

> No one has ever seen God. It is God the only Son, who is close to the Father's heart, who has made him known. (John 1:18)

> "Whoever has seen me has seen the Father," Jesus said to Philip. (John 14:9)

> The apostle Paul says, "He is the image of the invisible God." (Col 1:15)

The chief aim of the four Gospels is to show us Jesus and thereby to show us the most we will ever know of God this side of glory. The focus of every Gospel passage is to reveal Jesus. They combine to show him as a bright light in the gloom and darkness of his times. For us the New Testament is a master *signal* containing the many, many *signals*. It is vastly important, but only because by the work of the Holy Spirit, the Bible shows us Jesus our Lord and Savior, and through him our Father the Lord God.

I am fascinated by the Gospel accounts of Jesus' actions, his relationships with a wide variety of people, his teachings and the way he spoke and lived them. And so are most people who read the Gospels with even a minimum of attention. There is no section of Scripture that is not a deliberate *signal* to show us more than first meets the ear and startles the imagination. The birth narratives with their striking accounts of angels visiting a young girl, of an old man struck dumb, of an old woman who haunted the temple and prophesied, of a visit of Eastern astrologers, of the birth of a baby in a stable. This is not just the stuff of children's drama at Christmas time. These are the magnificent, odd and unusual break-ins of an otherwise invisible reality, a visit from the universe next door, we might say. And they are only harbingers. Two Gospels pay little attention to them because what comes when the child is a man beggars all comparison. The boy who at age twelve astonishes the biblical scholars becomes, over a decade later, the man who fulfills the ancient prophecies thus changing *signs* into *reality*. He will challenge the accepted meaning of the Scriptures, sweep through Palestine, casting out demons, healing the sick, changing ordinary water used for ritual foot washing into gourmet wine, walking on the lake, declaring himself the One who is to come from God to redeem his people, thus infuriating the religious leaders, and frustrating the government. He will be crucified, die, rise from the dead, ascend to heaven, and, in short, turn the world upside down.

We could consider in detail any of these aspects of Jesus' life and teaching. Each would count as a *signal of transcendence*. But I have chosen an event that Mark places early in his Gospel. It has drama, conflict and resolution, and it leaves the people involved astonished. It can leave us astonished today.

Jesus, Four Men and a Paralytic

> When he returned to Capernaum after some days, it was reported that he was at home. So many gathered around that there was no longer room for them, not even in front of the door; and he was speaking the word to them. Then some people came, bringing to him a paralyzed man, carried by four of them. And when they could not bring him to Jesus because of the crowd, they removed the roof above him; and after having dug through it, they let down the mat on which the paralytic lay. When Jesus saw their faith, he said to the paralytic, "Son, your sins are forgiven." Now some of the scribes were sitting there, questioning in their hearts, "Why does this fellow speak in this way? It is blasphemy! Who can forgive sins but God alone?" At once Jesus perceived in his spirit that they discussing these questions among themselves; and he said to them, "Why do you raise such questions in your hearts? Which is easier, to say to the paralytic, 'Your sins are forgiven,' or to say, 'Stand up and take your mat and walk'? But so that you may know that the Son of Man has authority on earth to forgive sins"—he said to the paralytic—"I say to you, stand up and take your mat and go to your home." And he stood up, and immediately took the mat and went out before all of them; so that they were all amazed and glorified God, saying, "We have never seen anything like this!" (Mark 2:1–12)

The richness of this story comes to us in very few words. In modern parlance it is shorter than a short short story, but it bristles with *signals*. First, the story is set in time and space; this is not a legend or a myth; these events really happened. Four people take special pains to bring a paralytic to Jesus. Their goal is to bring their friend to the newly famous healer. What does Jesus say?

First surprise: He says absolutely nothing about the man's physical problem. He responds as if the paralytic were standing before him hale and hearty and addresses him, not his disease. Jesus, of course, is not unaware or unconcerned. Rather, this was Jesus' way of shifting the event from the agenda of the paralytic and the four friends to his own primary mission and, in reality, to the paralytic's main problem as well, though the paralytic and his four friends didn't know it.

Second surprise: Jesus responded to the faith of the four friends, not to the faith of the paralytic. We don't see the paralytic's faith until he obeys Jesus, gets up, and walks away. Then we see his faith in action. The four friends had faith that Jesus would heal; the paralytic had faith that Jesus had healed.

Third surprise: The words Jesus spoke went directly to the heart of the matter. Like all people, the paralytic was a sinner needing forgiveness. So Jesus simply said, "Son" (thus holding him to his breast as one of his family), "Your sins are forgiven."

Fourth surprise: We are not told how the man first responded. Did he say to himself, "Hey! What's going on here? I want to stop suffering from paralysis!" My guess is that he hardly had time to think anything before Jesus made his second move. Maybe he saw right away that Jesus had not only solved his real problem, but that forgiving his sin was everything he really needed anyway. Maybe the story is not about the man or his healing or his being forgiven but about Jesus himself. Ah, that fits! That's the surprise.

Certainly we do know this: Jesus was hunting bigger game than a cure for paralysis. He knew by declaring the man's sins forgiven that he was encroaching on the territory of the priests. No prophet of Israel was in a position to forgive sins. God alone could do that, and this wasn't the way it was done. Forgiveness of sin involved the ritual sacrifices at the Temple; it was done within a religious system with which Jesus, like most prophets of Israel who were outside the priestly class, had nothing to do. If anyone in the room knew that Jesus had stepped outside the bounds of religious propriety it would be the scribes. They, however, are not the ones to break the silence and declare Jesus a blasphemer. Jesus responds to their concerns before they can openly articulate them.

Remember what sin is. Sin is basically a rebellion against God—a transgression of God's plans and goals for our lives. Sin often involves our harm to others, our lack of kindness, our breaking of relationships with our families, our greed and self-centeredness. But fundamentally our sin is about our rebellion against God. What is wrong with our behavior is that it does not reflect the holiness and purity and perfection of him in whose image we have been created. If we are to be forgiven, we must be forgiven by the one against whom we have rebelled. We need forgiveness not only from each other; we need forgiveness from God. That is, the religious leaders are right: Only God can forgive sins. In Jesus Christ God is present both in his judgment and his mercy.

Fifth surprise: Jesus is claiming to have God's ability to forgive sins. If he does not have this authority, he really is blaspheming. As C. S. Lewis would say, he is either a very bad man—a liar, perhaps, or a lunatic—or the Lord. Early in his ministry Jesus poses this dilemma (or trilemma) and never ceases to add to its force.

Sixth surprise: Jesus links his power to heal with his power to forgive sins. As Mark puts it early in his Gospel, Jesus came "proclaiming the good news of God and saying 'The time is fulfilled and the kingdom of God has come near; repent, and believe the good news'" (Mark 1:14). His mission involved the penetration of the realm of God into what we see as the ordinary workaday world. And so it is in this house filled with people from all around Capernaum. The kingdom of God, God's reign over the entire scope of human existence, both spiritual and physical health and welfare, is being realized in this time and this space.

Finally, no surprise: Everyone was amazed. No one had seen this sort of thing before. The *signal* of Jesus' healing had become the *reality* of God's compassionate forgiving presence. Justice and peace have kissed (Ps 85:10). Here, indeed, is transcendence—much, much more than meets the eye and even the imagination.

Jesus and His Parables

If one of the distinguishing features of a *signal* is the suddenness with which we perceive it as a *signal*, then Jesus' parables are certainly *signals*. If they bring to our consciousness the presence of more than meets the eye or our normal material understanding, they are *signals of transcendence*.[6] Many of Jesus' parables meet these criteria. Certainly this is true of the Parable of Good Samaritan.

> Just then a lawyer stood up to test Jesus. "Teacher," he said, "what must I do to inherit eternal life?" He said to him, "What

---

6. Novelist Ron Hansen says, Jesus' "favorite method of teaching seems to have been in parables because stories so well fuse the feelings of immanence and transcendence that are the two primary qualities of religious experience" (*Stay*, 21). I would say that parables fuse these feelings more than any other form of story.

is written in the law? What do you read there?" He answered, "You shall love the Lord your God with all your heart, and with all your soul, and with all your strength, and with all your mind; and your neighbor as yourself." And he said to him, "You have given the right answer; do this, and you will live."

But wanting to justify himself, he asked Jesus, "And who is my neighbor?" Jesus replied, "A man was going down from Jerusalem to Jericho, and fell into the hands of robbers, who stripped him, beat him, and went away, leaving him half dead. Now by chance a priest was going down that road; and when he saw him, he passed by on the other side. So likewise a Levite, when he came to the place and saw him, passed by on the other side. But a Samaritan while traveling came near him; and when he saw him, he was moved with pity. He went to him and bandaged his wounds, having poured oil and wine on them. Then he put him on his own animal, brought him to an inn, and took care of him. The next day he took out two dinarii, gave them to the innkeeper, and said, 'Take care of him; and when I come back, I will repay you whatever more you spend.' Which of these three, do you think, was a neighbor to the man who fell into the hands of the robbers?" He said, "The one who showed him mercy." Jesus said to him, "Go and do likewise." (Luke 10:25–37)

This is such a familiar story that readers today may miss the clever way Jesus often teaches more than we may first be aware. Did Jesus teach the lawyer something the lawyer did not know? Yes, but not what it first may appear to be. Let's look closely at the structure of the story.

What did you grasp as Jesus' main point? If someone were to ask you how Jesus answered the lawyer's question, how would you answer? Did he tell him to love God fully and love his neighbor like himself? Not really. He asked the lawyer what the lawyer himself thought, and then he approved of it. No surprise here. But this did not satisfy the lawyer. Why? because the lawyer had asked his question in order to test Jesus. He wanted to pose a question that would catch Jesus in a dilemma so that Jesus would either show that he didn't know the answer or that Jesus' answer was so outside the bounds of orthodox thought, he would fall afoul of the Jewish heresy patrol. But he had a limited way to proceed. He could not ask who is God or what does it mean to love him. That was too clear. He had to find a term that was somewhat ambiguous. Ah, he thought, *neighbor* should do nicely. So he asked, "Who is my neighbor?" He surely did not anticipate Jesus' response.

Jesus, however, was not baffled. As in the case of the paralytic, the lawyer's problem was not in his knowledge of the law but in what it might mean for his own life. The lawyer asked, "Who is my neighbor?" in order to escape having to obey the law's full implication. He expected Jesus to limit "neighbor" to one of his own kind, someone who lived nearby or belonged to the same Jewish clan. He did not expect Jesus to include the Romans or Greeks, and certainly not the Samaritans.

Jesus, however, wanted to do more than provide a technical, clerical answer to a typical lawyer class-conscious question. So he told a story. The hero turns out not to be one of the privileged classes of Jewish society but a person from the despised half-breed class of Samaritans. "Who proves neighborly?" he asked. Now the lawyer was trapped.

Jesus didn't ask the lawyer to answer the question the lawyer had actually asked. He asked a more appropriate question: Not "Who is my neighbor?" but "What does it mean to be a neighbor?" The issue was not what sorts of folk he had to love like himself, but what kind of person he had to be to fulfill the ultimate meaning of the law. "What does it mean to be a neighbor?" shifts the burden away from intellectual judgment (or casuistic reasoning). The burden of the law is on each person who tries to live by the law. It is the *virtue* of neighborliness that is at stake, not the logic-chopping identification of the people toward whom anyone is to be neighborly. I am—all of us are—to to be neighborly, no matter toward whom, period! The identification of one's neighbors is not relevant.

But think again about that second part of the law. One is to love one's neighbor as one's self. Put it personally: I love myself. This is a given. So if I am to love others as myself, I must first love myself and then treat others as I treat myself. That treatment I would like for myself is what it is to be neighborly. In other words, first I am a neighbor; then I treat others equally as neighbors. The point was already in the law. Whatever else Jesus did in responding to the lawyer, he remained completely within the framework of the ancient texts from Deuteronomy and Leviticus (Deut 6:5 and Lev 19:18). He unlocked the meaning already there and placed the lawyer, his disciples and even himself in the position of being responsible neighbors, neighbors who loved other neighbors without regard to class.

Jesus' rhetorical move was a brilliant *signal of transcendence*. The lawyer would go away, having his whole "testing" attitude revealed as being unneighborly. The lawyer was a sinner by his own standard. Only his own perversity or spiritual blindness would keep him from self-condemnation. He stood in the position of needing forgiveness. He needed Jesus as a savior, not just as a teacher. Did the lawyer realize this? We do not know.

Why would Luke, the storyteller of the whole story, not give us some indication? Because, I think, he was doing the same thing Jesus did—letting us realize that as readers we too may be categorizing people as neighbors and not-neighbors. In fact, we are off base even when we say that the meaning of the story is that everyone is our neighbor and we should love them. Quite simply, that is not the meaning at all. If we say it is, we buy into the intellectual casuistry of the scribe. So, since we are likely to think that the meaning of the story is that everyone is our neighbor, our fresh reading of the story acts as a *signal of transcendence*—especially if it leads each of us to ask ourselves what it means be a neighbor.

Notice, too, that this means we have to act like the despised Samaritan or maybe like someone in our community or society whose religion is not ours but who behaves neighborly anyway. Christians, consider this when you are "neighbored" by a Hindu, a Muslim, an atheist, a New Ager, a . . .

We know, by the way, that Jesus did not agree with either the Samaritan religious system or the ultimate completeness of the Jewish system (see John 4:19–26). But when he met the Samaritan woman at the well outside Jericho, he treated her in neighborly fashion and she responded in kind. Then for two days Jesus' disciples and the people of the village treated each other as neighbors and many came to believe in Jesus (John 4:27–42). *Signals of transcendence* can lead to personal and even societal transformation.

The Apostle Paul

Two events in the life of the Apostle Paul come to mind immediately–Paul's experience on the road to Damascus and his visit to the "third heaven." The initial signal event in Paul's conversion was, of course, his encounter with the risen Christ as he was on the way to Damascus to persecute the Christians. Luke tells the story:

> Now as he was going along and approaching Damascus, suddenly a light from heaven flashed around him. He fell to the ground and heard a voice saying to him, "Saul, Saul, why do you

persecute me?" He asked, "Who are you, Lord?" The reply came, "I am Jesus, whom you are persecuting. But get up and enter the city, and you will be told what you are to do." The men who were traveling with him stood speechless because they heard the voice but saw no one. Saul got up from the ground, and though his eyes were open, he could see nothing; so they led him by the hand and brought him into Damascus. For three days he was without sight, and neither ate nor drank. (Acts 9:3–9)

Meanwhile, a "disciple in Damascus named Ananias" received a vision and instructions from "the Lord" to go where Paul was staying and "lay hands" on Paul so that he could get his sight back. After the Lord assured Ananias that he would be safe and told him that Saul would be a great missionary to the Gentiles, Ananias did as he was told. Paul's sight was restored; he was baptized, received the Holy Spirit, and was called by Christ to be a witness to the Gentiles. This is the beginning of the drama of early Christian history—the spread of the Christian faith throughout the Roman Empire.

If repetition is a clue to the importance of this event, then this one is surely important. In Acts 22:1–22, Paul recounts the story to the Jewish and Roman authorities, to the consternation of both; Paul spent two years in captivity as a result. Later he tells the story to King Agrippa (Acts 26:2–23). Paul has no qualms about citing his personal experience as a part of his reasons for his own faith and behavior and for its relevance to varied audiences.

A Visit to the Third Heaven

In 2 Corinthians 12, Paul justifies his calling to be an apostle by listing his qualifications while, at the same time, making light of them, claiming as he does so that he is acting like a fool. He would much rather boast of his weaknesses and the suffering that has come to him by being an apostle than of his strengths and the glory they might seem to bring to him.

When he gets to "revelations of the Lord," he is especially reticent. He both wants to claim that he has them, but that he has nothing personal to boast about. Here is Paul in his own rather odd words:

It is necessary to boast; nothing is to be gained by it, but I will go on to visions and revelations of the Lord. I know a person in Christ who fourteen years ago was caught up to the third heaven—whether in the body or out of the body I do not know; God knows. And I know that such a person—whether in the body or out of the body I do not know; God knows—was caught up into Paradise and heard things that are not to be told, that no mortal is permitted to repeat. On behalf of such a one I will boast, but on my own behalf I will not boast, except of my weaknesses. But if I wish to boast, I will not be a fool, for I will be speaking the truth. But I refrain from it, so that no one may think better of me than what is seen in me or heard from me, even considering the exceptional character of the revelations. Therefore, to keep me from being too elated, a thorn was given me in the flesh, a messenger of Satan to torment me, to keep me from being too elated. Three times I appealed to the Lord about this, that it would leave me, but he said to me, "My grace is sufficient for you, for power is made perfect in weakness." So, I will boast all the more gladly of my weaknesses, so that the power of Christ may dwell in me. Therefore I am content with weaknesses, insults, hardships, persecutions, and calamities for the sake of Christ; for whenever I am weak, then I am strong. (2 Cor 12:1–10)

What shall we make of this piece of tangled rhetoric? Is he himself the man he knew fourteen years ago? Is he boasting by claiming not to be boasting? What is Paradise or the "third heaven"? Was he in the body or not? What did he see and hear? Was the experience important? To whom? What does this experience mean to us? I have puzzled over this, and here are my answers:

1. Yes, Paul is the man who had the experience of the third heaven.

2. No, he is not boasting, just trying to let people know he has had an experience that is very unusual and important, but only to him.

3. Paradise is probably the "third" and the highest of three heavens, likely the heaven to which the soul would ascend at death.[7]

4. Only God knows whether he was in or out of the body. Speculation about similarity with accounts of present so-called out-of-the-body experiences is just speculation.

5. We neither know nor can we know what he saw or heard.

---

7. Keener, *Bible Background Commentary*, 514.

6. This experience was important only to Paul. But the fact that he has had such an experience and will not speak about it means that he does not see it as a part of the gospel nor his justification for believing the gospel.

7. Paul did not seek these experiences. Rather he distrusted "elation" (ecstatic experiences) in his own life. The power in his life did not derive from his character but from the presence of Christ and his Spirit in his life, regardless of his personal experience of that power.

8. Paul's spare narrative is for us a caution not to take our own religious experiences as indications of the exalted nature of our own character. Pride lurks dangerously behind every profound experience of the holy.

I think we should take the seventh and eighth of these conclusions seriously as we contemplate the logical force of the many accounts of ecstatic religious experience we hear from others. These experiences may get in the way of honoring Christ himself.

Paul's account of his vision of Christ at his conversion is very different. This life-transforming personal experience was important in his presentation of the gospel. Some of us, including me, are reticent to tell our own sometimes dramatic conversion stories because we recognize our experience is only ours. It ought not have much compelling logical force; after all, my experience is only mine. Still everyone is likely to have some rather interesting elements in recounting their coming to faith. This can have rather compelling rhetorical power. Because we are all equally human, we may be surprised how much our lives are like the lives of others and thus how likely our own early encounters with Christ will stir a response in both the mental and emotional side of those to whom we proclaim Christ's power to save.

And On and On

Why stop here with examples of *signals of transcendence* in Scripture? No specific reason. We could go on and on and on. Of course there is a way we can do that. I can simply stop typing out stories and commentaries, you can simply stop reading this book, and both of us can pick up our Bibles and begin anywhere.

By the way, every day we should do that—that is, stop what we might well be doing, read the Bible, recognize and listen to the *signals*, glory in realizing the Presence of God and act on what we come to perceive. Yes, that's what we can do. Why not do it?

3

Am I Stepping on God?

A Philosophical Theology of Transcendence

O Thou, far off and here, whole and broken,
Who in necessity and in bounty wait,
Whose truth is light and dark, mute though spoken,
By Thy wide grace show me Thy narrow gate.

—WENDELL BERRY, "TO THE HOLY SPIRIT"

As will soon become apparent, *signals of transcendence* do not wear their philosophy or their theology on their sleeve. They are experienced by people of almost every intellectual and religious persuasion—theistic, deistic, pantheistic, panentheistic, even atheistic. As certain pointers to the biblical God, by themselves they are inadequate. Still, if we are committed to a Christian understanding of them, we need some explanation for both their ambiguity and their existence as pointing toward transcendence. We have that explanation in the traditional Christian doctrine of God.

I cannot give here even a summary of the full Christian doctrine of God. That would take us into a vast array of biblical texts and theological explanations. We can, however, focus on the essence of the issue.

The essence of theology relevant to *signals of transcendence* is this: God is both *transcendent* and *immanent*.[1] His utter otherness is at one with his utter thisness, his distance with his presence, his holiness with his mercy. Rather than beginning with a profound explanation of this seeming paradox or perhaps, some would say, genuine contradiction, let me recount my wife's encounter with my daughter's puzzled question as a five-year-old.

Standing in the kitchen of our four-room graduate-student apartment, Carol was curious. She believed there was a God, but she wanted to know more about him. At the time she and her mother were in the kitchen.

"Where is God," Carol asked.

"He's everywhere," her mother replied.

"Is he in the bedroom?"

"Yes."

"Is he in the living room?'

"Yes."

Carol began to look puzzled. "Is he here in the kitchen?"

"Yes," her mother repeated.

Carol looked around, eyes widened with awe. "Am I stepping on God?

My wife does not remember her own reply, but the answer now has to be "No, not really, not as you and I are in this room and as the room and we are part of his creation. But, Yes, God is here in a different way than you and I and the floor. He is here in a more basic dimension." Of course, if my wife had said this, Carol would have been just as puzzled as before, probably more so. The whole dialogue, however, can stand for us as a *signal of transcendence* that can lead us to pose a Christian understanding of *transcendence* itself, one that involves the *immanence* of God as coexistent with his *transcendence*.

Help from Hans Küng and Donald Bloesch

I normally do not consult Hans Küng for answers to my theological puzzlements, and I normally don't read atheist philosopher J. L. Mackie,

---

1. Hammond says, "Christianity is alone in uniting in its description of God, His 'transcendence' . . . and His immanence" (*In Understanding*, 44). Hutchinson agrees; see "Transcendence" in *Handbook*, 364.

but one of Mackie's essays appears in Christopher Hitchens's collection of arguments for atheism, and I was reading them to find how atheist philosophers might deal, as they sometimes do, with *signals of transcendence.*[2] Can I conclude that such a happenstance is not really coincidental? Maybe it is one of God's little ways of impressing us with his care for us and his creation. Perhaps this encounter with Christian theology through an anti-Christian critique was itself a *signal.*

In any case, Mackie rejects Küng's version of Christian theism, but I found Küng's explanation of *transcendence* and *immanence* both clear and convincing. Here is that explanation:

> God is in this world, and this world is in God. There must be a uniform understanding of reality. God is not only a (supreme) finite—as a part of reality—alongside finite things. He is in fact the infinite in the finite, transcendence in immanence, the absolute in the relative. It is precisely as the absolute that God can enter into a relationship with the world and man: a relationship not in the sense of weakness, of dependence, of relativity in a bad sense, but of strength, of unlimited freedom, of absolute sovereignty. God is therefore the absolute who includes and creates relativity, who, precisely as free, makes possible and actualizes relationships: God as the absolute-relative, here-hereafter, transcendent-immanent, all-embracing and all-permeating most real reality in the heart of things, in man, in the history of mankind, in the world.
>
> The Absolute in the world is therefore at once sustaining the world, maintaining the world and escorting the world: at once depth, center and height of world and man.
>
> That is, a world-immanent world preeminence of God: a modern, secular understanding of God.
>
> For man's being and action, this means that God is the close-distant, secular-nonsecular God, who precisely as sustaining, upholding us in all life and movement, failure and falling, is also always present and encompassing us. "God is beyond in the midst of our life," as Bonhoeffer puts it.[3]

2. Mackie, "Conclusions and Implications," 246–66.

3. Dietrich Bonhoeffer, *Letters and Papers*, 155, quoted by Küng, *Does God Exist?*, 185–86. It may seem strange for Küng to call this view of God "a modern secular" understanding. But Küng was writing in response to Bonhoeffer's much misunderstood concept of *secular* that had caused some theologians to talk about the "death of God" in a way totally out of sync with traditional theology. Neither Küng nor Bonhoeffer should be interpreted as doing that. In the present context, *secular* means within the frame of human beings' (Jesus being one) existence as "human." Actually, I did not

Theologian Donald Bloesch says something similar.[4] Like Küng, he begins his explanation of *transcendence* and *immanence* by recounting the way these concepts have been understood within Western philosophy and theology. Along the way, both point out when and where the church and its most influential thinkers have gone beyond the bounds set by Scripture. Bloesch sees two equal and opposite errors: deism overemphasizing the otherness and distance of God and pantheism overemphasizing God's presence or even his identity with nature. He calls his own view "dynamic transcendence." In his words,

> We must avoid the Charybdis of deism and the Scylla of pantheism by affirming a dynamic biblical theism that does justice to both God's otherness and his personalness. God is present to us but not inherent in us. He upholds us but is not identical with us. God is both the Wholly Other and the infinitely Near. He is both God transcendent and God *with* and *for* us. . . .
>
> If we conceive of God as infinitely other, we must at the same time envision him as infinitely close. If we picture him as wholly transcendent, we must at the same time allow for the truth that he is radically immanent in the sense of being present with us and for us. But he is never immanent without being essentially transcendent, just as he does not remain transcendent without making himself for our sakes immanent. God's immanence is an act of his freedom, not a quality of his being. Just as he freely relates to his creation, so he is also free to withdraw from his creation.[5]

Perhaps the simplest formulation of the biblical notion of the relationship between *transcendence* and *immanence* comes from John Henry Cardinal Newman:

> [Even though God as Creator is infinitely separate from his creation,] yet He has so implicated Himself with it, and taken it into His very bosom, by His presence in it, His providence over it, His impressions upon it, and His influences through it, that we cannot truly or fully contemplate it without contemplating Him.[6]

find anything in this essay that suggested how Mackie himself might deal with *signals of transcendence*.

4. Bloesch, *God*, 79–102.

5. Ibid., 99.

6. Newman, *Idea*, 37.

In short, the God of the Bible encompasses the totality of ultimate reality both as (1) uncreated, self-existent Creator, and (2) different from and continuously and intimately present in and to his creation.[7] This notion of God as "prime reality" is the ontological basis for some experiences that seem to point to a transcendent aspect of reality.

It also explains why the existence of God as the transcendent is not always obvious. God in his absolute sovereignty as creator can withdraw the obviousness of his presence as often and as long as he wishes. He can appear, as Pascal said, the *deus absconditus*—the hidden God—for those who are in moral or spiritual rebellion or for any other reason, as he does, for example, with Job.[8] Or he can appear as the awesome and unapproachable as he does to Pascal in his night of "fire."[9]

> If this religion boasted that it had a clear sight of God and plain and manifest evidence of his existence, it would be an effective objection to say that there is nothing to be seen in the world which proves him so obviously. But since on the contrary it says that men are in darkness and remote from God, that he has hidden himself from their understanding, that this is the very name which he gives himself in Scripture: *Deus absconditus* [the hidden God] [Is 45:15]; and, in a word, if it strives equally to establish these two facts: that God has appointed visible signs in the Church so that he shall be recognized by those who genuinely seek him, and that he has none the less hidden them in such a way that he will only be perceived by those who seek him with all their heart, then what advantage can they derive when, unconcerned to seek the truth as they profess to be, they protest that nothing shows it to them? For the obscurity in which they find themselves, and which they use as an objection against the Church, simply establishes one of the things the Church maintains without affecting the other, and far from proving their teaching false, confirms it.[10]

7. Augustine opens his *Confessions* with a long and profound meditation on God as both *transcendent* and *immanent*. Here is but a taste: ". . . you [my God] have made us for yourself, and our heart is restless until it rests in you . . . How shall I call upon my God, my God and Lord? Surely when I call on him, I am calling on him to come into me. But what place is there in me where my God can enter into me? 'God made heaven and earth' (Gen 1:1). Where may he come to me? Lord my God, is there any room in me which can contain you?" *Confessions* 1.1.2 (3–4).

8. Pascal, *Pensées*, no. 427 (155) and no. 781 (263).

9. Pascal, "Memorial," *Pensées*, 309–10.

10. Pascal, *Pensées*, no. 427 (155). Isaiah 45:1 reads: "Truly, you are a God who hides himself, O God of Israel, the Savior."

Küng and Bloesch draw their views of God from the rich lode of revelation of God in the Old and New Testaments and from the massive and complex reflections of the great theologians and Western philosophers before them. Küng's summary is a long list of contrasting, if not contradictory, characteristics that have been a part of Christian and Jewish theological interest for centuries. For our purposes, however, the pair of contrasts that are most significant are *transcendent* and *immanent*. Let's examine these terms separately.

Immanence and Transcendence

Immanence

To be *immanent* is to be here, at hand, present. The *immanent* need not be seen or seeable, heard or hearable, tasted or tasteable, felt or feelable, smelled or smellable, but it must be here. We may not have any sensation in the direct presence of electricity, but we have learned to detect its physical presence by instruments. Something immanent may be difficult to detect by any means we now have at hand. Subatomic, even atomic, parts were undetected until only a few years ago. Even now it takes special equipment to detect them. But they are here; they are immanent, nonetheless. For centuries there were those who thought that something like what we now know as atoms existed, but even our best conception of them were incomplete and inaccurate. There may be many things that are immanent that we do not now, or perhaps ever will, detect.

On a different, some might call a higher, plane ideas are immanent. They are a product of the workings of our mind. One knows that thoughts exist by their immediate detection. Descartes even "thought" that he could know that he existed as an independent being because he could immediately detect the presence of his thought. His famous formulation, "I think; therefore I am," whether understood as an argument or an intuition, may not carry a philosopher very far toward solving the riddle of knowledge, but it is an instance of our understanding that ideas can be immanent. They exist and we indubitably detect them by what we assume, at least at the moment we detect our thought.

We need not solve the mind-brain problem. Is the mind more than or different from the brain, a view held by most people usually without question? Or is the mind merely a function of the organic machinery of the brain? Either way, ideas are not necessarily in and of themselves transcendent. Even the idea of *transcendence* is immanent. For one thing, it leaves its tracks in documents like the one I am now typing and you are now reading.

Even what we sometimes call extrasensory perception may be immanent, if what we mean is that some of our actual perceptions seem to have no material explanation. Take the very rare but sudden instantaneous perception that someone emotionally close to us has died, say, on the battlefield thousands of miles away. Often these intuitions prove incorrect, but sometimes they don't. Maybe something "out of this world" has brought us the message, but maybe not. Maybe such ESP is a part of the workings of our material being. Maybe not. So there is much that happens in the immanent world that we may have never dreamed has or could exist. So immanence does not need to be known and maybe will never be known. The created physical order is far more complex than we can yet—or perhaps ever—know. Moreover, as Os Guinness has said, "There is more to human knowing than human knowing will ever know."

Transcendence

To be *transcendent* is to be apart from and other than what we normally understand as material or natural. We have no difficulty in believing, for example, that any being worthy enough to bear the label God must be *transcendent*. He or she or it or they must be of a different sort than even the most noble—the most wise, the most loving, the most good—of us. A god must have some attributes that are simply beyond any of the characteristics of which humans or animals or inanimate things are capable. Even a stone idol to which we might pray is more than mere stone if only in the mind of the worshiper. A god may be in many places at one time, or know more than a human can know, or be able to manipulate things in this world, or appear as human or animal or any *thing* if the god wishes. If a being can't do at least some of these things, it is not a god.

Often we use the word *spirit* to designate a being who is lesser than a god, perhaps if it can only do some of those god-like, unnatural things. It, too, is *transcendent* though, except as the Holy Spirit, it does not attain the status of a god. Many people believe such beings exist. They are labeled variously *angels*, *demons*, *jinns*, *spirits*, *ghosts*, and in other languages a host of names.

Immanent or Transcendent

Beyond what I've written above, things get sticky. We experience and speak of beauty, morality, love, hatred, intentions, design, wisdom, frustration, anger. Are any of these more than *immanent* in and of themselves? If so, do any of these require something *transcendent* to explain what they are, something more than is merely physical or merely an idea? If, for example, we notice and identify the moral value of *tender loving care*, can there be such a thing as that without something transcendent lying at the foundation of its existence? Is *beauty* only in the eye of the beholder? Or *tender loving care* only in the perception of the care giver or the care receiver; that is, is it only material behavior that we label *loving*? Or is *love* more than a physical sensation or a category into which some physical actions fall when we try to label them? More generally, is any *value*—love, wisdom, compassion, generosity, benevolence, even the negative *values* of hatred and miser—more than an immanent category of immanent thought? Or is *value* merely a subjective mental conception used only to organize immanent thoughts? Does *value* exist if there is no one to recognize it?

An analogy here may clarify the issue: If a tree falls in the forest uninhabited by a hearing-sensitive animal, does it make a sound? Yes, it sets up vibrations, but does it make a sound? Or does a rainbow exist if there is no one to see it? The question is as old as Plato, and the answer can only be given by assuming a larger framework of ideas, in short, a worldview.

Those who are atheists or naturalists must conclude that everything that exists is immanent. There is nothing other than brute reality—star stuff in its many constantly evolving manifestations. *Beauty, love, mercy, goodness, justice, intentionality, design*: these are all immanent, explicable, if explicable at all, in terms of physical stuff.

People holding most other Western worldviews believe that the physical word is undergirded by something else, something more fundamental, something "otherly"—*God*, the *gods, spirit, mind*—that is more than and beyond the physical. The worldviews of primal religions—so-called pagan religions—side with the West. Eastern worldviews introduce the concepts of illusion or samsara to explain notions indicating *value*, removing them from any transcendent existence in a different way from naturalists. All is One, say Hindus. Differences of truth or falsity, here or there, value itself (the difference between good and bad): these are all illusions. Zen Buddhists say that all of these so-called elements of human understanding do not actually exist anywhere beyond the musings of human beings who themselves are not even selves with valuable individuality. Humans are in some sense beyond analysis Not-Selves; they live in a reality that is utterly indeterminate and unidentifiable about which nothing can be conceived or said.

An Artist's Vision of Immanence

Annie Dillard, a writer whose major work, *Pilgrim at Tinker Creek*, we will examine later, is obsessed by the first fundamental worldview question: What is the really real?

In her short book *Holy the Firm* she turns this question over and over. She reflects on raw beautiful but cruel nature, agonizes over children who are violently burned by accident, and glories over the land, the sea, and a spate of islands in northwest Washington state. How does everything fit together? Is there a pattern hidden in the chaos of human time and the material universe of almost empty space? Is there a God? Who is he? How does he relate to the world he has created? Is he so *immanent* that reality is flat and Christ and his creation are one? Or is Christ so *transcendent* that he barely touches the top of a long hierarchy of matter?

Her suggestions are "only ideas, by the single handful." But they finally rest in what she calls *Holy the Firm*—a highly metaphoric conception of created reality. It would probably satisfy no philosopher or theologian, and may connect only with readers with poetic imagination. But perhaps she can help us to grasp, even with slippery fingers, something of the essence of reality as they see God's "right hand is clenching, calm, and round the exploding left hand of Holy the Firm."[11]

11. Dillard, *Holy*, 71.

Biblical Theology

We have seen the Scriptures, both Old and New Testaments, giving countless examples of *signals of transcendence*, stories demonstrating the interface between our material world and the spiritual or "otherly" world next door, a world so close that its presence is experienced both with and without surprise. We will now examine the "theological" or "philosophical" verbal revelations of reality's *immanent/transcendent* interface.

Old Testament

The most direct of these revelations is, I think, the glorious verses in Psalm 19, familiar to everyone who has been exposed for long to the Bible. They are the biblical cornerstone to this book.

> The heavens are telling the glory of God;
> and the firmament [dome of the heavens] proclaims his handiwork.
> Day to day pours forth speech,
> and night to night declares knowledge.
> There is no speech, nor are their words;
> their voice is not heard;
> yet their voice goes out through all the earth,
> and their words to the end of the world. (Ps 19:1–4)

This is an amazing text. The visible world, whatever it is, *speaks*. It proclaims *knowledge*. But it doesn't talk about itself, "Hey, look. I am here! Watch me!" It points beyond itself; it *declares* the glory, the magnificence, of God himself.

On a cloudless night as we lie on the dock of a lake in the North Woods far from city lights, a vast arena opens itself to us—beautiful, marvelous. Gazing into the firmament that in our scientific age we know as an almost infinite door into space, we marvel, we sigh, "Aaaah!" We stare, we ponder, we seem to see through and beyond the view before us. Its glory is staggering. And we say from the depth of our being, "How glorious you are, O God! O God! how glorious! O God . . ." And we forget about ourselves, our troubles, our earthly joys and sorrows. We sail into the heavens and we sink into the presence of the great Creator.

There is no speech, not even our own. Nonetheless, even without speech, without thought, we sense God's *transcendent* reality *immanent* in our world. This is what Küng means when he says, "*God is in this world, and this world is in God. There must be a uniform understanding of reality. God is not only a (supreme) finite—as a part of reality—alongside finite things. He is in fact the infinite in the finite, transcendence in immanence, the absolute in the relative.*"[12]

Psalm 19:5–6 continues its theology of *transcendence*:

> In the heavens he has set a tent for the sun,
> which comes out like a bridegroom from his wedding canopy,
>   and like a strong man runs its course with joy.
> Its rising is from the end of the heavens,
>   and its circuit to the end of them;
>   and nothing is hid from its heat.

The *transcendent* God as creator has fashioned the immanent world in which he has put his immanent sun that we experience directly anywhere and everywhere we are on earth. We live in God's complex cosmos of interpenetrating immanence and transcendence.

Following this text is the psalmist's account of God's self-revelation through Scripture. His laws, decrees, commandments and ordinances are conveyed through speech. They too are glorious—"More to be desired are they than gold, / even much fine gold; / sweeter also than honey, and drippings of the honeycomb" (Ps 19:10). These verbal revelations have a *transcendent* source with an *immanent* presence. They speak of more than can be known by our unaided human minds. But with our God-created human minds listening to these Scriptures, we can be "warned; / in keeping them there is great reward" (Ps 19:11). Psalm 19 ends then with the implications of God's *transcendence* and *immanence* worked out in the ongoing life of the psalmist. It is a prayer everyone can and should pray:

> Let the words of my mouth and the meditation of my heart
>   be acceptable to you,
>   O LORD, my rock and my redeemer.

---

12. Küng, *Does God Exist?*, 185.

New Testament

Near the beginning of his Gospel, Mark announces its central theme:

> Now after John was arrested, Jesus came to Galilee, proclaiming
> the good news of God, and saying, "The time is fulfilled, and the
> kingdom of God has come near; repent, and believe in the good
> news." (Mark 1:14)

"The kingdom of God"—the *transcendent* realm of God's rule over all of
reality—has in the presence of Jesus of Nazareth, approached the ordinary world of ancient Israel. The people of his time, then, observed in the
actions and *teachings* of Jesus the presence of the *transcendent* himself
and his sovereign rule. What is the character of the *transcendent*? Observe Jesus. Listen to what he says.

Do you want to see God? Then listen to Jesus' dialogue near the end
of Jesus' life on earth. He has just told his disciples that he is going away
to prepare a place for them. Here is an implicit reference to a *transcendent*
existence after death. Neither of the apostles, Thomas or Philip, understands. So Jesus explains, first to Thomas:

> Thomas said to him, "Lord, we do not know where you are go-
> ing. How can we know the way?" Jesus said to him, "I am the
> way, and the truth, and the life. No one comes to the Father
> except through me. If you know me, you will know my Father
> also. From now on you do know him and have seen him." (John
> 14:5–7)

Then he expands his explanation to Philip:

> Philip said to him, "Lord, show us the Father, and we will be
> satisfied." Jesus said to him, "Have I been with you all this time,
> Philip, and you still do not know me? Whoever has seen me
> has seen the Father. How can you say, 'Show us the Father'? Do
> you not believe that I am in the Father and the Father is in me?"
> (John 14:8–10)

Nowhere in the history of humankind is the *transcendent* God more revealed than in the *immanent* Jesus. Jesus is not a *signal of transcendence*.
He is the *transcendent* in the *immanent*. And in this section from John's
Gospel Jesus himself says this. For there in the midst of the disciples who
have walked and talked with Jesus for some three years, this man who
has never shown himself less than a man now makes a declaration about

himself that none of the disciples could have made about him. Yes, they have observed *signal* after *signal* (John's Gospel calls them *signs*) of his transcendence, but here is a direct philosophic statement: "I [this very material being you've seen and know well as a man in this material world] am in the Father [the one and only utterly holy and transcendent God] and he is in me." As Küng has said, "*He [God] is in fact the infinite in the finite, transcendence in immanence, the absolute in the relative.*"

Then, in this same upper room discourse, Jesus explains that he must go away, but that he will send an Advocate (NRSB) or Comforter (KJV) or Counselor (NIV), a Spirit of truth, to be with them and in them (John 14:16). In the traditional language of the early church, when the second person of the Trinity ceases to be materially present in the created physical world, the third person of the Trinity will become not only present (he has been present all along) but intimately present to each of Jesus' disciples. The *transcendent* will be *immanent* with and in Jesus' followers. The events of Pentecost (Acts 2:1–12) show something of the coming of the Holy Spirit predicted by Jesus. Speaking in foreign tongues and healing of the sick become the *signals of transcendence*, signals of the presence and the power of God.

Interestingly, what these *signals* point to is not so obvious that everyone interprets them properly. Those who were not within the community of Jesus' followers thought they were "filled with wine" (Acts 2:12). It took the Apostle Peter to explain what was happening and to refer to the Hebrew Scriptures as being fulfilled (Acts 2:14–21). Again, as Küng says, God as Holy Spirit is "*the transcendent in the immanent.*"

Human Transcendence

We, too, as human beings are open to the *transcendent* or put more accurately *self-transcendent*.[13] There is more to us than matter. Not only is there mind, but there is spirit. So to complete our theology of transcendence, we need to consider biblical anthropology.[14]

13. "Augustine was the first great thinker of the West to emphasize the reality of the transcendent self. He insisted that it was the self, or the 'I' which operated in all its faculties. 'It is I who remember in my memory, and understand in my understanding, and will in my will'" (Niebuhr, "The Self," 344).

14. For a more detailed exposition of biblical anthropology in general, see Sherlock, *The Doctrine of Humanity*; for a detailed study of the *image of God*, see Hoekema, *Created in God's Image*; for a focus on the spiritual character of human beings, see Macaulay and Barrs, *Being Human*.

The Image of God

The most fundamental statement about us as human is that we are all made in the image of God (Gen 1:26–28; 5:1–2; 9:6–7). We are like God, but not God. We display characteristics that no other creature displays at such a depth of profundity as we: We possess personality (i.e., self-awareness and self-determination), self-transcendence (ability, by the grace of God, to rise above our current sinful nature and be transformed ever more fully into the likeness of God), intelligence (capacity for reason and knowledge), morality (ability to recognize the difference between good and evil), gregariousness (desire and need for human companionship—community—especially represented by the "male and female"), and creativity (ability to imagine new things and endow old things with new significance). For most of these characteristics, *transcendence* over the otherwise strict cause-and-effect nature of the material world is necessary.

First, if we have *intelligence*, we must have the *transcendent* capacity to recognize when we have reached or come close to understanding things as they really are. If our minds consist only of the causes and effects of flowing blood and firing neurons, then our thoughts themselves are determined not by rational considerations but by the machinery of our brain. Reason itself requires *transcendence*, a freedom over what it is reasoning about.

Moreover, if we have the capacity to find *meaning* in life and make *significant decisions*, we must in some way *transcend* our selves. On this theologian Reinhold Niebuhr is eloquent:

> The problem of meaning, which is the basic problem of religion, transcends the ordinary rational problem of tracing the relation of things to each other, as the freedom of man's spirit transcends his rational faculties.
>
> This problem is not solved without the introduction of a principle of meaning which transcends the world of meaning to be interpreted. If some vitality of existence or even some subordinate principle of coherence is used as the principle of meaning, man is involved in idolatry. He lifts some finite and contingent element of existence into the eminence of the divine. He uses something which itself requires explanation as the ultimate principle of coherence and meaning. . . . The fact of

self-transcendence leads inevitably to the search for a god who transcends the world.[15]

Third, if we have the ability to be *moral*, we must be able, not only to make judgments about what we take to be good or bad behavior, but to recognize when something that *is* really *ought not* to be. The standards of *oughtness* by which we make those judgments must *transcend* both our own opinions (for our opinions differ widely) and the opinions of our community (for the opinions of communities differ widely). Morality itself requires *transcendence*, the existence of a "real" goodness.

Fourth, if we are able to be *creative*, we must be able to imagine the as yet unimagined. God, of course, has this limitless capacity. He can create the as yet uncreated. We can take his now created creation and fashion and refashion it, making it what it has not yet become. God's command to Adam and Eve in the garden confirms this: They were to tend the garden and bring it into a fuller expression of what the kingdom of God is intended to be. The botched job we have all made of this does not mean that our creative capacity has been removed. Creativity itself requires *transcendence*.

Body and Soul

From the very beginning, the Bible sees human beings as material but also as more than material. In Genesis 2 God takes dust, breathes into it the "breath of life" and "the man became a living being" (v. 7, NRSV) or "living soul" (KJV). As Old Testament scholar Derek Kidner says, "man neither 'has' a soul nor 'has' a body. . . . The basic truth is here: he is a unity."[16] This conception of body-soul unity (or body-soul-spirit unity) is the foundational notion of human beings through Scripture.[17] Still, the exact relationship between these terms—*body, soul, spirit*—has never been worked out to the agreement of most biblical scholars. It is certainly not necessary, however, for us to do so.[18] It is enough to say that human beings, like the rest of creation, not only have a *transcendent* origin,

15. Niebuhr, *Nature*, 162–65; quoted by Sommerville, *Decline*, 124–25.

16. Kidner, *Genesis*, 61.

17. E.g., 1 Thessalonians 5:23 refers to body, soul, and spirit, which theologians often interpret as body and soul (consisting of mind and spirit).

18. On the agreements and disagreements of biblical scholars, see Anderson, *On Being Human*, 207–14.

having been created by the *transcendent* creator, but their very nature is a complex of *transcendence* in *immanence* or the *immanent* interpenetrated by the *transcendent*.

New Testament texts that make reference to this complex unity are legion. We will look at two:

In Luke 8:40–42; 49–56, Jesus brings back to life a young girl who had died before he arrived at her bedside. It's too late, friends of the girl's father said. She has already died. But Jesus tells them that she's only sleeping. With three of his disciples and the girl's parents, he enters the room where she lay. "He took her hand and called out, 'Child, get up!' Her spirit returned and she got up at once. Then he directed them to give her something to eat." Then, showing that body and spirit were now again a unity, he asked her parents to give her something to eat.

In Luke 8:26–39, body, mind, and spirit are illustrated in the healing of the Gerasene Demoniac. "For a long time," Luke says, he had been possessed by demons. His raging through the tombs had only been partially controlled; he would break the shackles that the authorities used to keep him orderly. Then he met Jesus and Jesus cast out the demons. The townspeople heard about Jesus' power to cast out the man's demons, that they had entered a swine heard, and had then rushed into the nearby Lake of Galilee. "They found the man . . . at the feet of Jesus clothed and in his right mind" (Luke 8:35). The *transcendence* of the kingdom of God had become a reality in the event. Body, mind, spirit—the whole person of the demoniac—was brought into harmony with God's reign.

Sensus Divinitatis

In the above biblical anthropology, we have focused on ontology, *who* we are. But *who* we are enables us to *know* what we think we know. Being made in the *image of God* means that we have some God-like characteristics. God is the all-knowing knower of all things; so we can be the sometimes knowing knowers of some things. This ability includes the capacity to perceive through our five senses various aspects of the material world. Our reasoning ability allows us to understand what our senses perceive and to reason in both simple and complex ways toward a basic knowledge of our surrounding material world. Modern science is the capstone of the great monument we make to human reason.

Cardinal Christoph Schönborn puts it this way:

Next to the book of Bible, they [the scientists from Copernicus to Newton] recognize the book of creation, within which the Creator speaks to us in readable, perceptible language. What is overlooked in a material concept of science is the sense of wonder about the very readability of reality. Scientific exploration of nature is possible only because it gives us an answer. Nature is "built" such that our spirit can penetrate its structure and laws. . . .

The natural world is nothing less than a meditation between minds—the ultimate mind of the Creator and our limited human minds. . . . God speaks the language of his creation, and our spirit, which is likewise his creation, is able to perceive it, to hear it, to comprehend it.[19]

How, then, do we come to know or to believe that there is something else in the world beyond material? First, some ancient Greek philosophers, and Christian philosophers too, have constructed arguments for the existence of God from the existence and character of the material world and/or from the existence of ideas they perceived existed in their own minds. Second, traditional Christians and their predecessors in ancient Israel also believed that God chose to directly reveal himself to human beings through various prophets. Of course, we have already spoken of this and of the very, very special revelation of God in Christ. And, of course, these sources of the knowledge of God have been challenged. The arguments have been, so some say, refuted over and over (as each argument has been endlessly refined). And the revelations, the Bible, the Qur'an, and others have been subjected to scholarly study and explained as wishful thinking, clever imagination, and self-deception.

So we puzzle over the roots of our religious beliefs. How do the things our senses perceive and the conclusions our reasoning comes to lead us to believe in the ultimately immaterial? Are these "perceptions" that God or gods or spirits exist merely the faulty results of an inaccurately operating, perhaps deceiving brain? Are all these meanderings of the mind and the emotions mere fancy? Or does some other ability, say, imagination lead us beyond material perception to spiritual perception? The so-called Romantics of the late eighteenth century and early nineteenth century thought so. Among the poets Wordsworth and Coleridge made significant comments on such a capacity. But does such an ability—which we seem to have in abundance, given the vast spiritual world

19. Schönborn, "Reasonable Science," 25.

that human beings have concocted—tell us the truth? Are our profound theologies of God no more likely to be true than recent Flying Spaghetti Monster that some modern atheists have cynically suggested?

Sigmund Freud would, of course, agree with the cynics. For Freud, God does not exist. The idea of God, therefore, could not be innate, a result of human beings having been made in the image of God or their having received some revelation of God from God. The notion of God rather derives from the human need for consolation in a hostile world. It is a human invention. In fact, all religious doctrines are illusions, the result of wish fulfillment.[20] This does not mean, of course, that anyone is aware of how they acquired the notion of God. The idea may well have been acquired unconsciously. Religious ideas have "psychical origins":

> These, which are given out as teachings, are not precipitates of experience or end-results of thinking: they are illusions, fulfil- ments [sic] of the oldest, strongest and most urgent wishes of mankind. The secret of their strength lies in the strength of those wishes.[21]

But, unlike the notion of space or time or being, God is not a conception we must have before we think about God. The idea of God is more like the idea of a king. We can learn about kings without having any precon- ception of what a king is. So we learn about God from our social context. As Freud says,

> Think of the depressing contrast between the radiant intelli- gence of a healthy child and the feeble intellectual powers of the average adult. I think it would be a very long time before a child who was not influenced began to trouble himself about God and things in another world.[22]

In other words, Freud denies the existence of *signals of transcendence*. Whatever so-called religious experience people seem to have is not based on any perception of the divine; it is rather a delusion.

Christians, however, beg to differ. There are indeed solid ontologi- cal foundations for an understanding of *signals of transformation*. Both Thomas Aquinas and John Calvin take the notion of God to be a direct perception of God's existence, one unmediated by reason, by revelation,

20. Freud expands on this notion throughout *Future*, 36–56.
21. Ibid., 30.
22. Ibid., 47.

by society, or by psychological need. Aquinas says, "To know that God exists in a general and confused way is implanted in us by nature."[23] Karl Rahner calls this the *pre-apprehension* of God. And Calvin says that everyone has a *sensus divinitatis* (a sense of Deity):

> That there exists in the human mind, and indeed by natural instinct, some sense of Deity, we hold to be beyond dispute, since God himself, to prevent any man from pretending ignorance, has endued all men with some idea of his Godhead, the memory of which he constantly renews and occasionally enlarges, that all to a man, being aware that there is a God, and that he is their Maker, may be condemned by their own conscience when they neither worship him nor consecrate their lives to his service.[24]

Notice that it is not just God as abstract Being but as Creator that is grasped by the human mind. That would seem to include personhood as well. Alvin Plantinga, a philosopher who, in his own development of Reformed epistemology emphasizes the existence of the *sensus divinitatis*, adds this explanation: "The *sensus divinitatis* is a disposition or set of dispositions to form beliefs in various circumstances, in response to the sorts of conditions or stimuli that trigger the working of this sense of divinity."[25]

But this raises an interesting question. If Aquinas and Calvin are right, the naturalist has had, at least at one time, an intuitive grasp of

---

23. Aquinas, "Whether the Existence of God Is Self-Evident: Reply to Objection 1." Otto also emphasizes the direct apprehension of God: "No intellectual dialectical dissection or justification of such intuition is possible, nor indeed should it be attempted, for the essence most peculiar to it would be destroyed thereby" (*Idea*, 164). This notion leads Otto to dismiss rational justification (i.e., apologetics) of Christian faith (ibid., 190–91). Otto's views are discussed in more detail in chapter 1 above. Catholic philosopher-theologian Karl Rahner expands and explains Aquinas's view. Catholic philosopher Eric Lionel Mascall comments: "In all knowledge, Rahner tells us, there is a pre-apprehension (*Vorgriff*) of being, in which the existence of an Absolute being is also affirmed simultaneously; this is implicit, unformulated and 'unthematic.' And, in Rahner's own words, 'this is in no sense an "*a priori*" proof of God's existence. For the pre-apprehension and its "whither" can be proven and affirmed as present and necessary for all knowledge only in the *a posteriori* apprehension of a real existent and as the necessary condition of the latter'" (Mascall, *Openness*, quoting Rahner, *Spirit*, 181). In other words, God must be in order for us to know anything; any argument we construct rests on the existence of God. We pre-apprehend God as the condition for any knowledge.

24. Calvin, *Institutes*, 1.1.3 (43).

25. Plantinga, *Warranted*, 173.

the existence of God. They would use as the authority for this Romans 1:18–20:

> The wrath of God is revealed from heaven against all the un-
> godliness and wickedness of those who by their wickedness
> suppress the truth. For what can be known about God is plain
> to them, because God has shown it to them. Ever since the cre-
> ation of the world his eternal power and divine nature, invisible
> though they are, have been understood and seen through the
> things he has made.

If, for example, Freud or Dawkins no longer intuits the existence of God or concludes he exists from his observation of the world around him, it is because he has suppressed the truth through his own wickedness. According to a Calvinist worldview, then, Freud may *presuppose* the final reality to be the material world, he may even give reasons for this *presup-position*, but he is both wrong and responsible for being wrong. He could and should have known better.

Calvin would say that the confidence in the knowledge of the ex-istence of God goes beyond any argument for it. It is predicated on the God-given human ability to sense God directly. Freud's failure to sense God is not so much due to his intellectual as his moral failure. The truth is there, not just in front of him (as the phenomena of the world) but in him (as the *sensus divinitatis*). As Pascal so intriguingly said, "The heart has reasons of which reason knows nothing."[26]

The short version of the philosophical theology of *transcendence* is straightforward: a Christian understanding of God, the universe, and human beings easily undergirds the reality of *signals of transcendence* at all four levels outlined in chapter 1. There is meaning at every level from thoughtful understanding of material events and things (sirens sounding trouble in the road ahead) to the highly charged *mysterium tremendum* (sights and sounds or astounding beauty that trigger the intuitive grasp of the *numinous*, the presence, the very holiness of God himself).

Islam: A Huge Contrast

An integral part of any theism is that God is both *transcendent* and *im-manent*. In the case of Islamic theism, however, God's *transcendence* far

---

26. Pascal, *Pensées*, no. 423 (154); also see no. 110 (58).

outweighs his *immanence*.[27] Any notion of a possible relationship with Allah must respect this boundary. God and a human person can never meet on the same plane. In the (perhaps slightly overstated) words of Isam'il Ragi al Faruqi,

> Islam is transcendentalist. It repudiates all forms of imma-nentism. It holds that reality is of two generic kinds—tran-scendent and spatiotemporal, creator and creature, value and fact—which are metaphysically, ontologically unlike as different from each other. These two realms of being constitute different objects of two modes of human knowledge, namely, the a priori and the empirical. Consciousness of this duality of being is as old as man; but it has never been absolutely free of confusion, absolutely clear of itself, as in Islam. . . . Islam takes its distin-guishing mark among the world religions precisely by insisting on an absolute metaphysical separation of transcendent from the spatiotemporal.[28]

In Christian theism, as we have seen above, there is no direct contradic-tion between God's *transcendence* and his *immanence*. In fact, Christians maintain that an important aspect of what it means to be human is to have the capacity for an intimate relationship with God, namely to know him as we would know our brother or father. Even though the Qur'an allows us to know of Allah's presence and to recognize his guidance, his availability, and his kindness, it keeps a much wider gap between a per-son's relationship with Allah compared to Christian theism.

The Qur'an does state that God is close to us, but we also need to recognize what this means. "When My servants ask thee concerning Me, I am indeed close (to them): I listen to the prayer of my suppliant when he calleth on Me: Let them also with a will, I listen will, Listen to My call, and believe in Me: That they may walk in the right way" (Qur'an, 2:186).

Hammudah Abdalati asserts on the basis of this verse:

> God is High and Supreme, but He is very near to the pious thoughtful people; He answers their prayers and helps them. He loves the people who love Him and forgives their sins. . . . Be-cause He is so Good and Loving, He recommends and accepts

27. This section is based on Win Corduan's explanation of Islamic theism in Sire, *Universe*, 244–77.

28. Isam'il Ragi al Faruqi, "Islam," in *Great Asian Religions,* quoted in Sire, *Uni-verse,* 249.

only the good and right things. The door of His mercy is always
open to any who sincerely seek His support and protection.[29]

This verse is considered to be of great comfort to Muslims in the struggles
of everyday life, but we should also recognize the context and its overall
intent. The verse occurs in the midst of various rules concerning the ob-
servance of Ramadan. Its immediate predecessor enjoins fasting during
Ramadan and allows for those who are sick or on a journey to make up
their obligation later. It is followed by the instructions not to have sexual
relations during fasting hours and not to overindulge oneself during the
times when eating is permitted. In short, even though the verse carries
reassurance of God's presence, in its setting its primary purpose seems
to be to provide conditions under which believers' prayers will be heard
during Ramadan. Thus, it is a word of comfort, but it is also bound up
with an exhortation to obedience.

But of course, despite al-Faruqu's statement above, Islam does not
do away completely with the immanence of God. As we shall see below,
even from afar, he regulates the events of the universe, and he has consis-
tently revealed himself throughout human history. The most important
revelation from Allah is the Qur'an, but Islam even allows for a certain
amount of general revelation.

> Behold! in the creation of the heavens and the earth; in the al-
> ternation of the night and the day; in the sailing of the ships
> through the ocean for the profit of mankind; in the rain which
> God Sends down from the skies, and the life which He gives
> therewith to an earth that is dead; in the beasts of all kinds that
> He scatters through the earth; in the change of the winds, and
> the clouds which they Trail like their slaves between the sky and
> the earth;—(Here) indeed are Signs for a people that are wise.
> (Qur'an 2:164)

Note that the perception of these divine clues is already limited to those
people who are "wise," which is just another way of saying "people who
believe in Allah already." In fact, what follows this verse immediately is a
condemnation of anyone else who may see the signs, but winds up wor-
shiping them rather than Allah.

Still, the fact of revelation shuts the door on the idea that because of
God's transcendence we must be agnostic concerning Allah's attributes.
We can know some things about Allah. However, at all times we must

29. Abdalati, *Islam*, 5.

acknowledge that this knowledge is only general. We can know that Allah is merciful, but we should in no way pretend that we comprehend what this means sufficiently to draw implications from it.

The reason for noting this contrast between Christian theism and Islamic theism is to highlight that, at least theoretically, there is less likelihood that there will be Muslim accounts of *signals of transcendence* coming from direct experience of nature or human nature. Such *signals* will surely come from the Qur'an, for in its Arabic form it *is* the Word of God. It is already *transcendent*. But *signals* from the natural world are not likely; they are too dangerous, too apt to be seen as the *transcendent* itself.

The View from Christian Theism

The Christian basic philosophical theology of *transcendence* is straight-forward: A Christian understanding of God, the universe, and human beings easily undergirds the reality of *signals of transcendence* at all four levels outlined in chapter 1. As we have noted, there is meaning at every level from thoughtful understanding of material events and things (sirens sounding/trouble in the road ahead) to the highly charged *mysterium tremendum* (sights and sounds or astounding beauty that triggers the intuitive grasp of the *numinous*, the presence, the very holiness, of God himself).

4

Christ in Ten Thousand Places

Signals of Transcendence in Christian Experience

> As swimmers dare
> to lie face to the sky
> and water bears them,
> as hawks rest upon air
> and air sustains them,
> so would I learn to attain
> freefall, and float
> into Creator Spirit's deep embrace,
> knowing no effort earns
> that all-surrounding grace.
>
> —DENISE LEVERTOV, "THE AVOWAL"

All of us as human beings share the same reality. There is a "way things are." We may experience these things differently, but there is, in the final analysis, only one determinate thing. Water is composed of hydrogen and oxygen, two parts to one. That's either the way "water" is, or "water" is something else. The same is true of its components, hydrogen and oxygen. There is, indeed, so far as we know, only one universe, only one earth. How we understand that reality varies widely with our *worldview*. Let's take the most personal, existentially sensitive issue of anyone's worldview—our understanding of what happens at our death. Do we simply cease to exist as an entity (naturalism), move over to the Other Side as a disembodied spirit (occultism), become reincarnated (Hinduism, New Age), or become resurrected for a life with God in a condition that is most satisfying or for an existence without God in a most unpleasant state (Christian theism)? If any one of these is true, the others are false. Something happens at death to each human being. That's rock bottom; for all intents it's certain. But what is it? We disagree. So we can say the human *world* we live in varies with our worldview.

In this chapter we will see, I hope, something of how Christians have experienced *signals of transcendence* that point clearly to Christian theism. Certainly not all *signals of transcendence* deal with what happens at death, but all of them are relevant to the worldview that undergirds the Christian notion of the existence of heaven and, though not always, of hell. We are, in that sense, interested in *signals* that point to the existence and, more importantly, to the Presence of God as Father, Son, and Holy Spirit—Trinity.

Signals of transcendence as experienced by Christians can be categorized in several ways. One is to rank them, as in chapter one, by Levels 1 to 4, that is, to identify them by the depth of *transcendence* they signal. A second way is to divide them into (1) *epistemological signals* that stimulate a curiosity leading one to learn more about the *transcendent* dimensions of reality and (2) *ontological signals* that record a profound sense of the *presence* of *transcendence*. A third classification looks at the forms in which the deeply private experiences of *transcendence* are made public. Do we learn about them through (a) relatively straightforward narrative or prose or by (b) carefully crafted poetry? This chapter uses all three types of classification.

Because most Christians comment on the personal character of the *transcendent* that is signaled, most of these *signals* are at Level 3 or 4. Christians may have Level 2 experiences, but they need not be associated with a Christian worldview. They do, of course, fit with either a Buddhist or Deist worldview. Everyone has Level 1 experiences.

Beginning Simply

Signals of transcendence are received by human beings at every age in every path of life and every country in the world. The beginnings are often simple flash insights that open up amazing vistas or trigger profound thoughts. The first brief narratives that follow here are not complex, though the nature of the *transcendence* they signal can stimulate profound philosophical thoughts and reveal depths of reality that change or even transform lives.

A Young Boy on a Ranch [Level 4 (2) (a)]

One summer a young boy living in a little house on a prairie rode his pony to fetch the cows for milking. Three thunderheads rose higher and higher above the western horizon. As they approached him the air turned electric, a cool breeze shivered his spine, his little horse lifted its head. Where he was there were no cattle; they were grazing just over the edge of a nearby ravine. He was alone under the big sky in the vast reaches of ranchland. Suddenly he wondered and thought and *realized* he was being pursued by the Father, the Son, and the Holy Ghost. He continued his search for the cows and found them; the storm passed over but behind him, and he returned to the ranch house with a memory he would never forget.

As I said in the preface, I was that boy. What did I learn? I already had heard my mother teach me some very basic Christian truths. Not much, but the reality of the existence of God as Trinity, though I could certainly not explain the doctrine, became present to me. I have learned more about the Christian faith and experienced God's presence in other ways since then, but I have never forgotten that early sense of God's presence. I can explain it only as a *signal of transcendence*, awesome at the time, glorious in memory.

A Young Boy, His Mother, and a Heroic Grandfather [Level 3/4 (1) (a)]

Was the significance of those three thunderheads just my imagination? I don't think so. Certainly my imagination was not the source of other experiences of the holy. Take the time that my younger sister Marjorie and I were coming home from our country school in early spring. The weather was warm; we were carrying our jackets. We had already ridden our pony a couple of miles when we heard a tremendous roar coming from the valley where our ranch house was.

"What's that?" I exclaimed, a bit frightened. When we reached the top of the hill above our house, there, east and west and below us in the valley, Eagle Creek, bloated with water from the melting ice upstream, stretched out like a lake. South, ahead of us, Honey Creek spread wide and sparkled in the declining sun. Even after heavy rains, I had never seen the Eagle or the Honey so full of water. When we reached our house in the valley, my terrified mother explained it all. The roar was coming from the sudden cracking and breakup of the frozen stream. An ice dam had formed a few hundred yards above our house. It would not long remain in place. If it broke to the south, our house and barn and outbuildings would be saved. If it broke to the north, we would be flooded. That, however, was not her present concern.

The channel in front of our house still remained frozen. But almost our entire herd of Registered Herefords was on the other side. A small stream had already broken to the south; so they were trapped on a newly formed island. My grandfather and my mother called to them (my father was still in O'Neill where he worked as County Assessor). The cattle milled around sensing danger but had no idea what to do. So my mother and grandfather called to them. "Hyah, Come Bossy, Hyah, Hyah!" over and over. They stirred but did not dare step into the water that now ran a foot or so above the solid ice beneath.

So my grandfather hitched the team to our two-wheeled utility cart, drove across the ice and tried to drive the cattle back across the stream. But to no avail. I stood by my mother.

"Pray, Jim, pray!" she said. "Pray like you've never prayed before!" I did. But nothing my grandfather could do would budge the cattle. So he gave up and drove back across the ever deepening stream. And the cattle followed.

The next morning, the temperature had dropped and Mom bundled up us three kids. The former main channel of the Eagle was now little more than a trickle. During the night the ice dam above the house had broken and the river had cut a channel to the south. Huge blocks of ice from the broken ice jam now littered the island where the cattle had been. Had they not followed my grandfather and his team of horses, perhaps sixty cattle would have been crushed and slaughtered. As it was, we kids stood up on the huge blocks of ice taller than we were, and Mom took our pictures. I remember the reality far more than the photos.

"I lift my eyes to the hills," says the psalmist. "From where will my help come?" And he is quick to answer: "My help comes from the LORD who made the heaven and the earth" (Ps 121:1–2). Indeed it was not the hills that helped. It was their maker—a lesson I learned early and have not forgotten. The hills have, however, provided the context for profound hints that God is there and not completely silent.

A Child at Prayer [Level 3/4 (2) (a)]

In the early Sunday afternoons we sometimes went to church held in a schoolhouse six miles up the road from my school. Lutheran or Methodist pastors from Spencer, twenty miles away, came to lead worship and preach. What was it all about? I wondered. What happened when we prayed? I felt funny, weird; the schoolroom was eerie. If I looked up, would I see little tongues of fire above the heads of others, or maybe angels? I never peeked. But I knew something special, something holy, must be going on. There were *signals of transcendence* here, though I would have no idea what that meant if I had heard the term then. I know it now.

A First-year College Student [Level 2 (1) (a)]

Once, while leading a class discussion on *signals of transcendence*, I asked if anyone in the group had ever experienced one. Jim Gray, a retired chemist, responded. He was raised in a moderately Christian home, he said. His parents only occasionally went to church. As a beginning student at Beloit College, he shared a suite with two other freshmen; they had individual bedrooms and a common study room. It was not long before a conflict appeared to be developing.

One of his roommates said to the other, "I want your desk."

The other replied, "Okay. You can have it."

Jim was astonished. Why would his roommate respond with such congeniality? He eventually discovered that it simply reflected his character. His roommate was a Christian who knew what he believed and lived by his belief. That stimulated Jim's interest in the Christian faith, and he took it in gradually as a whole package, not struggling over, for example, the difficult-to-believe miracles such as the resurrection. Jim has been an active Christian ever since.

A College Student Who Would One Day Be a Philosopher [Level 3 (1) (a)]

After being raised in a staunch Calvinist family with a father who was a professor at a Christian college, Alvin Plantinga was awarded a scholarship for a term at Harvard. There he "encountered serious non-Christian thought for the first time."[1] Impressed with what he encountered, he says, "My attitude gradually became a mixture of doubt and bravado."[2] Then came a life-transforming experience:

> One gloomy evening (in January, perhaps) I was returning from dinner, walking past Widenar Library. . . . It was dark, windy, raining, nasty. But suddenly it was as if the heavens opened; I heard, so it seemed, music of overwhelming power and grandeur and sweetness; there was light of unimaginable splendor and beauty; it seemed I could see into heaven itself; and I suddenly saw or perhaps felt with great clarity and persuasion and conviction that the Lord was really there and was all I had thought. The effects of this experience lingered for a long time; I was still caught up in arguments about the existence of God, but they often seemed to me merely academic, of little existential concern, as if one were to argue about whether there has really been a past, for example, or whether there really were other people, as opposed to cleverly constructed robots.[3]

Plantinga has gone on to become a highly regarded philosopher, once in the vanguard of Christian philosophy, now, to some extent due to his influence, only one of many highly regarded Christian philosophers.

A Philosophy Major Who Would One Day be Both a Philosopher and a Priest [Level 3 (1) (a)]

Marilyn McCord Adams had been drawn into Christian faith in her childhood, but her highly active religious and philosophic curiosity had pitched her faith up and knocked it down as she read her way through the major philosophers in her teenage years. In college, she writes, "I attended the complex high church worship services for about a year before I found myself believing in God again." Here is her story:

1. Plantinga, "Christian Life," 50.
2. Ibid., 51.
3. Ibid., 51–52.

> I was sitting in the library reading Alasdair McIntyre's early (and bad) essay "Visions" (which ridicules the evidential value of religious experience) when my if's, and's, and but's about God ran out. None of my questions had been answered, but I was filled with an overpowering sense of the real presence of God right there in the library. Nor was it a fleeting presence. God remained a given in experience, just as He had been in my childhood, along with sunshine, green grass, and the vast Midwestern skies. I was overjoyed.[4]

Her curiosity was not curbed by this experience, and she continued to puzzle and struggle over her commitment both to God and philosophy. The story of her continued religious experiences is fascinating.[5] Today she holds a PhD in philosophy and is a priest in the Episcopal Church.

An Evolutionary Paleobiologist [Level 3 (1) (a)]

Simon Conway Morris, a professor at Cambridge University, focuses his scientific attention on "evolutionary convergence: the recurrent tendency of biological organization to arrive at the same 'solution' to a particular need." The "camera-like eye," for example, "has evolved independently at least six times."[6] In the penultimate chapter of *Life's Solutions*, Morris lists five main observable facts that *signal* the presence of a *transcendent* source for the universe he studies as a scientist: (1) "the overwhelming sense of purpose" that characterizes the human species; (2) the universal moral sense that, for example, declares "Thou shalt not steal"; (3) the suitability of the universe for the emergence of human life; (4) "life's ability to navigate to its solutions"; and (5) the inability of philosophic naturalism to account adequately for these observations.[7]

As is clear from this list of *signals*, only the first two of them are directly perceived, that is experienced without rational reflection. Nonetheless, they are each *signals* that trigger Morris's sense that this material world in all its various physical and human aspects cannot be explained without reference to a transcendent source.

4. Adams, "Love of Learning," 144.

5. Ibid., 137–61.

6. Morris, *Life's Solutions*, xii.

7. Ibid., 313, 315, 327–28; the fifth of these five reasons is developed throughout the entire chapter entitled "Towards a theology of evolution?," 311–30.

A Lecturer at Moscow State University [Level 3 (1) (a)]

From a letter written by Brad Wathen, when he attended a conference sponsored by the International Fellowship of Evangelical Students in Russia:

> While out for a walk in Siberia, I saw a hawk in the sky above me. For the next few minutes I watched spellbound—not once did he flap his wings. He just effortlessly glided on the air currents, the perfect picture of grace and freedom. Later, I wondered if God had sent me a "sign." So often I feel as if my experience is the very opposite of the hawk's—as if I'm beating my wings furiously just to stay airborne.
>
> The image of the hawk was a gentle yet powerful reminder from God that he offers us a better way. We can ride the "wind" of his Holy Spirit and experience amazing freedom and life and power in ministry, or we can strive along in our own strength, *perhaps even working against his Spirit,* and experience frustration in life and ineffectiveness in ministry. Let us learn to get quiet before him, to wait on him, so that we more fully cooperate with him. 'Cuz I believe we're meant to soar just like that hawk.[8]

Going to the Heights and the Depths

My file of accounts of *signals of transcendence* is fairly large, but I know of none that goes emotionally or theologically deeper or that conveys more of the mind and heart of the recipient than Pascal's "Memorial." It ranks just below the accounts of Moses at the burning bush and on Mt. Sinai, and Isaiah in the temple, and the disciples at the empty tomb and on the road to Emmaus, and Paul's encounter with Christ on the road to Damascus. It is indeed a full-blown example of Rudolf Otto's *numinous* and *mysterium tremendum.* Are there other accounts of Christian experiences so deep? Not many, I would venture.

The mystery of the "Memorial" is heightened by our lack of details about how Pascal came to have the experience. We know the date; we know the time. The "Memorial" records an actual experience. Pascal's mere imagination as such is not involved. Moreover, the focus of the "Memorial" is not on Pascal qua Pascal but on the *transcendent* God himself in all his Trinitarian Presence.

8. Wathen, Newsletter.

Born in 1623 and raised in Paris by his father to be "an aristocratic man of culture, civility, self-sufficiency, and discernment," Pascal first learned Latin and Greek and then mathematics.[9] Here his mental ability soared into action; a life of the mind was his in both his heritage and his accomplishment. His original mathematical and scientific research focused on such issues as conic sections, projective geometry, atmospheric pressure, vacuum, and calculating machines (he invented the first one). Despite his life-long bouts with illness, for many years he lived the aristocratic life his father wished, engaging in the pleasurable pursuits of aristocratic culture. Then in 1646 he encountered Jansenism, "an Augustinian reform movement in Catholicism" and experienced a conversion from wine, women, and song to serious Christian faith, though as Douglas Groothuis says, "he was not irreligious before this time."[10] In 1654, however, Pascal was moved by a profound sense of the presence of God. Somewhat oddly, even though he wrote many *pensées*—short comments and a few short essays—toward a full work of Christian apologetics, he never spoke publicly of this experience.

After his death in 1662, however, an astounding short, poetic note on paper and a parchment copy were found stitched inside his jacket. Apparently the note was written quickly, perhaps, as Groothuis says "in order to record accurately the significance of what is described."[11] The parchment copy makes a few additions and variations. At this point for Pascal, his life of the mind of science and mathematics with its contribution to the world's grasp of physical reality was mere prelude. After November 23, 1954, his heart and mind were tuned to the spiritual movements of the God of Abraham, Isaac, and Jacob. His was a Level 4 (1/2) (b) experience.

Each time I read "The Memorial," I feel both its expressive power and its status as a *signal of transcendence* for me as well. I both long for and fear such an encounter with the Lord of the Universe. If you have not previously read "The Memorial," I suggest that you do so slowly and repeatedly until you sense the spiritual and emotional flow of ideas

9. Groothuis, *On Pascal*, 8. In addition to Groothuis's short introduction to Pascal, I recommend a full reading of his *Pensées*, Krailsheimer's Introduction and especially *Pensées* nos. 68, 110, 148, 149, 199–201, 382, 414, 418, 423–24, 429, 460, 620, 781, and 913; also see Émile Cailliet's classic study, *Pascal*.

10. Groothuis, *On Pascal*, 9–10.

11. Many of his *pensées* were scribbled "in feverish haste" in order to capture the immediate sense of the thoughts themselves (Krailsheimer, "Introduction," in Pascal, *Pensées*, 18).

and images and begin to grasp with both heart and mind something of what Pascal is trying to express. Then, if you can do so, proceed with my comments.

Pascal's Memorial [12]

> The year of grace 1654.
> Monday, 23 November, feast of St. Clement, Pope and Martyr, and others in the Martyrology.
> Eve of St. Chrysogonus, Martyr and others.
> From about half past ten in the evening until about half past midnight.
> Fire
> 'God of Abraham, God of Isaac, God of Jacob,' not of philosophers and scholars.
> Certainty, certainty, heartfelt, joy, peace.
> God of Jesus Christ.
> God of Jesus Christ.
> *My God and your God.*
> 'Thy God shall be my God.'
> The world forgotten, and everything except God.
> He can only be found by the ways taught in the Gospels.
> Greatness of the human soul.
> 'O righteous Father, the world had not known thee, but I have known thee.'
> Joy, joy, joy, tears of joy.
> I have cut myself off from him.
> *They have forsaken me, the fountain of living waters.*
> 'My God wilt thou forsake me?'
> Let me not be cut off from him forever!
> 'And this is life eternal, that they might know thee, the only true God, and Jesus Christ whom thou hast sent.'
> Jesus Christ.
> Jesus Christ.
> I have cut myself off from him, shunned him, denied him, crucified him.
> Let me never be cut off from him!
> He can only be kept by the ways taught in the Gospel.
> Sweet and total renunciation.
> Total submission to Jesus Christ and my director.
> Everlasting joy in return for one day's effort on earth.
> *I will not forget thy word.* Amen.

12. Pascal, *Pensées*, no. 309 (309–10). The main text is translated from the French; the italic phrases from Latin.

Note the specific secular date and its relation to the church year and to the specific time, both beginning and end. Pascal is nailing this note to both the secular and Christian calendars. The occurrence is a vital piece of history.

Fire. We must not miss this first word—*Fire*—the triggering *signal of transcendence*, perhaps even a *transcendent* itself. In Pascal's note version the word is surrounded by short lines emanating from it like flames around a burning log. Word and image. Metaphor and symbol. There is, of course the fire of the burning bush (Exod 3:1-6), the pillar of fire by night, the fire and the Holy Spirit with which John the Baptist says Jesus will baptize, and the "tongues, as of fire" that rested on each of the followers of Jesus at Pentecost. So for Pascal, *Fire* was the sensual and sacramental center of his spiritual, emotional, and intellectual experience.

We ourselves are, of course, left to our own imagination in seeing and feeling that fire. It was not a word meant for us but a memorial meant for him. The word strikes our imagination; we sense the intensity of what will follow. And we are silent. We must be. Then we must listen.

The God of Abraham, Isaac, and Jacob. The first words identify the God who is now Present to him: Pascal's God is not just a vague and fuzzy feeling of generic *transcendence*. He is the awesome God of the Hebrews, the specific God who identified himself to Moses at the burning bush (Exod 3:6) and said, "I AM WHO I AM" (Exod 3:14), declaring among other things his sole uniqueness as Sole Personal Being, without compare. Here is the *numin* of the *numinous*, stirring the ultimate experience of *mysterium tremendum*, Rudolf Otto would say. We know that Pascal was deeply familiar with the Bible; his *Pensées* are replete with allusions to Scripture. We can imagine that everything we today know of the biblical God through our own reading and experience is present in Pascal's mind as he jots the biblical phrase.[13] It will be a touchstone as he proceeds.

Not the God of the philosophers. To Pascal God was not an abstraction, not an intellectual idea summarizing the best that had been thought about the divine. Let Aquinas and Descartes speak philosophically about such a denuded reduction of the awesome personal God of Scripture. Let them replace him with a mere construction of the intellect. We should note, however, that Pascal's rejection of the professional thinkers' notions of God did not keep Pascal from constructing his own apologetic for the

---

13. Pascal was, of course, not aware of the coming Enlightenment and modern critical reading of Scripture, nor the response of traditional Christian scholars.

Christian faith. What it did do was to assure that Pascal would concentrate on those arguments that would acknowledge the mystery of God and yield to him his right to be whoever he would be. God cannot be put in a philosophical box, and Pascal will not try to do so.

Certainty, certainty. Now comes his reaction to God's presence. *Certainty* is first. All doubt is gone. Skepticism already had a long history in philosophy and theology. Stemming from Socrates, Pyrho, and Sextus Empiricus, it had been addressed by Christian philosophers from Augustine to Pascal's contemporary, Descartes. In overdone logic and cleverness, Descartes, whom Pascal twice met, thought he had answered the nagging doubts that Christians or anyone else might have. Pascal would have nothing of Descartes' individualist, anti-traditional and purely rationalist approach. His direct experience was all he needed. How did he know the God of the Bible existed? "The heart has its reasons of which reasons knows nothing," he wrote.[14] God had been in his conscious presence for two hours. He had been in his life forever, known or unknown.

Heartfelt, joy, peace. His intellectual problems solved by utter certitude, Pascal yields to heartfelt joy and a peace that passes all understanding. We sense here the great solution to all Pascal's wonderings and worries. Can we imagine him resting at this point in silence, then plumbing further the God who is present?

God of Jesus Christ. Further flames of the fire flare as God is identified with God (the Father) of Jesus. This is not only the distant and puzzling God who sometimes frightens and disturbs but the one who has now brought peace. This is the God of Jesus who brought God the Father into the historical present, into time and space. Pascal thus seems both to identify God as separate from Jesus and to declare his identity with Jesus. This is the view of Jesus himself, who while standing among them declared to his disciples, "I and the Father are one" (John 10:30). Neither Pascal nor we can think of God in Christ or Christ in God without thinking theologically, even if we insist that we are not doing so.

My God and your God. Is Pascal now bringing in his own community of faith or the church community down through the ages? He is certainly declaring him *his own.* Is he also reflecting instead, or in addition, to Jesus who found himself forsaken by his own Father God as he hung dying on the cross: "My God, my God, why have you forsaken me?" (Mark 14:34).

---

14. Pascal, *Pensées,* no. 423 (277).

The world forgotten and everything except God. Here Pascal falls securely into the hands of God. He is conscious of nothing else. He is alone with God. Remember: two hours will pass before the fire will burn low and go out. What did he do? What does it matter? He is alone with God.

He can only be found by the ways taught in the Gospels. Does Pascal begin to think? Does he reflect on how it is he can be conscious of *what* he is being or even *be* what he is being? Has he turned to apologetics in his reverie? Or is he, rather more simply, realizing that only through the testimony of the Gospels is he able to realize what is happening to him? How would he ever know that the God into whose presence he has come is the God who first met him in Scripture unless he had been exposed to Scripture? Or are my questions a bit of double think? Whatever is the case, Pascal has clearly stated a truth. The God of the Gospels must come only through the Gospels.

We might reflect on that ourselves. Will we find the God of the Gospels in the Qur'an? Or in *The Da Vinci Code*? Let's not fool ourselves.

Greatness of the human soul. Ah! the paradox of biblical anthropology. The human soul is great. We are made in the *image of God*. We are *like* God (that's great) but we are not God. Pascal is here grasping in a phrase the paradox of biblical anthropology that we noticed in chapter 3. But does he do so well?

'O righteous Father, the world had not known thee, but I have known thee.' The source of this phrase is John 17:25. They are the words of Jesus for his disciples. Jesus is talking to his Father God about his own knowledge of God and the lack of such knowledge by the world, that is, by those who are not his disciples. But for Pascal the words are life itself.

Joy, joy, joy, tears of joy. Pascal either understands this phrase as one he himself can say, or he is associating himself with the disciples to whom Jesus is speaking. In either case, he rejoices in the riches of his own knowledge of God and in seeing himself as not among the people "of the world." All he can say is *joy*. Words fail him. All he can do is weep. Weeping for joy, this is another paradox of human nature. Think again of Pascal solitary and silent. The joy of the Lord sweeps over him. Then suddenly joy turns to surprised grief, agony, even terror.

I have cut myself off from him. What have I done? No, no, no, it can't be! But yes, I have lost my deep connection with God. And I have done it to myself. With this recognition all Pascal's sins fall back on his own shoulders, triggered by his blasphemy—triggered by his taking to himself what is only characteristic of Jesus. Only Jesus knows the Father so completely. Pascal now feels severed from the God of Jesus Christ.

They have forsaken me, the fountain of living waters. This phrase is a small segment of "the word of the LORD" that came to Jeremiah (Jer 2:1–13) and that Jeremiah in turn passed on to Jerusalem, its intended audience. It is recorded in Jeremiah 2:13; here is its immediate context:

> Be appalled, O heavens, at this,
>> be shocked, be utterly desolate,
>>> says the LORD,
>> for my people have committed two evils:
>> they have forsaken me,
> the fountain of living water,
>> and dug out cisterns for themselves,
> cracked cisterns
>> that can hold no water. (Jer 2:12–13)

Pascal sees himself as the heir of Jerusalem, repeating its errors and bringing about the same results in his own life and spirit.

'My God wilt thou forsake me?' He has cut himself off from God. But, and this is worse: Will God now abandon him? The quotation reflects Jesus' words on the cross, "My God, my God, why have you forsaken me?" (Matt 27:46). See the logic of Pascal: If God has abandoned his holy, sinless son . . . (one shudders at the completion of the logic) . . . then there is no reason for God not to abandon Pascal's sinful self.

We know too that Pascal was both fascinated and troubled by the paradoxical Scriptural theme of *deus absconditus*, the hidden God, which Isaiah 45:15 cites: "Truly, you are a God who hides himself." God both reveals and conceals—reveals to those who sincerely seek him, conceals from those who, like Bertrand Russell, refuse to see what could be seen if they would only pay attention to what is already in front of them.[15]

Let me not be cut off from him forever! And so the desperate plea. Remember, Pascal has just basked in the joy of God's presence; now he

---

15. "The great atheist philosopher Bertrand Russell was once asked what he would say if he found himself standing before God on the judgment day and God asked him, 'Why didn't you believe in Me?' Russell replied, 'I would say, "Not enough evidence, God! Not enough evidence!"' (Craig, "Evidence"). Pascal has a response: "God has appointed visible signs in the Church so that he shall be recognized by those who genuinely seek him, and that he has nonetheless hidden them in such a way they will only be perceived by those who seek him with all their heart, then what advantage can they derive when, unconcerned to seek the truth as they profess to be, they protest that nothing shows it to them?" *Pensées,* no. 427 (194). See also *Pensées,* no. 242 (545).

feels himself abandoned. Will God exercise his absolute right to let Pascal stay where he is? That is his fear. "The eternal silence of these infinite spaces fills me with dread," Pascal wrote.[16] If he could be terrified by the silent emptiness of infinite space, how much more would he be terrified by the absence of God?

'And this is eternal life that they might know thee, the only true God, and Jesus Christ whom thou hast sent.' But Pascal is reminded of how God administers his salvation. It is in knowing Jesus Christ. It is in taking Christ as the center of one's life. It is, in the final analysis, not in doing anything. Salvation is by grace, as Pascal has long known by his association with the Jansenists and their great predecessor, Augustine. Christ is the redeemer. And so he turns his attention from the just God the Father to the gracious God the Son. Of course, he does not do this by disassociating the Father from the Son so that the two cease to be One with the Holy Spirit. But Pascal's focus is on the Son as Jesus the Messiah, the one who came to save sinful Jerusalem and sinful Pascal.

Jesus Christ. Jesus Christ. I take it that here as above, Pascal has no words to convey his thoughts, or that his thoughts are more like contemplation, silent, wordless attention to Jesus Christ and only to him. His association with the nuns and brothers of the Port-Royal convent would have furnished him with ways in which to contemplate in silence and solitude. Something happens during the two hours he is in the presence of God, which he is despite his sense now that he is not.

I have cut myself off from him, shunned him, denied him, crucified him. What are the results of his contemplation of Jesus Christ? First, it intensifies his sense of guilt. He sees himself like the disciples. They first shunned him and denied him. Then they were silent and far off beyond the crowd when he was crucified. They would know later that their own sinfulness would require Jesus' death as he bore the penalty for their own sins and the sins of the world. So they too *crucified* Christ. So did Pascal. And, if as Christians readers we follow the logic of Pascal and the church, we too have shunned, denied, and crucified Christ.

Let me never be cut off from him! Does this repeated prayer now offer a glimmer of hope? Has Pascal seen through his contemplation of Christ that it will be Jesus who will bring him back to God? I think so.

He can only be kept by the ways taught in the Gospel. Now Pascal confirms that his knowledge of God comes in the teaching and encounter

16. Pascal, *Pensées*, no. 201 (95).

with Jesus Christ in the New Testament, especially the Gospels, though the word *Gospel* could include the teaching of the whole New Testament Scriptures as understood by the creeds and tradition. Given Pascal's embroilment in many of the theological controversies of his time, I think *Gospel* should be understood as the four Gospels. He will do and believe as the Jesus of the Gospels teaches and commands.

Sweet and total renunciation. Total submission to Jesus Christ and my director. The break is made. Pascal's self-will, his pride in seeming to grasp the very being of God as the result of his joy in being in the presence of the very God of very God—this pride is relinquished. He falls at the feet of Jesus and he opens himself to the instructions of his spiritual director.[17] He will be obedient. As Dietrich Bonheoffer has so famously said, "Only those who believe obey, . . . and only those who obey believe."[18] This is an unbreakable bond. Pascal has accepted it.

Everlasting joy in return for one day's effort on the earth. Has Pascal suddenly substituted works salvation for grace? I think not! He has rather looked back on his two hours of fire with its ecstasy and its agony, its pride and its submission. He has done no "work," but he has been through the fire of self-awareness. This in itself is an "effort," a time which has depleted his energy and left him drained but full of joy. This time it is not *joy, joy, joy* (only three temporal times); it is *everlasting joy*.

I will not forget thy word. Amen. Then comes the pledge, almost as an afterthought. Life from now on will be lived under the tutelage of Jesus Christ. So be it!

Though "Pascal's Memorial" was written in a quasi-poetic free-verse form and, like a poem, stirs aesthetic, emotional, intellectual, and spiritual reactions, it was certainly not intended for anyone other than its author. We will look now at a couple of Christian poets who knew they would have an audience, even if one of them expected an audience of only one. The first is Gerard Manley Hopkins. The second is Wendell Berry.

17. "Pascal had been a proud, ambitious, and celebrated man as well as an acclaimed prodigy and genius. He had initially opposed [his sister] Jacqueline's admission to Port-Royal des Champes. Now he himself would go on retreats and submit to a spiritual director at Port-Royal, although he would not become a full-fledged solitary there" (Groothuis, *On Pascal*, 13–14).

18. Bonhoeffer, *Cost*, 68.

Gerard Manley Hopkins

Though Gerard Manley Hopkins (1844–89) wanted his poetic works to be destroyed on his death, he sent his poems to his friend poet Robert Bridges who, when the time came, denied his request. While Hopkins died in 1889, his poems were not published until 1919, at which time they went against the grain of "modernist poetry" such as that of T. S. Eliot, and they had a major impact on how poetry would be written in the next few decades.

Hopkins was raised an Anglican. While he was a student at Oxford, he came under the influence of the Anglo-Catholic Tractarian Movement, and in 1866 he followed John Henry Newman into the Catholic Church. In 1868 he became a Jesuit and in 1877 a priest, subsequently serving as a parish priest and then as a teacher. Throughout his life, he read, studied, and wrote poetry, but very little of it was published until almost thirty years after his death.

The story of Hopkins the man is fascinating but not a part of our present interest. Our focus is on the art of his poetry, not the character of his biography. We start with "God's Grandeur," one of Hopkins's most glorious, most loved and most frequently anthologized poems. As in all the poems we will examine, this one expresses a Level 4 (2) (b) grasp of *transcendence*. The first line states its subject—the world as a *signal of transcendence*.

> The world is charged with the grandeur of God.
>   It will flame out, like shining from shook foil;
>   It gathers to a greatness, like the ooze of oil
> Crushed. Why do men then now not reck his rod?
> Generations have trod, have trod, have trod;
>   And all is seared with trade; bleared, smeared with toil;
>   And wears man's smudge and shares man's smell: the soil
> Is bare now, nor can foot feel, being shod.
>
> And for all this, nature is never spent;
>   There lives the dearest freshness deep down things;
> And though the last lights off the black West went
>   Oh, morning, at the brown brink eastward, springs—
> Because the Holy Ghost over the bent
>   World broods with warm breast and with ah! bright wings.[19]

19. Hopkins, *Poems*, 66.

"God's Grandeur" is, first of all, a poem written completely within the Christian worldview. Many of the major concepts of that worldview are presented in bold relief—God as creator of a world that reveals his glory, the rebellion of human beings and their pollution of his glorious creation, and the restoration of the world through the work of the Holy Spirit. The poem, in fact, is a Christian take-off on the central theme of Psalm 19: to wit, that the skies and the material world bristle with *signals of transcendence*. "The heavens declare the glory of God," says the ancient poet. And Hopkins echoes: "The world is charged with the grandeur of God."

Then the poem's brilliant flashing images point sacramentally to a realm beyond the material world. Material reality—the universe as a whole (lines 1–3a) and human beings in particular (3b–9)—*signal* the existence of the biblical God. Even in its fallen and broken condition, the world is not left to itself but is being renewed by the Holy Spirit (lines 9–14).

The poet sets fallen human beings firmly in their place as rebels against God, and, long before the Green movement, as polluters of the earth. Nonetheless, the earth is not lost. It will be reborn not by human effort but by the Holy Spirit, who sustains it, mothers it, and fosters its return to its rightful place in the kingdom of God.

This poem embodies Christian theology at a profound level and testifies to the truth of the Christian faith. This is the way it is, the poem says. And the artifice of the poem—its rhymes and images and sprung rhythm—reinforces the message. If we read this poem well, we will gain an aesthetic experience of what it would be like to believe that the world is like this.

But this poem is more than literature. It is an icon. We look through it into the mystery of God himself. Not only is the world charged with the grandeur of God, but so is the poem. Taken as a whole, the poem actually states in poetic form the argument from beauty: "There is the poetry of Gerard Manley Hopkins / Therefore there must be a God. / You either see this or you don't."[20]

---

20. The seventeenth out of twenty arguments Kreeft and Tacelli give for the existence of God is this: "There is the music of Johann Sebastian Bach. / Therefore there is a God. / You either see this one [argument] or you don't" (*Handbook*, 81). Also see Wiker and Witt, *Meaningful World*, 15–82, where a similar aesthetic argument is worked out in more detail.

At least as philosophic (both in ontology and in epistemology) and theological is Hopkins's "Hurrahing in Harvest." But here it is also personal:

> SUMMER ends now; now, barbarous in beauty, the stooks rise
> Around; up above, what wind-walks! what lovely behaviour
> Of silk-sack clouds! has wilder, wilful-wavier
> Meal-drift moulded ever and melted across skies?
>
> I walk, I lift up, I lift up heart, eyes,
> Down all that glory in the heavens to glean our Saviour;
> And éyes, heárt, what looks, what lips yet gave you a
> Rapturous love's greeting of realer, of rounder replies?
>
> And the azurous hung hills are his world-wielding shoulder
> Majestic—as a stallion stalwart, very-violet-sweet!—
> These things, these things were here and but the beholder
> Wanting; which two when they once meet,
> The heart rears wings bold and bolder
> And hurls for him, O half hurls earth for him off under his feet.[21]

For those readers who may be stumbling through Hopkins's sprung rhythm and convoluted syntax, let me offer a simplistic paraphrase to get you started. You must not leave your reading with my paraphrase. I guarantee that if you take the time to read well, your heart will half hurl earth off under your feet.

Here is the paraphrase: Summer is ending; the birds are rising and soaring among the fluffy clouds in the windy sky. I walk out in the early autumn and gaze skyward to pick up in the last vestiges of summer the presence of the Lord our Savior. How full is the scene with the response of God and his creation! The very azure hills outline the shoulder of the creator-sustainer-savior Christ. Stunning! But the immanent presence of the transcendent God needs his human creation to be there to grasp his presence. When both are there, the very heart of the human beholder turns over in ecstatic joy and praise.

There is so, so much more captured in these fourteen lines! So much emotion, insight, theology, and art! Again, as in "God's Glory," Hopkins combines the biblical ontology of God as both *immanent* and *transcendent* with sacramental epistemology: The created order of the world speaks. Material things are *signals of transcendence*. It is possible to know

21. Hopkins, *Poems*, 70.

God through nature, to perceive his glory, to sense his presence, to find oneself suspended in worship and praise even in the ordinary world of nature, for nature itself is not really ordinary. As God's creation, it is lifted into the extraordinary kingdom of God.

Almost every one of Hopkins's poems exhibits in some way *signals of transcendence*. We will look at two more, the first much like those above and one very different but nonetheless filled with *signals*.

The final lines of the sonnet beginning "as kingfishers catch fire" are at the heart of Hopkins's conception of reality. Here is the poem:

> As kingfishers catch fire, dragonflies draw flame;
>   As tumbled over rim in roundy wells
>   Stones ring; like each tucked string tells, each hung bell's
> Bow swung finds tongue to fling out broad its name;
> Each mortal thing does one thing and the same:
>   Deals out that being indoors each one dwells;
>   Selves—goes itself; *myself* it speaks and spells,
> Crying *What I do is me: for that I came.*
>
> Í say more: the just man justices;
>   Keeps gráce: thát keeps all his goings graces;
> Acts in God's eye what in God's eye he is—
>   Chríst. For Christ plays in ten thousand places,
> Lovely in limbs, and lovely in eyes not his
>   To the Father through the features of men's faces.[22]

This time I will let you as readers work out the meaning of this poem for yourselves. Any hard labor you do will be rewarded many times over. Suffice it to say that the final three lines capture the sacramental nature of reality as Christians understand and experience it. God the Word is somehow in his own creation, not as equated with it, but as reflected in its structure and the human meaning of this structure. He is as close to us as the men and women we meet every day. Of course, there is the human fall into sin and the corruption of the earth that follows as a consequence, but God's creation is redeemable and has been redeemed by God the Savior. We are born to bear the nature of God, and in the final analysis God will not let us cease to do that.

"The Grandeur of God," "Hurrah in Harvest" and "As kingfishers catch fire" are glorious poems, a delight on every level. But not every Hopkins poem is lit so brightly. Take this sonnet, often referred to as one

22. Ibid., 90.

of the "terrible" sonnets, not terrible as poems but terrible in content. Sometimes readers with minimal understanding of the Christian view of human nature think these poems indicate Hopkins's loss of faith. Quite the contrary; they represent the deep depression of a soul sensitive to its own depravity and its own lack of saving power.

> I WAKE and feel the fell of dark, not day.
> What hours, O what black hoürs we have spent
> This night! what sights you, heart, saw; ways you went!
> And more must, in yet longer light's delay.
>
> With witness I speak this. But where I say
> Hours I mean years, mean life. And my lament
> Is cries countless, cries like dead letters sent
> To dearest him that lives alas! away.
>
> I am gall, I am heartburn. God's most deep decree
> Bitter would have me taste: my taste was me;
> Bones built in me, flesh filled, blood brimmed the curse.
>
> Selfyeast of spirit a dull dough sours. I see
> The lost are like this, and their scourge to be
> As I am mine, their sweating selves; but worse.[23]

The Christian worldview is displayed no less here than in "God's Grandeur." But in this sonnet the consequences of sin focus on the sinner rather than on the natural world that *signals* the presence of God or the world that suffers for human sin. The final line is a crushing but keen insight into what hell must be like. The *numinous* is dark, the mystery of depression is tremendous.

A tour through Hopkins's poetry enriches a reader with profound grasps of God, the universe and humankind. As a presentation of and witness to the Christian understanding of reality, they all but scream the argument: There is the poetry of Gerard Manley Hopkins; therefore there is a God.

The case I am trying to make now, however, is not only that Hopkins's poetry *signals* the existence of God because it embodies the Christian worldview. Rather, I am trying to show that the art of Hopkins's poetry, its very aesthetic character, points to the existence of God. His poetry as poetry is a *signal of transcendence*. The two are, of course, entangled with each other. The art is appropriate to the content; it helps us feel with

23. Ibid., 101.

Hopkins what it is like to perceive the world from a Christian point of view. But the art, the beauty of the poem itself, points to the existence of the *transcendent*.

Perhaps it would be better to turn this around and say that God reveals himself through the art of poetry as well as through the content of Hopkins's poetry. This places the proper emphasis on the priority of being to knowing. We know God first, not because of our own epistemic equipment (our ability to know anything at all), but because God reaches out to us. He speaks. In Hopkins's language he *charges* the world with *his grandeur*. It is because of that charge, that speaking "without words" (as Psalm 19:3–4 says), that we can hear and see him through the world, through poetry, and the art of the artist.

Wendell Berry

Wendell Berry (1936–) has been a Kentucky farmer for some forty years. Kyle Childress gives us a quick overview of his life:

> Berry is technically a member of New Castle Baptist Church, where he was baptized; he attends worship with his wife, Tanya, at Port Royal Baptist Church. . . . After receiving his bachelor's and master's degrees in English from the University of Kentucky, he married Tanya and studied creative writing at Stanford University with Wallace Stegner. An aspiring writer, he traveled for a year in Europe, after which he wrote and taught in New York. Then he decided to move back to Kentucky. Most of his friends and colleagues thought he was crazy. He bought a small, marginal farm and reclaimed it, took care of it, and farmed it using traditional methods.[24]

Berry's literary work consists of novels, poems, and essays, the general tone of which reflect his commitment to treating the earth and its people with love and respect. This has brought him the great admiration of many Christians and environmentalists and the frustrated charge of being an anti-technology radical whose vision of the good life is as impossible to bring about as it is backward looking and foolish.

But in all of this two things are clear: He is steeped in biblical understanding, and he is a remarkable poet of the *immanence* of the *transcendent* God. This comes out in almost all his work, not only in his writing

24. Childress, "Good Work," 28–33.

but in his life. He lives his vision. Readers who want an introduction to his life and mind could well start with his first novel, *Nathan Coulter* (1960), and a later novel, *Jayber Crow* (2000), his Sabbath poems in *A Timbered Choir* (1998), and his early essays in *The Unsettling of America: Culture and Agriculture* (1977) and *The Gift of Good Land* (1981).[25] We will be examining a couple of his Sabbath poems. They illustrate one who, in practicing Sabbath rest, regularly experiences the Presence of God among the forests of his Kentucky farmstead.

Each year from 1979 to 1997, Wendell Berry wrote poems celebrating the Sabbath. The Sabbath itself—a rest from work—is both an event occurring every seventh day and a sacrament, an embodied *signal* in *immanent* human reality of a *transcendent* spiritual reality characteristic of God. God took the first Sabbath, resting after six days of creation. More than a mere symbol or metaphor, each Sabbath is a temporal realization of eternal *Being* in the *being of the world*.

Berry says this about the poems comprising *The Timbered Choir*:

> These poems were written in silence, in solitude, mainly out of doors. A reader will like them best, I think, who reads them in similar circumstances—at least in a quiet room. They would be most favorably heard if read aloud into a kind of quietness that is not afforded by any public place. I hope that some readers will read them as they were written: slowly, and with more patience than effort. . . . The poems are about moments when heart and mind are open and aware.[26]

As physical reality speaks of eternal reality, the words of his poems speak the Word of God, not as Scripture but as human response to God and his creation. But this is getting all too abstract. We need to be concrete. So here is one of Berry's early Sabbath poems:

> Another Sunday morning comes
> And I resume the standing Sabbath
> Of the woods, where the finest blooms
> Of time return, and where no path
>
> Is worn but wears its makers out
> At last, and disappears in leaves
> Of fallen seasons. The tracked rut
> Fills and levels; here nothing grieves

25. Bonzo and Stevens in *Wendell Berry* summarize and critique Berry's life, work, and vision.

26. Berry, *Timbered Choir*, xvii–xviii.

In the risen season. Past life
Lives in the living. Resurrection
Is in the way each maple leaf
Commemorates its kind, by connection

Outreaching understanding. What rises
Rises into comprehension
And beyond. Even falling raises
In praise of light. What is begun

Is unfinished. And so the mind
That comes to rest among the bluebells
Comes to rest in motion, refined
By alteration. The bud swells,

Opens, makes seed, falls, is well,
Being becoming what it is:
Miracle and parable
Exceeding thought, because it is

Immeasurable; the understander
Encloses understanding, thus
Darkens the light. We can stand under
No ray that is not dimmed by us.

The mind that comes to rest is tended
In ways that it cannot intend:
Is borne, preserved, and comprehended
By what it cannot comprehend.

Your Sabbath, Lord, thus keeps us by
Your will, not ours. And it is fit
Our only choice should be to die
Into that rest, or out of it.[27]

Readers familiar with poetry—especially those for whom poetic language forms the warp and woof of their thought—will, I think, be immediately drawn into the poem. A first reading will not yield even the poem's basic surficial meaning, but it will stop the good reader from turning immediately to the next poem. There is too much going on in the poem—the trees, leaves, and flowers of external nature are triggering and tracking the memories of the past, the momentary movements of the present

27. Ibid., 6–7.

conscious mind and the imaginative projecting of the future. There is more here than the emotion stimulated by a "pretty" vista; there is as well a scent of philosophy—more than meets the eye, maybe even more than meets the mind. In the final analysis, I think, we find that the *human being* of the poet is being struck by the *being of the world* that has been created by *Being* that is God so that Berry and his readers are brought into the very Presence of that final *Being*. This is a lot to claim. Let me try to justify it by looking more closely at the details of the poem.

The poem opens with the setting, the time, and place:

> Another Sunday morning comes
> And I resume the standing Sabbath
> Of the woods, where the finest blooms
> Of time return, and where no path
>
> Is worn but wears its makers out
> At last, and disappears in leaves
> Of fallen seasons. The tracked rut
> Fills and levels;

A new Sunday has arrived and the poet walks, as he often does (it is a "standing" practice), into the woods in a deliberate act of resting. There he "stands" with the "standing" trees and absorbs the reality that presents itself to him. The forest is regenerating with its "finest blooms." The woods have been worn down, tracks have been beaten through the trees, but the tracks have been refilled with relentlessly accumulating dead and decaying leaves. Yes, the woods have been dying, but their death has provided the food for new life. There is no mourning, no "grieving / Over Golden grove unleaving," as in Hopkins' poem "Spring and Fall."[28] Rather,

> here nothing grieves
>
> In the risen season.

That is because in the *being of the world* new life always comes from the old. There lives "the freshest deep down things," says Hopkins.[29] And Berry agrees:

> Past life
> Lives in the living. Resurrection
> Is in the way each maple leaf

28. Hopkins, *Poems*, 88.
29. Ibid., 66.

> Commemorates its kind, by connection
>
> Outreaching understanding. What rises
> Rises into comprehension
> And beyond.

Slowly Berry introduces both elements of *human being* (understanding and comprehension) and elements of the *Being* that is God (what "out-reaches" understanding and goes "beyond" comprehension). At work in the resurrection of physical nature is the super nature that transcends the *being of the world.*

> Even falling raises
> Its praise of light. What is begun
>
> Is unfinished.

In these lines, Berry returns to the natural, noting that, even in the physical decay and fall of the leaves and even the trees, the light (of *Being*?) returns to the forest to work again its rejuvenation. Then he shifts back to the mind of *human being* in which he sees a paradox. The mind "rests" in "motion," a motion, however, that is not its own but the motion of the *being of the world.*

> And so the mind
> That comes to rest among the bluebells
> Comes to rest in motion, refined
> By alteration. The bud swells,
>
> Opens, makes seed, falls, is well,
> Being becoming what it is:

In the very ebb and flow—death and resurrection—of the forest, the *being of the world* is birthing itself. It is becoming what it *is*. And what it *is* is both a "miracle," that is, a mysterious power to resurrect, and a "parable," a story with a dual meaning. And that dual meaning is a paradox because it is a "meaning" that exceeds thought by its "immeasurable," that is transcendent, character.

> Miracle and parable
>
> Exceeding thought, because it is
> Immeasurable; . . .

Actually, it is that "immeasurable" character of the *being of the world* that *signals* that the *being of the world* is not all the being there is; the *being of the world* is held in being by the *Being* that is God.

In order to understand the *being of the world*, the "understander"—that is, Berry and the reader—reduces the *being of the world* to human size. But there is something in the *being of the world* that is beyond the compass of the mind of *human being*. Knowledge—at least human knowledge—is always less than being. We dim the light by trying to understand it.[30]

> the understander
> Encloses the understanding, thus
> Darkens the light. We can stand under
> No ray that is not dimmed by us.

If we are to take the Sabbath rest with Berry, we will find that we are rested by others, rested by both the *being of the world* and the *Being* that is God.

> The mind that comes to rest is tended
> In ways that it cannot intend:
> Is borne, preserved, and comprehended
> By what it cannot comprehend.

In Berry's Sabbath we are tended and comprehended by God. In entering the woods we have entered his Presence. Or, better, in entering the woods, God has entered us; the *being of the world* has mediated the *Being* that is God. So, in turn, we turn to God, recognizing that without the Sabbath rest he brings, we are lost. The future comes to us in the present; it is not our task to make that future; we can only accept or refuse the rest. To put the meaning in theological terms, it is only by grace that we are saved.

> Your Sabbath, Lord, thus keeps us by
> Your will, not ours. And it is fit
> Our only choice should be to die
> Into that rest, or out of it.

Berry, I think, knows what so many of us do not. We do not grasp God; God grasps us. So our search for Being is futile unless it becomes a rest

30. Elsewhere Berry writes about the "ravenous intellect" (*Timbered Choir*, 30), a remark that could be taken as anti-intellectualism. But this and other similar comments are rather apt descriptions of the intellect and its natural limitations. In other words, Berry is being no more anti-intellectual than Pascal.

from the search. It is when we let go and let God—a concept I was once told is unbiblical—that God comes, that is, when we perceive that God has been here all the time.

In another powerful Sabbath poem written the following year, Berry writes about walking in the forest without his "eager dog" who now "lies strange and still." When alive he thrashed about in the woods and made a "ruckus." Now, with the woods to himself, the poet goes "more quiet"; other animals now make themselves known:

> For as I walk the wooded land
> The morning of God's mercy,
> Beyond the work of mortal hand,
> Seen by more than I see,
>
> The quiet deer look up and wait,
> Held still in quick of grace.
> And I wait, stop footstep and thought.
> We stand here face to face.[31]

Man and deer, face to face, only because God's grace holds both in *being* and man is quiet. Here, then, in the woods of Berry's farm are thin places where earth and heaven come so close together that they meet there, face to face to Face.

A Long Journey Home

This chapter has taken us from narratives and literary works written by Christians who have experienced the intrusion and the presence of God—from a young boy, a first-year college student, a Christian minister, a scientist/apologist, and two stellar poets. This is merely a tiny sample of the great number of accounts of deep religious experience. Almost every Christian has one of his or her own. But these narratives and poems serve to illustrate the rich and varied character of *signals of transcendence* as experienced by Christians. Some are quick in coming, quick in leaving; some are the result of meditation and Christian reflection over long periods of time. Some are simple prose; others are complex poetry.

But one need not look long before it becomes obvious that many Christians claim to have had experiences that for them provide ample justification for their belief, not only in the basic tenets of the Christian

---

31. Berry, *Timbered Choir*, 26.

worldview, but in the reality of the existence of the God of the Bible—the one who makes himself known not only in the contemplation of the beauties of nature but in the art of artists, the poems of poets, the novels of novelists, in the sudden appearance of the *numinous* accompanied by Otto's *mysterium tremendum* and in the terror of spaces empty of God. These *signals* strike Christians not only with the beauty, love, and compassion of God but with a righteous jealousy that brooks no equation of the self with God. There are the terror of the *deus absconditus* of Pascal and the sense of infinite distance when Hopkins "feels the fell of dark, not day."

Christians believe that their religious experience alone can and does justify a commitment to Christ. But atheists object. Yes, many of them often have odd experiences some of which are like those received by Christians and other religious people. But they make no such connection with religious belief. We turn now to their anti-religious understandings of these striking sensations.

5

Darkness Out of Light

Signals Rejected, Naturally

I think that sometimes, out of the corner of an eye, "at a moment
which is not of action or inaction," *one* can glimpse the true scientific vision;
austere, tragic, alienated, and very beautiful. A world that isn't
for anything; a world that is just there.

—JERRY FODOR, *IN CRITICAL CONDITION*

Men have 'em, Women have 'em. Everybody in the world has 'em.
Let's have one now. So we might sing if we were silly celebrants of
sappy *pseudo-signals of transcendence*.

Still we would be noticing the near universality of the phenomena.
Sudden ecstatic experiences really do strike us. Perhaps not often, but
they come, sometimes with great intensity, sometimes with misty subtle-
ty. What shall we do with them? We have lots of options. We can dismiss
them as insignificant and simply to pay no attention to them at all. We
can dismiss them as mere insoluble anomalies or maybe odd misfirings
of our mental spark plugs. We can submit them to Freud and see them
as embedded psychic memories of our emerging human life in a swampy
prehistoric jungle.[1]

1. Freud saw the oceanic feeling as the expression of a "'limitless narcissism,' which
he attributed to a 'primitive phase of the sense of self.'" (Comte-Sponeville, *Little Book*,
154).

Still, disregarding them is like disregarding the guilt we feel when we have told a white lie. We are guilty and we know it. The feeling will not go away. Neither will the signals. How can we explain these experiences without any reference to anything *transcendent*?

Poets, Philosophers, Novelist

Robinson Jeffers (1887–1962) was a poet, atheist, contemplative, and haunter of California's glorious Big Sur south of San Francisco. His poetry stuns me. I, too, have been captured by his powerful vision of life without God in a world of great beauty. "The Place for No Story" is an example. Here the poet stands transfixed by the scene before him—the stark, dark bluffs, the long extension of the ocean, cattle and hawks, all greater than, but foreign to, human presence. There is only material reality, and it is enough to know that and to see it as all there is. What is just is. No signal detected. But looked at by a poet who knows only this, its grandeur is still there.

For fellow poet and novelist, Steven Crane, the hollow edge of nothingness lies close to the "tattered coat" of human being:

> If I should cast off this tattered coat,
> And go free into the mighty sky;
> If I should find nothing there
> But a vast blue,
> Echoless, ignorant,—
> What then?[2]

Fear, a powerful potential *signal of transcendence,* does not lead Crane to any hope for human kind, as any of his brief poems, short stories, or novels clearly attest. *Transcendence* is desired but missing.

In the poetry of naturalist Philip Larkin, too, *transcendence* is frequently suggested and then dismissed. In "To Write One Song, I Said" the poet is surprised as he goes to a graveyard "to visit the dead." There, as the morning sun suddenly hits the stones "above a sodden grave," they "would shine like gold." But the possible *transcendence* of this brief moment remains a distant memory.[3] Scholar Don W. King notes that this

2. Crane, *Black Riders*, LXVI.
3. Larkin, *Collected Poems*, 291; King, "Sacramentalism," 60–61.

is much like the experience Thomas Hardy depicts in "The Darkling Thrush."[4]

Simon Blackburn, a modern atheist and philosopher writes, "It is hard to confess, but I can enjoy religious music, and even religious poetry," and the "*Book of Common Prayer* and the King James Bible."[5] For him, however, such potential *signals* are transcendentally minimal [Level 2 (2) (b)]. "The nave of Durham, the Taj Mahal, Stonehenge, Lindisfarne make moral demands because they testify to the human spirit that deserves some admiration, and even awe." But he adds, we do not have to respect "the beliefs that lay behind them."[6]

Fellow philosopher Stewart Shapiro, "once or twice, particularly when in the stunningly beautiful highlands of Scotland, or the northern regions of Israel," felt a faint memory of his earlier faith, but these stirrings [Level 2 (2) (a)] didn't last long. As he says, "All I had to do was to start to think about it."[7]

Psychologist Roberts E. Ornstein in his studies of human consciousness has concluded that human consciousness includes the consciousness of both normal and paranormal reality: "Man is not so closed a system as the western scientific community once thought. We are sensitive and permeable to subtle sources of energy from geophysical and human forces which often lie unnoticed in the brilliance of day." While never affirming the existence of a genuine transcendent as the source of paranormal consciousness, his conclusions remain fully within a naturalist worldview.[8]

Novelist Virginia Woolf knew what *signals of transcendence* were supposed to be—striking indications that, despite the meaninglessness of life as she experienced it, these moments of insight should remove despair and lead one forward to life-giving meaning. We find descriptions of such experiences in her novels, but they lead nowhere, and the characters in her novels who experience them are worse off for having them. We will look in more depth at her novel *The Years* in what follows

4. King, "Sacramentalism," 61.

5. Blackburn, "Religion," in *Philosophers*, 185.

6. Ibid., 286.

7. Shapiro, "Faith and Reason," 3–4.

8. Ornstein, *Psychology*, 184. Keeping his explanations within the confines of naturalism, for example, he writes, ". . . [T]he exercises of meditation . . . are . . . techniques designed to cultivate a certain mode of operation of the nervous system, at a certain time, within a certain context" (104). See also Targ and Puthoff, *Mind-Reach*.

below. But first we will examine the interesting treatment a noted scientist gives these signals.

Steven Weinberg: A Pointless Universe

Nobel Prize-winning physicist Steven Weinberg not only rejects any implication that experiences of awe and wonder are *signals of transcendence* but explains why they are totally natural in their source and their meaning. His comments, made over the course of several decades, deserve a closer look. First, notice what he writes at the end of his popular book *The First Three Minutes* (1977). There he admits that many people do have experiences that seem to demand a *transcendent* verdict:

> It is almost irresistible for humans to believe that we have some special relation to the universe, that human life is not just a more-or-less farcical outcome of a chain of accidents reaching back to the first three minutes [after the big bang], but that we were somehow built in from the beginning.

Then immediately he demurs:

> As I write this I happen to be in an airplane at 30,000 feet, flying over Wyoming en route home from San Francisco to Boston. Below, the earth looks very soft and comfortable—fluffy clouds here and there, snow turning pink as the sun sets, roads stretching straight across the country from one town to another. It is very hard to realize that this all is just a tiny part of an overwhelmingly hostile universe. It is even harder to realize that this present universe has evolved from an unspeakably unfamiliar condition, and faces a future extinction of endless cold or intolerable heat. The more the universe seems comprehensible, the more it also seems pointless.[9]

In the next paragraph Weinberg, then, contradicts what he has just said:

> But if there is no solace in the fruits of our research, there is at least some consolation in the research itself. Men and women are not content to comfort themselves with tales of gods and giants, or to confine their thoughts to the daily affairs of life; they also build telescopes and satellites and accelerators, and sit

---

9. Weinberg, *First Three Minutes,* 154; quoted by Wiker and Witt in *A Meaningful World,* 23; it was Wiker and Witt who first pointed out to me the contradiction between these paragraphs.

at their desks for endless hours *working with the meaning they gather* [emphasis added]. The effort to understand the universe is one of the very few things that lifts human life a little above the level of farce, and gives it some of the grace of tragedy.[10]

Fifteen years later in *Dreams of a Final Theory* (1992), Weinberg says his statement about the pointlessness of the universe did not mean that the "universe is pointless but rather that the universe itself suggests no point."[11] But surely in a world where nothing is truly transcendent (no god, no non-material realm), then, if there is meaning of any kind (whether suggested by the part of the universe that is being observed or manufactured—imagined, dreamed, hypothesized—by a scientist's mind), it still comes from a mind (brain). And a brain is a part of the universe. In other words, if there is any meaning of any kind at all—meaning that is true or false, misguided or on the right track—it is stimulated by the universe.

One of Weinberg's scientist colleagues suggested that what triggered the sense that the universe does have meaning was Weinberg's own nostalgia "for a world in which the heavens proclaimed the glory of God." Weinberg agreed with his colleague, but whether seriously or not is not clear. Perhaps his agreement was offered as an ironic attempt to dodge the embarrassing inconsistency.[12]

One attempt to avoid the metaphysical implications of ecstatic experiences is to make meaningful experiences, including ecstatic ones, goals in themselves.

Philosopher Anthony Simon Laden, for example, rejects *metaphysical transcendence* ("transcendence as a property of objects"), but argues

---

10. Weinberg, *First*, 154–55.

11. Weinberg, "What About God?," 375.

12. Ibid. Weinberg admits his closing statement in *The First Three Minutes* has given him endless trouble with critics. Weinberg's actual sentence from which the section quoted above is taken does not itself express what I think he means. He says that a colleague at the University of Texas thought the remark was "nostalgic." Weinberg commented, "Indeed it was—nostalgic for a world in which the heavens declared the glory of God" (ibid.). But how can a statement be "nostalgic" without expressing the "nostalgia" of its author? I have thus attributed the nostalgia to Weinberg himself. Moreover, is it not the case that nostalgia is a signal of transcendence? Nostalgia is a desire for something valuable that one has had but has no more. Is nostalgia, then, not a version of the "argument from desire" that plays a major role in C. S. Lewis's *Surprised by Joy*?

for what I call *immanent transcendence* ("transcendence as a property of experience").[13]

An object has the property of transcendence insofar as it exceeds, in some way, the ordinary human realm. Similarly, experiences have the property of transcendence when they somehow go beyond our ordinary experiences, when they somehow draw us out of and beyond ourselves.[14]

But notice how being drawn "out of and beyond ourselves" cannot actually be what the metaphoric language suggests. There is no "out and beyond" to be drawn to. We are machines; our selves are entirely within us and always will be. Any sense of being drawn "out and beyond" is illusion, a trickery of our consciousness. So when Laden attempts to give a liveable reason for our being significant, he indulges in semantic mysticism. "I am interested," he says, "in showing how a life without God can nevertheless be infused with transcendent experiences that give it value and meaning."[15] Even with this hope, Laden's "bracing" vision is chilling:

> In the absence of God, all there is left to human life is human action and interaction with ourselves and each other and other aspects of the natural world, and the only meaning any of it has is the meaning we manage to give it. Our existence is thus one long walk on a tightrope over a yawning abyss and there is nothing to catch us should we fall into meaninglessness or isolation or even mere ordinariness. But that is exactly what I find so exhilarating about being an atheist. Life is up to us; there are no safety nets. That's a bracing thought. It's also a reason to live."[16]

Weinberg, too, comes to a similar solution to the threat of nihilism and despair.

Weinberg is fascinated enough by *signals of transcendence* and human significance to address the issue again in "Without God" in *The New York Review of Books* (2008).[17] Here he explains why he has been able to reject potential *signals of transcendence*.

First, he recounts the now standard story told by anthropologists. For primal humans the notion of transcendent beings of some sort

13. Laden, "Transcendence," 129.

14. Ibid., 132.

15. Ibid., 129.

16. Ibid., 142.

17. Weinberg, "Without God," 73–76; "This essay," he writes, "is based on the Phi Beta Kappa Oration given at Harvard University on June 3, 2008, and draws on some of my other lectures" (73).

derived from "the observation of mysterious phenomena—thunder, earthquake, disease—that seemed to require the intervention of some divine being."[18] Nymphs and dryads were in every brook and tree. But Descartes, Newton, and modern science in general were able to provide natural explanations for these phenomena. "The important thing," Weinberg says, "is that we have not observed anything that seems to require supernatural explanation."[19] Darwin and modern evolution now give all the explanations needed to satisfy our understanding of human beings, even human *consciousness* itself. Some people do not accept these naturalistic explanations, but, says Weinberg, "I can imagine how disturbed they will feel in the future, when at last scientists learn how to understand human behavior in terms of the chemistry and physics of the brain and nothing is left that needs to be explained by our having an immaterial soul."[20]

We should note that this is a *hope* requiring *faith*; it is not a present reality. It is a version of the mañana argument: Science does not know the answer today, but it will know tomorrow.[21] Nonetheless, Weinberg combines his hope with a modern stoic plea to live as if life has meaning:

> We know that we will never get to the bottom of things, because whatever theory unites all observed particulars and forces, we will never know why it is that the theory describes the real world and not some other theory.
>
> Worse, the worldview of science is rather chilling. Not only do we not find any point to life laid out for us in nature, no objective basis for our moral principles, no correspondence between what we think is the moral law and the laws of nature, of the sort imagined by philosophers from Anaximander and Plato to Emerson. We even learn that the emotions that we most treasure, our love for our wives and husbands and children, are

18. Ibid., 73.

19. Ibid.

20. Ibid., 74.

21. The mañana argument is itself a mirror image of the "god of the gaps" argument so excoriated by secular critics of Christian critiques of evolution. For the naturalist, evidence is imagined; for the Christian, agency is perceived (concluded?). In the increased ability of science to explain complex phenomena there is some evidence for the hope of science to explain all, just not enough to be so certain as scientists often seem to suppose. Note Weinberg's phraseology: "when [not if] scientists learn." In fact, Weinberg does admit that scientists cannot in principle get to "the bottom of things." This humility is both admirable and justified. Still Weinberg follows this admission with a determination to be much more than ordinarily human!

made possible by chemical processes in our brains that are what they are as a result of natural selection acting on chance mutations over millions of years.[22]

Then comes the Nietzschean or existential move—the manufacture of meaning:

> And yet we must not sink into nihilism or stifle our emotions. At our best we live on a knife-edge, between wishful thinking on the one hand and, on the other, despair. . . .
>
> Living without God isn't easy. But its very difficulty offers one other consolation—that there is a certain honor, or perhaps just a grim satisfaction, in facing up to our condition without despair and without wishful thinking—with good humor, but without God."[23]

Weinberg has been writing about religious experiences in general and explaining how they have come to be and what they really mean. What sorts of them has he experienced? Has he ever stood transfixed by a mountain vista or felt awe-ful tremor as a thunderstorm came crashing through his family's campsite in the North Woods? If he has, he was not impressed: He says he is simply unable to see such supposed signals as *signals* at all.[24] Rather he sees Berger's *signals of transcendence* as totally natural behavior that can allow us to live. They include "sympathetic merriment at ourselves, trying to live balanced lives on a knife-edge, . . . ordinary pleasures of life, . . . pleasures of the flesh, . . . [and] pleasures brought by the high arts.[25] The purely natural is enough: "We who are not

22. Weinberg, "Without God," 76.

23. Ibid. Neuhaus comments on this move by secularists to manufacture morality and meaning: "Proponents of a scientific doctrine of materialistic determinism may depict themselves as Stoics bravely accepting the grim truth about reality, but they, too, are encountered by 'signals of transcendence.' In nature, in laughter, in scientific wonder, and, above all, in love. They too protest wrong and condemn evil, implicitly recognizing that there is Right and Good by which reference to which wrong is wrong and evil is evil. They too are possessed of an irresistible intuition that all of this is part of an infinitely greater More. They, too, ask in every present moment, 'What next?' And know that the question is unending" (*American Babylon*, 247–48).

24. Nonetheless, Weinberg closes his essay "The Missions of Astronomy," 22, with this quotation from astronomer Claudius Ptolemy c. AD 60—c. 168) in *The Greek Anthology*: "I know that I am mortal and the creature of a day; but when I search out massed wheeling circles of the stars, my feet no longer touch the Earth, but side by side with Zeus himself, I take my fill of ambrosia, the food of the gods."

25. Ibid.

zealots can rejoice that when bread and wine are no longer sacraments, they still will be bread and wine."[26] It is nonetheless true that

> the more we reflect on the pleasures of life, the more we miss the greatest consolation that used to be provided by religious belief: the promise that our lives will continue after death, and that in the afterlife we will meet people that we have loved. As religious belief weakens, more and more of us know that after death there is nothing. This is the thing that makes cowards of us all.[27]

So, we must conclude, if we do not wish to be cowards, each of us must become a brave Nietzschean *Übermensch*, a maker of our own morality, God of our own Godhood.[28] But that will never happen. To the extent it is tried, it threatens to lead, as it has before, to personal madness and, perhaps, social chaos such as we have seen where it has been tried—Nazi Germany, Stalinist Russia, and North Korea now. It is not that Weinberg would ever be party to such notions, but, given his naturalism as a foundation for his sense of morality, there is no rational justification for his not doing so.

Virginia Woolf: Darkness out of Light

With Virginia Woolf (1882–1941) we will begin at the end of her novel *The Years* (1937) and not far from the end of her own life.

The novel itself ends just as dawn is breaking over one of God's most gloriously beautiful islands. But instead of the beauty and hope that

26. Ibid. Weinberg rejects as immoral the story of Abraham and his willingness to sacrifice his son Isaac, and he fails to consider any more acceptable and pleasant experiences that people often have when they read the New Testament, especially the Gospels. He never considers Jesus as either a revelation of a personal God or a *signal* that there is any god at all.

27. Ibid. Though there is recent scholarly evidence for a decline in religious belief among emerging adults (age 18–23) in America, there is a lot of counter-evidence for Weinberg's assumption that religious belief is declining. See Smith and Snell, *Souls*, and Jenkins, *Next Christendom*. Globally, Weinberg himself may be wishfully thinking.

28. Literally, *Overman* or *Man beyond man*, sometimes translated as *Superman*. One who has by his or her (we must be politically correct, even though Nietzsche was not) own will self-transcended his or her humanity, not to become a supernatural being but to replace in all ethical and so-called spiritual aspects the God of Christians or, we could add, any truly transcendent being, there having been none in the first place.

is literally expressed in the final lines of *The Years*, there is nothing but darkness and despair.

> The sun had risen, and the sky above the houses wore an air of extraordinary beauty, simplicity and peace.[29]

These lines are laced with irony—as deep as any in the entire, often ironic corpus of her work. A party has brought together the major figures of the Pargiter family whose saga Woolf has been tracing from 1880 to 1937 (the present). The party has not gone well. No one can say what they would like to say, no one quite means what they do say, those who have had epiphanies of self-understanding are being self-deceived, no one knows either themselves or others, nor do they have even the faintest grasp of any significance in their long lives. When the children of the caretaker are brought in and asked to brighten the party with children's *joie de vivre*, their words are unintelligible, their voices harsh, their accent hideous:

> There was something horrible in the noise they made. It was so shrill, so discordant, and so meaningless. . . . The contrast between their faces and their voices was astonishing; it was impossible to find one word for the whole.[30]

There is a disturbing inevitability to the course of the story Woolf tells. Every character is trapped in his or her own skin, bound by their unique subjective awareness, unable either to understand themselves or to understand each other.

Virginia Woolf is rarely easy to read. Without one's full attention, the story quickly disintegrates. I can imagine many readers do not get past the first few pages. But, while her novels demand attention, they repay it four-fold, none more than *The Years*. Here Woolf, now a master portrayer of intricate human relationships, recounts events in the life of the Pargiter family over some sixty years and does so by stringing together eleven chapters, each recounting the events of only one day. The settings of these scenes are unrelentingly spare. She does not sketch the scene, identify the characters and then describe the details of the day. Rather she records snippets of conversations, constructs streams of consciousness, and alludes to past events and characters. The result is a meaning that is first obscure, only to become clear pages later, if then. Moreover, she creates and invades the minds of her cast of characters seemingly without

29. Woolf, *Years*, 435.
30. Ibid., 430–31.

pattern. I say seemingly because with lots of attention and thought, one sees a pattern emerge.

She has described this narrative method rather well in her essay "Modern Fiction," written some eighteen years earlier. Reflect, she says, on the experience of an ordinary day:

> The mind receives a myriad impressions—trivial, fantastic, eva-nescent, or engraved with the sharpness of steel. From all sides they come, an incessant shower of innumerable atoms; and as they fall, as they shape themselves into the life of Monday or Tuesday, the accent falls differently from of old; the moment of importance came not here but there; so that if a writer were a free man and not a slave, if he could write what he chose, not what he must, if he could base his work upon his own feeling and not upon convention, there would be no plot, no comedy, no tragedy, no love interest or catastrophe in the accepted style, and perhaps not a single button sewn on as the Bond Street tai-lors would have it. Life is not a series of gig lamps symmetrically arranged; but a luminous halo, a semi-transparent envelope sur-rounding us from the beginning of consciousness to the end.[31]

There is no implicit or obvious order to experience. It comes to us willy-nilly. We make of it what we will. So the novelist, if not bound by conven-tion, would depict life. Woolf seems to set for herself just such a task:

> Let us record the atoms as they fall upon the mind in the order in which they fall, let us trace the pattern, however disconnected and incoherent in appearance, which each sight or incident scores upon the consciousness.[32]

Late in her life she seems more bent on discovering and in her novels depicting the significant patterns of life.

> Perhaps this is the strongest pleasure known to me. It is the rap-ture I get when in writing I seem to be discovering what belongs to what; making a scene come right; making a character come together. From this I reach what I might call a philosophy; at any rate it is a constant idea of mine; that behind the cotton wool is hidden a pattern; that we—I mean all human beings—are con-nected with this; that the whole world is a work of art; that we are parts of the work of art. *Hamlet* or a Beethoven quartet is the truth about this vast mass that we call a world. But there is no

31. Woolf, "Modern Fiction," 154.
32. Ibid., 155.

Shakespeare, there is no Beethoven; certainly and emphatically there is no god; we are the words; we are the music; we are the thing itself. And I see this when I have a shock.

This intuition of mine—it is so instinctive that it seems given to me, not made by me—has certainly given its scale to my life ever since I saw the flower in the bed by the front door at St. Ives.[33]

Still, in the final analysis, that pattern, while it does show an implicit order under the chaos of events and thoughts, ends up being as meaningless as chaos itself. Take the several epiphanies that occur throughout *The Years*. Early in the morning, Kitty Malone, now Lady Lasswade, walks in the woods near her manor house somewhere north of London:

Suddenly she saw the sky between two striped tree trunks extraordinarily blue. She came out on the top. The wind ceased; the country spread wide all round her. Her body seemed to shrink; her eyes to widen. She threw herself on the ground, and looked over the billowing land that went rising and falling, away and away, until somewhere far off it reached the sea. Uncultivated, uninhabited, existing by itself, for itself, without towns or houses it looked from this height. Dark wedges of shadow, bright breadths of light lay side by side. Then, as she watched, light moved and dark moved; light and shadow went travelling [*sic*] over the hills and over the valleys. A deep murmur sang in her ears—the land itself, singing to itself, a chorus, alone. She lay there listening. She was happy, completely. Time had ceased.[34]

This Level 2 (2) signal comes in 1914. We never hear of this epiphany again. For Kitty the transient, ephemeral, ever-shifting world of impressions that had once seemed to become one returns to its daily character. Confusion returns. Meaning vanishes.

Eleanor Pargiter, too, has an epiphany at Level 2 (2). In the midst of the Great War with bombs bursting in London, partly as a result of wine, she sees a pepper-pot as a "dark moor":

A little blur had come round the edges of things. It was the wine; it was the war. Things seem to have lost their skins; to be freed from some surface hardness; even the chair with gilt claws, at

---

33. Woolf, "Sketch," 72.
34. Woolf, *Years*, 277–78.

which she was looking, seemed porous; it seemed to radiate out some warmth, some glamour, as she looked at it.[35]

Later, the feeling returns and intensifies:

> She lay back in the chair. Everything seemed to become quiet and natural again. A feeling of great calm possessed her. It was as if another space of time had been issued to her, but robbed by the presence of death of something personal, she felt—she hesitated for a word—"immune?"[36]

The destruction of war has missed her; she is, and will be, preserved from death. But, of course, only for a time. Nicholas, a mysterious alien figure in the novel, has envisioned a New World, and Eleanor is captivated:

> . . . [W]hen will this New World come? When shall we be free? When shall we live adventurously, wholly, not like cripples in a cave? He seemed to have released something in her; she felt not only a new space of time, but new powers, something unknown within her. . . . We shall be free, we shall be free, Eleanor thought.[37]

She even contemplates Virginia Woolf's own sense of a pattern beneath the chaotic surface:

> Does everything then come over again a little differently? she thought. If so, is there a pattern; a theme, recurring, like music; half remembered, half foreseen? . . . a gigantic pattern, momentarily perceptible? The thought gave her extreme pleasure: that there was a pattern. But who makes it? Who thinks it? Her mind slipped. She could not finish her thought.[38]

Dangling conversations, dangling thoughts, course through *The Years*. Scenes begin *in medias res* and end there. Slices of life, literary critics call them, slices that, pared from their context, hang precipitously till the next slice, a segment preceded by a gap, appears. She could not finish her thought partly because this is a dinner party and other guests impinge on thoughts and conversations, but finally because a thought, like the one Eleanor has begun, can never be completed.

35. Ibid., 287.
36. Ibid., 293–94.
37. Ibid., 297.
38. Ibid., 369.

Her niece Peggy, though, does not yet realize this. At the same party, she becomes bored, picks up a book, and opens it at random and reads:

> "La médiocrité de l'univers m'étonne et me révolte," she read. That was it. Precisely. She read on. ". . .la petitesse de toutes choses m'emplit de dégoût . . ." She lifted her eyes. They were treading on her toes. ". . . la pauvreté des êtres humains m'antéantit." She shut the book and put it back on the shelf. Precisely, she said.[39]

Set to thinking such dour thoughts, she is interrupted. Eleanor has suddenly burst forth with joy [(Level 2 (2)]: "'I feel . . .' she stopped. She put her hand to her head 'as if I'd been in another world! So happy!' she exclaimed. 'Tosh,'" says her brother-in-law Renny, accusing her of "always talking of the other world." No, she replies, "I meant, happy in this world—happy with living people."[40]

This sets the young Peggy to thinking again. How can people in this world be happy? "On every placard at every street was Death; or worse—tyranny; brutality; torture; the fall of civilization; the end of freedom." Peggy, the younger generation, the one in whom all peoples of all times place their confidence, despairs of thinking:

> Why must I think? She did not want to think. She wished that there were blinds like those in railway carriages that came down over the light and hooded the mind. . . . Thinking was torment; why not give up thinking, and drift and dream? But the misery of the world, she thought, forces me to think. Or was that a pose?[41]

She cannot trust her thinking, even her thinking about thinking. Laughter around her makes her thought dangle. It is never completed: "she tried to think herself away into the darkness of the country. But it was impossible; they were laughing. She opened her eyes, exacerbated by their laughter."[42]

The laughter, however, has a strange effect upon her. It produces an epiphany, a *signal of transcendence*:

39. Ibid., 383. The French reads in translation: "The mediocrity of the universe astonishes and revolts me. . . . The pettiness of all things fills me with disgust. . . . the poverty of human beings destroys me."

40. Ibid., 387.

41. Ibid., 388.

42. Ibid., 389.

It had relaxed her, enlarged her. She felt, or rather she saw, not a place, but a state of being, in which there was real laughter, real happiness, and this fractured world was whole; whole, vast, and free. But how could she say it?[43]

Like all "oceanic experiences," senses of cosmic consciousness, the insight is incommunicable, hers alone. She tries to articulate it, but what comes out is an insult to her brother. The epiphany is belied. A few minutes later she realizes this: "Yes, it was over; it was destroyed, she felt. Directly something got together, it broke. She had a feeling of desolation."[44]

She would have to start over. And so would Woolf in the novel. She does so by turning to the thoughts of North, Peggy's brother who has spent the past few years as a farmer in Africa. North does not fit into the company of the dinner party; he has been gone from England too long. Most of those he meets at the party are either foreign, as is Nicholas, or a generation ahead of him. As far as he is concerned, the English upper-middle class of his relatives fritters their lives away talking about money and politics. He would talk "about the past and poetry,"[45] but no one, not even his uncle Edward, an Oxford Greek scholar, would do so. As he watches the bubbles rise in his wine, he is left to his own ruminations. He does not want life with a pattern, but life "modeled on the jet (he was watching the bubbles rise), on the spring, of the hard leaping fountain,"[46] not a place in an orderly world of money and politics but a way to "make a new ripple in human consciousness, be the bubble and the stream, the stream and the bubble—myself and the world together."[47] This he thinks to himself and wants to say it to others, but he falters. He can't speak out or even continue with his thoughts, for, he questions himself, "how can I . . . unless I know what's solid, what's true; in my life, in other people's lives?"[48] But a few moments later he is feeling like "he had been in the middle of a jungle; in the heart of darkness; cutting his way towards the light; but provided only with broken sentences, single words, with which to break through the brier-bush of human bodies, human wills and voices, that bent over him, binding him, blinding him."[49] A moment later, he

43. Ibid., 390.
44. Ibid., 392.
45. Ibid., 408.
46. Ibid., 410.
47. Ibid.
48. Ibid.
49. Ibid., 411.

is again optimistic, seeing "the fruit, the fountain that's in all of us,"[50] and a moment after that down in the dumps:

> A block had formed in his forehead as if two thoughts had collided and had stopped the passage of the rest. His mind was a blank. He swayed the liquid from side to side. He was in the middle of a dark forest.[51]

By now, I think we are to assume, Woolf wants us to see that whether up or down, North is under the influence not of his own clear thought but the bubbling wine. In any case, Woolf leaves him pondering the fear that separates all of us from one another and struggling with the knot in his forehead: "Thinking alone tied knots in the middle of the forehead; thinking alone bred pictures, foolish pictures."[52]

Asked to speak the truth, a truth the younger generation—he and his sister Peggy—could tell, he flounders. He cannot do it. He feels "again the constriction of the knot in his forehead."[53] He wants "someone, infinitely wise and good, to think for him," but there is no one.[54] All he can do is to blurt out what he has heard from one even younger than himself earlier in the evening: ". . . To live differently . . . differently."[55] Then as the bubbles cease and the wine goes flat, North is reduced to solitary thought: "Stillness and solitude, he thought to himself, silence and solitude . . . that's the only element in which the mind is free now."[56]

With this North slips slowly, dreamily into unconsciousness:

> And he was floating, and drifting, in a shallop, in a petal, down a river into silence, into solitude . . . which is the worst torture, the words came back to him as if a voice had spoken to them, that human beings can inflict. . . .[57]

He, too, never gets beyond a Level 2 (2) experience.

Unrelenting, Woolf drives home the emptiness of the lives of her characters. They are interesting in their own right. We come as readers to

50. Ibid., 412.
51. Ibid., 413.
52. Ibid., 414.
53. Ibid., 423.
54. Ibid.,
55. Ibid.
56. Ibid., 424, Woolf's ellipses.
57. Ibid.

feel for them, but we see in them a vast desert, a wasteland of triviality, not because they wish to be trivial but because they cannot help but be so and, in the case of the major characters, are aware of that fact. The coup de gras is Woolf's picture of Eleanor's final epiphany.

At the end of a dinner party, Eleanor, like North, in a semi-drunken, sleepy stupor, yearns for an escape from this life to a better one:

> There must be another life, here and now, she repeated. This is too short, too broken. We know nothing, even about ourselves. We're only just beginning, she thought, to understand, here and there. . . . [S]he felt that she wanted to enclose the present moment; to make it stay; to fill it fuller and fuller, with the past, the present and the future until it shone, whole, bright, deep with understanding.[58]

But she cannot have what does not exist in the world of Virginia Woolf:

> It's useless, she thought. . . . For her too there would be the endless night; the endless dark. She looked ahead of her as though she saw opening in front of her a very long dark tunnel. But thinking of the dark, something baffled her; in fact it was growing light. The blinds were white.[59]

As the novel closes, the sun is rising. But the spiritual reality for Eleanor remains dark. In the final irony of Woolf's perhaps most ironic novel, day dawns as spiritual night looms large.

This is the truly depressing aspect of *The Years*. So much effort to construct a unified novel with such seemingly disjointed parts, so much depth to the characters themselves, so much effort on the part of the reader. And withal so little to satisfy either the characters of the novel or the readers, or, shall we sadly say, the novelist herself who, not long after she had written the novel, succeeded in committing suicide, an act attempted unsuccessfully in the novel by Rose Pargiter.

Virginia Woolf, we would say as Christians, is wrong about the absence of God. Rather, she is blind to the light of the Son. And it is being aware of the presence of the Son—not just as the pattern that orders the seeming chaos of the world, but as the one who by taking on the pain of the world is the answer to the pain in the world; not just as the source of life a long time ago but as the sustainer of life today, the one who is the

58. Ibid., 427–28.
59. Ibid., 428.

true fountain, who alone knows just what kind of living differently would be a proper goal of life—that is what banishes depression and brings a reasonable hope to all of life.

Weinberg and Woolf—two articulate voices from the world of naturalism—with one conclusion: there is in life only the meaning we human beings give it. But that meaning is temporary, often painful, and in the end utterly illusory. Still, let us look at some recent attempts to explain why we have these illusory experiences. We turn then to the neuroscientists and those attempting to understand the philosophical implications of the results of their research.

Transcendence as an Action of the Brain

There is now a growing body of literature addressing the ancient mind-brain problem from the perspective of neuroscience. Is the mind only brain? If not, what is mind and how is it related to brain? As usual, with such yet unresolved intellectual questions, there is great disagreement. That disagreement is reflected in modern views of *signals of transcendence*.

At one extreme are the Eastern-oriented mystics who take the brain as an illusion of the mind. Neither brain nor mind gives accurate explanations of ultimate reality. They are useful for getting around in the material world, but neither does each alone or both together lead a person to ultimate or objective truth. We will examine a few examples of this notion in chapter eight.

At the opposite extreme are the naturalists who hold that the brain is the mind in the sense that once one has understood the full material nature of the brain, the mind itself will be explained. At the moment this view, as nearly as I can discern, is held only by those scientists and philosophers who are entirely certain that matter is all there is in the world. That is, they are committed to a naturalist world view; so, when challenged, they assert their atheism as fundamental. As Carl Peraino puts it, "I guess I'm just tethered to 'natural world' logic."[60]

Many neuroscientists either ignore the issue as out of bounds for scientific analysis or make no claim that science does now or will in the future rule out some unique non-natural character to the mind or to ultimate reality. In some cases this seems to be proper humility; in others just a way to avoid a public display of the religion vs. science controversy.

60. Sire and Peraino, *Deepest*, 40.

For an overall presentation of some of these options, I suggest "How Our Brains are Wired for Belief," a transcript of the May 2008 Pew Foundation Forum on Religion and Public Life, hosted by Michael Cromartie. As Christian intellectual Cromartie said, "recent advances in neuroscience and brain-imaging technology have offered researchers a look into the physiology of religious experiences."[61]

Neuroscientist Andrew Newberg made the key presentation. *New York Times* columnist David Brooks responded by explaining the broader public significance of the findings. Newberg focused on the physiological changes in the brain as people who were meditating felt what they identified as religious experiences. Brooks noted how the research has seemed to strengthen the arguments of intellectuals who no longer believe that human beings have free will.

Brooks, however, challenged the view that human beings do not possess free will. Moreover, he believes that for a host of reasons neuroscience has actually strengthened the notion that human beings are in some sense spiritual beings, a view which he shares. One reason he cites is that recent scientific studies have given physical evidence of "elevated states" or "moments of transcendence," experiences I have been calling *signals of transcendence* at Levels 3 and 4.[62]

Scientific studies now make it difficult to maintain the traditional duality of mind and body. Mind and body are seen as inextricably entwined. Brooks remarks: "Where the research winds up ultimately is, frankly, at Buddhism. . . . soft-core Buddhism." We will return to this issue again as we look at Eastern views of *signals*.

Several journalists invited to this forum then raised questions for Newberg and Brooks. The gist of the ensuing comments addressed scientism (in which material science claims be the only valid way to know?), humility (the attitude required of scientists not to claim more certainty for their interpretations than can be rationally sustained), emotions (how they factor in relation to belief), human nature (is it universal?), faith (its

61. "How Our Brains are Wired for Belief."

62. Brooks,"Neural Buddhists." Brooks suggests that the challenge to theism in the future will not come from atheism. Rather neural "science and mysticism are joining hands and reinforcing each other." Actually, "The real challenge is going to come from people who feel the existence of the sacred, but who think that particular religions are just cultural artifacts built on top of universal human traits. It's going to come from scientists whose beliefs overlap with Buddhism." Notice the parallel with philosopher André Comte-Sponville's movement from Western atheism to a Western form of Buddhism, discussed in chapter 5.

role in scientific reasoning), the existence of God (as not necessarily in conflict with the findings of material science), and similarity of aha moments in science and in religion.

The transcript goes on for many pages, but near the end, perhaps it is the scientist who puts the main point best: "It's very, very difficult to be able to nail something down with such determinism that people would be able to say, 'There's no free will,' or 'There is no God.'" We may conclude, then, that while some scientists, philosophers, and intellectuals show great confidence in their rejection of any transcendent signaling, they have by no means convinced many of their colleagues and the public in general to agree with them. In short, neuroscience has not disproved the existence of the transcendent. Rather it may have strengthened the biblical notion that human beings are a unity of body and soul or body, soul, and spirit.

Zapping as Capricious

I have often discussed *signals of transcendence* with scientist Carl Peraino. He says, "I experience a powerful sense of awe and affirmation at the realization that I am made of stardust and starlight and am an integral part of the universe in all its vastness and diversity."[63] Nonetheless, he has never felt that these experiences signal anything beyond the universe. So he also says, "As one who has not been zapped by signals of transcendence, I am essentially in complete agreement with Steven Weinberg. For me, the discarding of religion was an intellectually and emotionally liberating experience that was triggered by education."[64] Carl then notes that some scientists, like Francis Collins, seem to have faith-affirming transcendent experiences, but as far as he can tell there seems to be no reason for their appearance. "Apparently belief in God comes and goes in a rather capricious manner." He then encouraged me to "deal with these particular dy-

63. Personal communication, April 9, 2009, used by permission from Carl Peraino. Carl, biochemist and my neighbor, co-authored with me *Deepest Differences*. Samuel Beckett, too, was tone-deaf to any hint of the spiritual: "I . . . seem never to have had the least faculty or disposition for the supernatural." *Letters of Samuel Beckett*, as quoted by Coetsee, "Making of Samuel Beckett," 14.

64. Personal communication, September 24, 2008, used by permission from Carl Peraino. Carl's attitude is much like that of Carl Sagan who, in the video version of *The Cosmos*, stands in awe in front of huge photographs of the skies and speaks in religious tones of billions and billions of stars.

namics as I discuss *signals of transcendence* in your next book. Thus, how is the sensitivity to such *signals* gained or lost? Is this sensitivity governed by the presence or absence of 'spiritual blindness'? Whence cometh the latter malady?"

This general issue is, of course, the topic of this book. But I will address one of his specific questions now. Do these signals really come capriciously, or do we just not know why they come? If capriciously, then their cause(s) will not be able to be understood; in fact, they are not understandable. If naturalism is true, the signals are caused naturally and should at least be subject to being understood, if not now at least in principle. If they only appear to be capricious, they have cause(s) which we do not yet understand. Naturalists should, I think, not easily yield to their being capricious. It puts their trust in the sufficiency, if not the autonomy, of human reason, in doubt. If that is in doubt, then maybe the notion of the non-existence of God is one of those matters, like signals, which is grasped capriciously. If that is so, then the case for either atheism or theism (or any other understanding of fundamental reality) is so suspect as not to be trusted at all.

On the other hand, Christians, being theists, have an a priori explanation for why the *signals of transcendence* seem capricious (to wit, that our finite epistemic abilities rest on God's infinite epistemic ability and are limited by the fact that our relationship with God has been broken and our epistemic powers not just limited by their finitude but by our *fallenness* as well). Indeed, then, Christians have a plausible explanation for *signals of transcendence* appearing capricious without their actually being so.

Then too, as Peraino points out, for Christians there is always the explanation of spiritual blindness to fall back on.[65] We can make a case for both our limited epistemic powers and our spiritual blindness. It is a case that does not rest on either the complete sufficiency or the autonomy of our reason. Of course, all intellectual "cases" (from either a naturalist or a theist standpoint) rest on some notions which, in the final analysis, cannot in principle be fully proven. That is, our conclusions cannot be understood to be so certain as to be without a doubt or a possible objection.

Charles Taylor in *A Secular Age*, his massive historical and sociological study of the rise of secularism in the West, mentions the frequent

---

65. "Spiritual blindness" is my term, not his.

incursion of intense religious experience into secular life.[66] At the same time, he notes the "strong incentives to remain within the bounds of the human domain, or at least not to bother exploring beyond it." Here is why.

> The level of understanding of some of the great languages of transcendence is declining; in this respect, massive unlearning is taking place. The individual pursuit of happiness as defined by consumer culture still absorbs much of our time and energy, or else the threat of being shut out of this pursuit through poverty, unemployment, incapacity galvanizes all our efforts.
>
> All this is true, and yet the sense that there is something more presses in. Great numbers of people feel it: in moments of reflection about their life; in moments of relaxation in nature; in moments of bereavement and loss; and quite wildly and unpredictably. Our age is very far from settling in to a comfortable unbelief. Although many individuals do so, and more still seem to be on the outside, the unrest continues to surface. Could it ever be otherwise?[67]

What? Me Worry?

What, then, are the alternatives? The first is to take these experiences as signaling a true metaphysical transcendence. Another is to glory in the seemingly transcendent feeling, as does Douglas Hofstadter, letting those occasional feelings of a moment suffice for all time:

> Perhaps my lifelong training in physics and science in general has given me a deep awe at seeing how the most substantial and familiar of objects or experiences fades away, as one approaches the infinitesimal scale, into an eerily insubstantial ether, a myriad of ephemeral swirling vortices of nearly incomprehensible mathematical activity. This in me evokes a cosmic awe. To me, reductionism doesn't "explain away"; rather, it adds mystery.[68]

Francis Schaeffer would call such "mystery" *semantic mysticism*. He would say the same thing of the words of neo-Darwinist W. H. Hamilton who "expressed a wish when he died to be laid out on the forest floor

66. Taylor, *Secular Age*, 5–7, 338, 342, 367–68, 606–8, 700–701, 727–72.

67. Ibid., 727.

68. Hofstadter, "Reductionism," 434, as quoted by Taylor, *Secular Age*, 368.

in the Amazon jungle and interred by burying beetles as food for their larvae:

> Later, in their children, reared with care by the horned parents out of fist-sized balls moulded [*sic*] from my flesh, I will escape. No worm for me nor sordid fly: rearranged and multiple, I will at last buzz from the soil like bees out of a nest—indeed buzz louder than bees, almost like a swarm of motor bikes. I shall be borne, beetle by flying beetle, out of the Brazilian wilderness beneath the stars."[69]

A third response is to acknowledge despair, like Weinberg, Nietzsche, Woolf, and Dr. Rieux in Camus' *The Plague*, and then gut out a local and temporary existence. A fourth is to pay no attention to why reality appears to be what it appears to be, and to enjoy as best one can what comes along.

Before he became concerned for his own significance, before his night of Fire, Pascal followed the nonreflecting, non-thinking crowd and engaged in wine, women, song, and gambling. His modern counterparts add to this exercise, shopping, sports, television, texting, twittering and MP3 (or 4 or 5 by the time this book is published). For them *Mad Magazine's* legendary Alfred E. Neuman may have been the truly wise one: "What? Me worry?"

---

69. Quoted over Hamilton's open grave by Louisa Bozzi from "No Stone Unturned: A bug-hunter's life and death," cited by Richard Dawkins, "Forever Voyaging."

6

Bright Footprints of God

The Role of Signals in Conversions
from Atheism to Christianity

Atoms dead could never thus
Stir the human heart of us
Unless the beauty that we see
The veil of endless beauty be,
Filled full of spirits that have trod
Far hence along the heavenly sod
And seen the bright footprints of God.

—C. S. Lewis, "Song"

One of the more interesting and, for Christians, joyful events to witness even from afar are the conversions of adults from firmly held non-Christian worldviews to full-bodied faith in Jesus Christ and to fully Christian worldviews. Sometimes the move is in the other direction. Christians lose their faith and shift their worldview or, more usually, shift their worldview and lose their faith. We will not, however, be considering these moves. We will stick with, for Christians, the joyful shift. And we will do so by considering a few people who have done this at least in part through *signals of transcendence*.

C. S. Lewis: Balder Is Dead

C. S. Lewis would be an ideal choice for a detailed analysis, but so many readers know so much about him that it is not necessary to retrace our way over such familiar territory.[1] I will make his story much briefer than the one he himself tells in *Surprised by Joy*. That story begins with intense childhood interest in the land of *faerie*, in the characters and tales of Nordic mythology, and his developing interest in Greek and other pagan mythologies. The world they signaled beyond this one fascinated him; it entered his imagination and triggered a powerful longing for a reality beyond his grim, staid, Northern Irish surroundings.

He read, for example, a few lines from an English translation of *Tegner's Drapa*:

> *I heard a voice that cried,*
> *Balder the beautiful*
> *Is dead, is dead—*

> I knew nothing about Balder; but instantly I was uplifted into huge regions of northern sky, I desired with almost sickening intensity something never to be described (except that it is cold, spacious, severe, pale, and remote) and then . . . found myself at the very same moment already falling out of that desire and wishing I were back in it.[2]

He encountered this primitive, Level 2, *signal of transcendence* as a young child, and, except during ages ten to thirteen, when his imagination slept, it accompanied him throughout his growing doubt of the Christian faith and his turn to atheism.[3] During prep school in England he again began to feel the pull of the northern myths. Once as he read the title *Siegfried and the Twilight of the Gods*, his whole sense of Northerness and the world of Balder that had so struck him in his childhood imagination returned—"a vision of huge, clear spaces hanging above the Atlantic in the endless twilight of Northern summer, remoteness, severity. . . .

1. Those who want details should first read Lewis's *Surprised by Joy* (1955). Corbin Scott Carnell's *Bright Shadow of Reality* is a sustained analysis of Lewis's concepts of Joy and *Sehnsucht* (the latter being a German word Lewis adopted to label his intense nostalgic longing—his early childhood sense of missing something of immense value and importance, something that was beyond his reach but which also stimulated his highly charged imagination).

2. Lewis, *Surprised*, 23.

3. Carnell, *Bright Shadow*, 41.

[T]he distance of the Twilight of the Gods and the distance of my own past Joy, both unattainable, flowed together into a single unendurable sense of desire and loss."[4] He devoured the music of Wagner and the Nordic myths, captivated by what he called *Sehnsucht,* a mystical and romantic longing for something that transcends the present that beckoned him on toward the future. At the same time, he began to doubt his childhood Christian faith, gradually moving deep into atheism in which he persisted for some twenty years, through his early years as a scholar and college teacher of English literature.

Nonetheless, throughout this period *Sehnsucht* persisted, rising to the surface, for example, in these lines from *Spirits in Bondage* (1919), a collection of lyric poems that border on nihilism:

> I cried out for the pain of man
> I cried out for my bitter wrath
> Against the hopeless life that ran
> Forever in a circling path
> From death to death since all began;
> Till on a summer night
> I lost my way in the pale starlight
> And saw our planet, far and small
> Through endless depths of nothing fall
> A lonely pin-prick spark of light
> Upon the wide, enfolding night.[5]

And yet there are glimpses of hope, desperate hope, but hope nonetheless. These glimpses are clearly at Level 2 *signals of transcendence*:

In the poem "Dungeon Grates" he writes of "the strange power / Of unsought Beauty" that can lead one out of the "strife and storm" of life:

> We know we are not made of mortal stuff.
> And we can bear all trials that come after
> The hate of men and the fool's loud bestial laughter
> And Nature's rule and cruelties unclean,
> For we have seen the Glory—we have seen.[6]

Moreover in these lines from "Song" his childhood love for *faerie* floods in:

---

4. Lewis, *Surprised,* 74–75.
5. Lewis, *Spirits,* XI, ll., 1–11.
6. Ibid., XV, ll., 37–41.

> Fairies must be in the woods
> Or the satyr's laughing broods—
> Tritons in the summer sea,
> Else how could the dead things be
> Half so lovely as they are?
> How could wealth of star on star
> Dusted o'er the frosty night
> Fill thy spirit with delight.[7]

And look especially at the final words of this poem:

> Atoms dead could never thus
> Stir the human heart of us
> Unless the beauty that we see
> The veil of endless beauty be,
> Filled full of spirits that have trod
> Far hence along the heavenly sod
> And seen the bright footprints of God.[8]

The imagined world of *faerie* is not the world of the Bible, but neither is it the world of mere materialism. Lewis's poetry displays both the bitterness of his atheism and betrays that bitterness with bursts of Joy, striking displays of *Sehnsucht*.

Lewis's trek toward full Christian theism is long and convoluted; it involves his scholar friends in the academy (including the Catholics Hugo Dyson and J. R. R. Tolkien and the anthroposophist Owen Barfield), his relationships with his brother and his housekeeper, and, of course, his reading. This included not only the classics in which he was trained and taught but his specific academic specialty, medieval literature, and the relevant theological and philosophic texts. Plato, Aristotle, Augustine, and Aquinas stand out as most influential. Then too he enjoyed the writings of George MacDonald and G. K. Chesterton. Given the close parallel of *Sehnsucht* to the *numinous* and the *mysterium tremendum*, it is easy to see why the philosophical theology of Rudolf Otto's *Idea of the Holy* also contributed to Lewis's own concern with *signals of transcendence*.[9]

Lewis's conversion to full-orbed Christian theism did not take place all at once. Nor did it come to him as something he wanted. His academic

7. Ibid., XXVI, ll., 1–8.

8. Ibid., XXVI, ll., 19–25.

9. Carnell, *Bright Shadow*, 96, notes, "The idea of the numinous long interested Lewis; indeed it was instrumental in his conversion to Christianity" and he drew on Otto's work in *The Problem of Pain*.

background, his long adherence to atheism, the awkwardness of being one of the few Oxford scholars who was a convinced Christian, and his own stubborn willfulness stood in the way. But through his friends, his Christian reading, and his persistent longing for Joy, he sensed that God himself was pursuing him. It was a sense he tried hard to resist. There were, in fact, at least two distinct turning points. The first was his conviction of the truth of theism. This took place in his room at Magdalen College, Oxford. Lewis writes:

> You must picture me alone in that room in Magdalen, night after night, feeling, whenever my mind lifted even for a second from my work, the steady, unrelenting approach of Him whom I so earnestly desired not to meet. That which I greatly feared had at last come upon me. In the Trinity Term of 1929 I gave in, and admitted that God was God, and knelt and prayed: perhaps, that night, the most dejected and reluctant convert in all England.[10]

Though, as Carnell says, he was "both anti-ecclesiastical and constitutionally inept at anything 'churchy,'" he began attending an Anglican church, feeling that he really should "fly one's flag," that is be open about his changed belief. But he was yet to be a full-blooded Christian. He didn't even believe in a life after death. He had yet to realize just who this pursuing God is—not just sovereign and righteous but personal, intimate, and revealed in Jesus as the Son of God.

There had to be a second major turning point: "I was driven to Whipsnade one sunny morning. When we set out I did not believe that Jesus Christ is the Son of God, and when we reached the zoo I did."[11]

Now lest we think that this move from mere theism to Christian theism was a result of either conscious thought or deep religious emotion, Lewis immediately adds: "Yet I had not exactly spent the journey in thought. Nor in great emotion. . . . It was more like when a man, after long sleep, still lying motionless in bed, becomes aware that he is now awake."

Lewis does not make the connection I will mention now, but his descriptions of these two conversion experiences are much like what we would expect if we were to take seriously Calvin's notion of a *sensus divinitatis*. Is he not speaking of a direct, unmediated encounter with reality? We see someone coming into a room, not just a person, a woman. We

10. Lewis, *Surprised*, 215.
11. Ibid., 223.

haven't seen her for years, but we know her and we name her in our mind as we say without thinking and with surprise, "Helen! Is it really you?" And it is. Emotion and thought come after the recognition.

Here is another way to put this: A siren sounds, we suddenly see the scene of the accident, the car is still burning, bodies are lying just outside the car, our senses heighten, our emotions flare, our mind races. Only later do we reflect, evaluate, and deal with the implications for ourselves and others.

When I told my friend Phil that Illinois Governor Blagojevich had been arrested for something I thought was fraud, he said, "My word! There is a God." He jumped immediately from his belief that the controversial governor was something of a skuz bucket to his being guilty of something illegal; then he jumped to the sudden appreciation that justice may finally be done; then he leapt to the intuitive connection between justice and the existence of God. Of course, he was trying to be funny. But wasn't his humor based on a sort of *sensus jus*?

Albert Camus: Transcending Nihilism

The story of Albert Camus' conversion is much less known and is hard for some to believe. Though Camus was baptized as an infant in a Catholic church in Algeria where he was raised, none of his published work suggests that he ever moved from his adult atheism. Rather he responded in short stories, novels, essays, and longer philosophic works to the cultural despair set in motion by what Nietzsche called the death of God. As Camus put it, "A literature of despair is a contradiction in terms. . . . In the darkest depths of our nihilism I have sought only for the means to transcend nihilism."[12] Living in the face of the absurd, creating one's own meaning in a socially responsible way though society could not do this for itself, saying no to violence, working against all that plagues human existence: All these were noble goals that earned Camus the respect of intellectuals across the world. Some, despite his direct words, thought him to be a Christian in spite of himself. But it wasn't so. Not until the lure of the beautiful art of the organ drew him to the American Church in Paris did he seriously consider a specifically Christian understanding of himself and the world around him.

---

12. Camus, *L'Été*, quoted by Cruickshank, *Albert Camus*, 3.

One summer in the 1950s Camus waited at the end of the Sunday service to speak with the American Methodist guest pastor for a few weeks. He introduced himself to the Reverend Howard Mumma and then explained: "For these past Sundays, I came to hear Marcel Dupré play, but today I came to hear you. Would you have lunch with me tomorrow?"[13] Their dialogues extended over the course of several years as Mumma served as summer pastor.

"I am searching for something I do not have, something I'm not sure I can even define," he told Mumma.[14] Camus questioned him about the stories in the Bible. What is the Bible? Why do you call it the word of God? Is the Genesis story of the Garden historical? When Mumma asked him if he had read the Bible, he said no. In fact he didn't have a Bible. So Mumma gave him one, and the content of the dialogues deepened. Camus explained why he was attracted to the writings of Simone Weil and Mumma answered Camus's puzzlement over the problem of evil by explaining C. S. Lewis's views in *The Problem of Pain*. Camus openly spoke of his own despair and from the beginning made his interest clear.

Mumma traces the pattern of their dialogues over several summers. Finally at the end of the summer of 1959 Camus asked two questions: What is the meaning of baptism? and What does it mean to be born again? Satisfied with Mumma's answer, he said, "Howard, I am ready. I want this. This is what I want to commit my life to."[15]

Camus asked Mumma to baptize him, but Mumma was reticent. Camus had been baptized as a child. That baptism was effective, Mumma said. Moreover, Camus wanted the baptism to be private; too many of his friends, admirers, and detractors would make a fuss about it, and he did not want to become a part of a church. At the end of the summer, Camus accompanied Mumma to the airport. They parted with the intention of continuing their discussion the following year. Mumma would be reconsidering the possibility of a private baptism, and Camus would further ponder his changing beliefs. For Camus that summer never came. He was killed in a car accident January 4, 1960. It was not a suicide, as some have thought. Camus was riding in the back seat with a train ticket in his pocket. With him as well was a partially written autobiographical

13. Mumma, *Albert Camus*, 7.
14. Ibid., 9.
15. Ibid., 89.

manuscript of a novel that has subsequently been published as *Le Premier Homme* (*The First Man*).

There they were—multiple *signals of transcendence*. First was great music well performed, a striking non-verbal signal; second, human longing for significance in a world that, if God is dead, is not really possible; third, sermons that suggested there was more to be known; fourth, Scripture with its own multiple signals and its thoughtful and convincing answers to existential longing.

I once gave a talk on the history of ideas at the Nansen Dialogue Centre in Podgorica, Montenegro. Few questions were asked. So on the spur of the moment, I said, "I don't know what you will think of this story, but I am going to tell you about how Albert Camus changed his own mind about the matters I have been presenting." I then recounted the events above. Verbal chaos ensued. No one wanted to believe Camus had become a Christian. He committed suicide, some said. What does that say about his conversion? Unfortunately, I did not have good documentation for a response. So the objections kept coming. During the following few days the controversy was played out in the newspapers. Camus' conversion that could itself be a *signal of transcendence* was for some a stumbling block to rational thought, let alone spiritual insight.

Wallace Stevens: The Palm at the End of the Mind

"In my view," philosopher Simon Critchley says in his detailed and fascinating study, "Wallace Stevens is the philosophically most interesting poet to have written in English in the twentieth century."[16] Indeed Stevens's trek from his early poems in the tradition of romanticism through a series of aesthetic and philosophic transitions has garnered the attention of thousands of lovers of poetry, philosophers, and literary critics. But few of the most talented of these readers are able to agree on the specific philosophic views Stevens manifests. There are, however, two matters on which all critics agree.

First: Wallace Stevens's poetry is immensely difficult to understand. Dip anywhere into the 698 pages of the poems in Stevens's *Collected Poetry and Prose*. Pick any poem. The simplest and shortest baffle, intrigue, and fascinate, but none of them wears its meaning anywhere near the surface as do many poems by, say, Stevens's contemporary, Robert Frost.

16. Critchley, *Things*, 15.

In other words, Stevens's works are almost ripe-for-harvest by intellectuals bent on understanding what Stevens really means or what, instead of intending to mean, he thinks he is doing in his poems—expressing the inexpressible, writing music in words, speaking mostly to himself about himself, or, perhaps, posing insolvable puzzles in free verse.

Second: Wallace Stevens was an agnostic or atheist until near the very end of his life. He was raised in a Christian home and attended a Presbyterian Sunday School and a Lutheran grammar school, but when he was at Harvard, his "reading . . . focused on Coleridge, Nietzsche, and Bergson." Moreover, "He was emphatically averse to traditional Christianity."[17] His early poetry was written in the shadow of the death of God as conceived by Nietzsche and manifested in the psyche of the twentieth century. "Sunday Morning," frequently anthologized and well known to most of his readers, recapitulates the musings of a woman who has known but long ago abandoned conventional spirituality. "We live in an old chaos of the sun," she muses as a "flock of pigeons . . . sink / Downward to darkness."[18] Among the "Thirteen Ways of Looking at a Blackbird" there is no "way" that points to anything transcendent. In fact, throughout his whole *oeuvres* I have found nothing that signals anything Otherly (*numenous*). "Anecdote in Tennessee" suggests that art or perhaps human culture itself gives all the necessary order the wilderness of Tennessee needs or can have. There is only either the hard rock of physical reality or the speaker's immediate perception (the *phenomenal*). As Stevens writes, "in the absence of a belief in God, the mind turns to its own creations and examines them . . . for what they reveal, for what they validate and invalidate, for the support they give."[19]

As I just said, the complexity of Stevens's poems makes them ripe for sophisticated readers not only to admire but to unpack and fill volumes with critical interpretation. Yes, but not quite. In the spring of 1955, Stevens, now in a hospital suffering from terminal cancer, sought the visits of Father Arthur Hanley. A few months later, again in the hospital, Stevens made a private expression of Christian faith, took communion and was baptized, saying a few days later, "Now I'm in the fold."

What gives a critic trouble is two-fold. Stevens left his readers no poems written after his conversion. Moreover, this conversion was only

17. "Wallace Stevens."
18. Stevens, *Collected Poetry and Prose*, 56.
19. Stevens as quoted by Scott, Jr., "Wallace Stevens' Route," 13.

made public twenty-two years later. Some readers, notably Critchley, dismiss his conversion with a wave of the hand: "Although, in the final days of his illness from cancer, he was converted to Catholicism, I see this as the act of a dying, lonely man who confessed to 'a certain emptiness in his life' and who hadn't been on speaking terms with his wife for years."[20] One twenty-five-page biography doesn't even mention his conversion, nor does the eleven-page chronology in *Collected Poetry and Prose*.[21] But the evidence belies such a blasé attitude to what is clearly a conversion of a man who always knew what he was doing.[22]

What, then, is the result of this late twist in the intellectual and spiritual life of this most complex of poets? Some critics see in his poetry anti-realism and solipsism (Alan Bloom and Joseph Riddel), others see a *contracted* or *transfigured* sense of the real or, perhaps, a *transcendent realism* (Sebastian Gardner).[23] Simon Critchley's detailed view of Stevens's philosophic and poetic meanderings is perhaps most succinctly stated here: "Stevens is attempting to write poetry of reality, where imagination touches reality, transfiguring the reality that it touches."[24]

Other readers emphasize the Zen-like character of some of his poems and conclude that he took a Buddhist-Christian path especially toward the end of his life.[25] There are arguments for assessing Stevens's early and even some of his late poems as purely secular, nihilistic or, for that matter, Zen-like. But this leaves his conversion to be dismissed as shallow, illusory or perhaps invented by well-wishing Catholic readers. If it is a genuine conversion, it would also mean that Stevens made a sudden radical u-turn in both philosophy and spirituality. To a man who constantly transfigured his deliberate thinking into his best poetics, such a sudden radical reversal is highly unlikely. Nathan A. Scott, Jr. sees in Stevens's poetry the idea that being (or Being) is that "*transcendens* which,

20. Critchley, *Things*, 21.

21. Stevens, *Collected Poetry and Prose*, 659–69.

22. See the summary of various interpretations of Stevens's conversion in Hall, "Wallace Stevens's Spiritual Voyage," 280–82, "Wallace Stevens's Alleged Deathbed Conversion"; and Cirurgao, "Last Farewell and First Fruits."

23. Critchley, *Things*, 26–30, documents these views.

24. Ibid., 61.

25. Hall, "Wallace Stevens's Spiritual Journey," 277–304. The lines of Stevens's very last poem, "The Palm at the End of the Mind," do indeed have the feel of a haiku by Matsuo Basho, but they also support a very different completely Christian reading.

as the enabling condition of everything that exists, is 'wholly other' than and distinct from all particular beings, even in their totality."[26]

The reading given by Nathan A. Scott, Jr. is to my mind the most perceptive of those I have considered. He takes seriously both their obvious philosophic import and their literary form; then he adds a brilliant exegesis of a few of Stevens's late poems seen through the light of the poet's Catholic conversion.

So what then shall we make of "Of Mere Being," the final poem in Stevens's last volume of poetry?

I quote it here and follow with four distinct "readings" of the worldview it reflects:

> The palm at the end of the mind,
> Beyond the last thought, rises
> In the bronze distance,[27]
>
> A gold-feathered bird
> Sings in the palm, without human meaning,
> Without human feeling, a foreign song.
>
> You know then that it is not the reason
> That makes us happy or unhappy.
> The bird sings. Its feathers shine.
>
> The palm stands on the edge of space.
> The wind moves slowly in the branches.
> The bird's fire-fangled feathers dangle down.[28]

A Zen Buddhist Reading

In Zen Buddhism fundamental reality cannot be known or understood by the human intellect, and since in Zen Buddhism there is no God, that is, no transcendent being, there can be no knowledge of fundamental

26. Scott, "Wallace Stevens' Route," 37.

27. The text in Stevens, *Collected Poems*, 476, reads "bronze decor"; this is the text interpreted by Critchley and Peraino. "Bronze distance" derives from the text in the first edition of Wallace Stevens, *Opus Posthumous* (1957), 141; see *Collected Poems and Prose*, 1004; this is the text interpreted by Scott and my versions of a Buddhist and a Christian reading.

28. Stevens, *Collected Poetry*, 476–77.

reality. Buddhists sometimes give a name to this *reality* that must now not be thought of as any "thing" or being at all. Buddhists call *reality* the Void (Emptiness) or Plenum-Void (Full Emptiness) or Not-Being. But these are *attempts* to label for matters of discourse what cannot be labeled. Poets, especially those in the tradition of Matsuo Basho (1644–95), seem to me the most able to suggest this state of affairs that is not a state of affairs. And they do so by indirection.

A modern frog leaps into an ancient pond and makes the sound of water, writes Basho. But in Japanese the word for "sound of water" is not onomatopoetic. It is simply "sound of water." At the precise moment when a frog jumps into the pond, there is no sound. Such is reality. It is full of potential (plenum) but it is nothing (void). Or take the classic Japanese Zen question, "What is the sound of one hand?" (Note: in Japanese, the word "clapping" does not appear.) So what is the sound of one hand? Exactly: nothing! Poised for making a sound but not doing so: empty and full.

Now take this background into a reading of Stevens's poem.

Stanza one: Like a Zen conundrum, *the palm* is at the *end of the mind*. It is *beyond the last thought* (the furthermost element not of physical reality but of thought) *in the bronze* distance (a beautiful background color with no detail).

Stanza two: *A gold* (a word *loaded* with sight imagery and suggestion of supreme value) *feathered* (it is something now seen physical) *bird* (birds are frequent in Zen haikus) *sings* (now there is sound) but without *human meaning* (without a word there can be no linguistic or intellectual meaning) and without *human feeling* (no emotion as well as no thought). The *song* is *foreign* (not domestic, but thoroughly unidentifiable, no name, only sound, color, and plumage).

Stanza three: *You know* (the intellect appears) *then* (logically therefore and chronologically next) *that it is not reason that makes us happy* (we know this because we are happy and our reason has not been involved in making us happy, only in making us realize we are happy). Now the *bird sings* (end of sentence indicates a break; don't go forward, reader, till you see what has just been said). *Its feathers shine* (like Basho's frog it simply does what it does; it calls attention to what it appears to be; this is the language of phenomenology; what the bird appears to be is all that can be known about it).

Stanza four: Now *the palm stands on the edge of space* (mind and space are one and the same). *The wind moves slowly* (we have almost reached the stage of full being; but the wind is still slowly moving; it will have to appear to stop before anything reaches full emptiness) *in the branches* (this is a tree of some kind after all; the language is now realistic, not merely phenomenal). *The bird's fire-fangled* (brightly lit by the non-visible [and non-real?] sun) *feathers dangle down* (not moved by the wind which is now quiet).[29]

The poem reaches its end as the whole scene empties and fills with reality at the same time.

A Nihilist Reading

Notice that in the Buddhist reading and the nihilist reading no mention is made of the title. The reason is that rarely are these seventeen-syllable (minimalist) poems given titles. The poem itself—the lines, the image(s), internal labels, and often incomplete sentences—is all there is. The poem thus directs attention to one usually visual point that itself disappears when the poem is contemplated, and the contemplator finds himself or herself to be a not-self in not-Being, not conscious, not unconscious, but beyond consciousness, that is, beyond being able to be spoken or intellectually thought.

In a nihilist reading the title may or may not be significant; it will depend on the type of nihilism that is mirrored in the poem. *Mere* is ambiguous; it can mean "only," that is, the poem is about "Being" and nothing else. Or it can be read "pure or unadulterated"; that is, the poem is about Being in its purity. Neither a Zen Buddhist nor an *ontological nihilist* would hold that there is anything about final reality that can be spoken or labeled. So *mere* could not mean either *only* or *pure*, for this would imply that there is something that can be called Being.

But there also nihilists who hold that something may be known about the world we live in. There may be an exception for the nihilist who denies that the world we live in has any final meaning but does not deny that humans have genuine knowledge of the material world. The cosmos exists but for no reason that can be discerned; if there is to be

29. I do not know what Hall would make of my reading; she argues her case from a different and much larger set of poems and she does so from both the early and the late ("Wallace Stevens's Spiritual Voyage," 277–304).

a meaning, it will have to be given it by meaning-givers (i.e., humans).[30] So this form of nihilism does not deny our ability to know that there are things, though it does force us to recognize that our so-called knowledge is only local, confined to beings who use language. This type of *epistemological nihilism*[31] can incorporate the word *mere* (meaning "only") but not the word *mere* (meaning "pure") into his grasp of the poem.

Aside from the title then, what might *be* a nihilist reading of "Of Mere Being"? For such a reading we do not need to make an exhaustive image-by-image analysis. We need rather to read the language of negation and nothingness as primary and straightforward, not as an indication that that which is not mentioned is transcendent. In stanza one thought is transcended but not replaced with anything. In stanza two there is neither *human meaning* nor *human feeling*. Even the *song* is outside one's comprehension. There is only a *bird* that appears to exist only in the mind (so it doesn't really exist). It *stands* (exists) on the edge of space ready to fall into complete oblivion. Finally the bird sits motionless—bright but motionless and illusory.

The techniques of Buddhist meditation are intended to help one cope with life, to deal with its inequities, pains, and sorrows. In the West interest in Buddhism blossomed in the 1960s and 70s as the death of God played in the background of everyone who was paying attention to the counterculture. Buddhism still bears cultural fruit today. This nihilist reading of Stevens's work, even as it takes a reading similar to Buddhism, denies any consolation. The universe is one empty place without, in the final analysis, being or meaning. Cold comfort this is!

30. Note that I use here the word *humans* rather than the more natural *human beings*, because this linguistic formulation would be self-refuting if it were used of people who were in the final analysis creatures created by language itself, as some forms of *postmodern thought* come close to implying. "Truth," wrote Nietzsche, "is a mobile army of metaphors"; it is constructed by our language and its reality is only linguistic. See "On Truth and Lie in an Extra-moral Sense," 46.

31. Thielicke (in *Nihilism*) would call "epistemological nihilism" *ciphered nihilism*; "it makes a virtue of the breakdown of reality" (63); that is, we can know those individual palms and birds as palms and birds, but it denies the transcendent that makes them *to be*. Being makes things to be and, if it wishes (since for Thielicke Being is God) continues to hold them in being. In Peraino's interpretation of Stevens's poem, there is only the physical world; the meaning we make of it vanishes with us.

A Humanist Reading Ending in Nihilism

Maybe I have been too hasty in concluding that there is no comfort in a nihilist reading. Maybe the poem inspires the reader to move beyond what is expressed. That is, maybe Stevens intends us to recognize the import of the poem as richly humanist: though particulars in a godless world, we are valuable because we give ourselves value. Perhaps, therefore, we should read the poem something like it is read by my friend, Carl Peraino, a scientist and an admirer of Stevens's poems.

Peraino sees in the first stanza "the jarring image of dimensionless 'mind' enclosed within a dimensionless constrained environment," and then continues:

> Thus, the workings of the mind may be considered a journey along a path (infinitely tortuous and difficult, as evidenced by the history of biological and cultural evolution) toward some greatly anticipated culmination, the holy grail of ultimate understanding. Metaphorically inching around precarious ledges and slashing through dense thickets, we suddenly come upon a clearing at the end of the path and find . . . a simple palm tree in a featureless bronze setting.
>
> Initially we are shocked and frightened by our conception of the "mereness" of this stark image—is this the nirvana of true meaning toward which we endlessly strive? Our apprehension rapidly dissipates, however, as Stevens's artistry guides us toward deeper understanding. A sense of comfort grows as we gaze upon this unprepossessing palm; it carries soothing connotations of tropical freshness and vitality, and its bronze surround lends the scene an aura of grandeur and majesty. The archaic meaning of "mere" begins to emerge in our consciousness.
>
> In the second stanza we find that the palm is inhabited by a gold-feathered bird singing a song that, the poem signifies, we can never hope to understand. We are disquieted by the realization that we are faced with a mystery that will never be fully resolved. Perhaps the most important message, however, is not the obscurity of the song's content, but rather that the bird is beautiful, and it is singing.
>
> Viewing this scene we realize, in the third and fourth stanzas, that by encompassing the totality of the poem's imagery we achieve the larger awareness that our true destiny is simply the journey through existence and "mere being" is the ultimate reality. Some may recoil from this revelation—Stevens embraces

it. "The bird sings. Its feathers shine." The branches of that un-imaginably terrible but also curiously benign palm are stirred by a gentle wind, and the beauty of the bird that sings in these branches shimmers through a cascade of alliteration at the poem's conclusion.[32]

Now we come to the sticky part. Is the *ontological nihilist* (one who believes there really is a world out there, not just constructed by our imagination by way of our language) really a nihilist? Peraino would say no. The beauty of the final scene of "mere" palm, bird and wind are enough:

> The growing understanding that we are an integral part of the universe, composed literally of stardust and starlight, and that our capacity to contemplate all this is an emergent property of the universe's purely physical workings just feels right and beautiful to me.[33]

The answer, however, is yes. Peraino's flattening of reality to the merely physical, even if it appears to recognize the aesthetic effect of that reality, is really *ciphered nihilism*. Here I am following the analysis of theologian Helmut Thielicke. The notion that there can be meaning without transcendence is illusory. If all reality is *mere* (only) matter; if the mind is only the brain at work; if thought, emotion, sense of value (right and wrong), and sense of beauty are not given an existence outside the physical, then we have only a world of *is*. *Mere being* becomes, not the *Being* that creates and upholds the universe, but another name for the collection of the world's particulars. Reality becomes stuff (mere matter in motion), with no way to judge whether any particular stuff among the great pile of stuff (things and actions) is good or bad, beautiful or ugly, lovely or despicable, and no way to be confident that our mind that thinks in terms of good and bad, beautiful or ugly, loving or despicable is trustworthy. In fact, there is no way to make the terms true and false any more than the opinion of each person who makes such a determination. In other

32. Carl Peraino, personal correspondence, May 20, 2009. Peraino's reading of "Of Mere Being" is similar to Critchley's general understanding of Stevens's last poems.

33. Personal correspondence, September 24, 2008, used by permission from Carl Peraino. Then he adds this: "The aesthetic to the unity between our 'mere' physicality and that of the rest of the universe is sullied by the gratuitous introduction of the discontinuity embodied in the concept of God or any other supernatural essence. The latter is not only superfluous, it's like a cancer eating away at our ability to understand how things work, the dynamics of which is part of the overall aesthetic of our existence."

words, *epistemological nihilism* is just as nihilistic as *ontological nihilism*, for while it admits the world exists, it can make no *epistemological* judgments that have any reason to be thought valid by anyone—either the one who makes the judgment or the community who responds to it. In other words *ontological nihilism* incorporates *epistemological nihilism*.

Whether Stevens is or is not a Buddhist or some sort of nihilist or Christian in his poetry is an interesting question. We would like to know the answer. But there are more important matters afoot. We can hope that there is some way out of this impasse for the rest of us. Perhaps we will see even in the negativity of Buddhism and the despair of nihilism a *signal of transcendence*. If we were to do so, we would be following the path of C. S. Lewis and Albert Camus.

But now back to the intellectual and possibly spiritual path of Wallace Stevens.

A Christian Reading

We will first follow the trail blazed by Nathan A. Scott, Jr. in "Wallace Stevens's Route Downward." Scott sets his reading in the context of Nietzsche's declaration that God is dead:

> The long meditation recorded by his [Stevens's] poetry [from 1915 to 1954] . . . is one whose enabling principle derives from a deep sense of ours being indeed a time of dearth, for this poet takes it for granted that we have seen "the gods dispelled in midair and dissolve like clouds"—"as if they had never inhabited the earth."[34]

What shall we do in the absence of the gods, or worse, the absence of the one and only transcendent God of Christian faith? Wallace answers: "the mind turns to its own creations and examines them . . . for what they reveal, for what they validate and invalidate, for the support they give."[35]

Art, poetry, music—these human creations stand in the place of the gods, grasping reality by the imagination and bringing order to otherwise wild and chaotic reality. Scott traces Stevens's endless permutations of imagination and how they relate to reality. Stevens's shifting views are all expressed in proverb-like ruminations and poetic images and language

34. Scott, *Visions*, 10, quoting *Opus Posthumous*, 290.
35. Ibid., 13, quoting *Opus Posthumous*, 186.

that wrench the mind well before clarifying it. In fact, I think that only the critic, the philosopher, or the most astute of readers will be able to see the order Stevens's work actually brings to reality. Scott, fortunately, is one of these. So I follow his lead.

The key to seeing Stevens's poems, especially the ones in his last volume, as Christian is to recognize that, like Aristotle, Aquinas and Kant, Stevens's "Being is not *a* being but, rather, that informing élan or power, that 'dearest freshness deep down things [Hopkins],' that enables all the various particular things of earth to be what their inner entelechies intend them to be."[36] This notion, with a little help from Heidegger, explains why Stevens, in directing attention to particular things, is in fact showing forth or expressing his trust in Being itself, that is, that which lies as the creative ground of all beings. In my view, then, the "palm at the end of the mind" is not nothing, not merely the most far out edge of physical reality or the edge of thought. It is a *signal of the transcendent.* The mode of expression, however, is not a transcendence upwards but, again in Scott's terms, a transcendence downwards.

If this sounds a bit like the mental and verbal gymnastics of Zen, so be it. It is not Zen. It is the Christian understanding of the *totaliter aliter* of God, the *mysterium tremendum*, that we have seen in the philosophical theology of Rudolf Otto. The God who creates and sustains "the tree at the end of the mind" is not only immanent (God with us), he is God beyond, below, and above us, beyond our ken, immortal, invisible, God only wise.

As Scott puts it, Stevens in the poems of *The Auroras of Autumn* (1950) has shifted "from his earlier view of the imagination as the principle of ultimacy to his final view of ultimacy as resident in nothing less than Being itself."[37] The role of the poet, then, is to show forth the things and creatures of earth "in the starkness and strangeness of their being what they are." He teaches us to revel in their particularity, in their *presence*, in the marvelous inner cohesion whereby they manage to be what they are, rather than something else.[38]

To put it more directly, Being itself, that is God, is our creator and sustainer. In Scott's words: "Being itself is steadfast, reliable, gracious, and

36. Ibid., 28, quoting Hopkins, "God's Grandeur."
37. Ibid., 31.
38. Ibid., 35, quoting H. D. Lewis, "Revelation and Art," 212.

deserves our trust: it is to say that the Wholly Other, the uncreated Rock of reality, is *for* us, not against us."[39]

Any hint of nihilism or Zen or pantheism or aestheticism, any taint of despair and meaninglessness, any notion that Stevens is only juggling words to give the impression of an insight too keen for others to grasp, is to be rejected. Stevens is a serious poet on a serious mission. It is a delight to Christian readers to find that he finally found that Being forgives and blesses and gives eternal life.

So, then, how shall we read this latest of his late poems? I suggest this:

Stanza one: The first two lines set the stage—a specific *palm at the end of the mind.* In fact, it's *beyond the last thought* (the final particular in a cosmos of "billions and billions" of particulars). This tree *rises* (i.e., it appears despite its being unthought) *in the bronze distance* (beyond, one might say, the setting sun).[40]

Stanza two: *A gold-feathered bird* (a brilliantly colored bird of great value and great beauty) *sings in the palm without human meaning* (because this bird is not the Word made flesh, but the enigmatic Word before being spoken in human language). Its singing is also *beyond human feeling* (i.e., in an enigmatic emotional stance), *a foreign song* (a Word before intelligible human speech).

Stanza three: *You* (the reader? or the viewer?) *know then* (both by logic and by chronology) that the human intellect is not in charge of its happiness.

Then the *bird sings* again (this time the bird expresses its being the Word, and, by that expression, the palm and the bird come to be). When the Word expresses itself, the bird's *feathers shine* (i.e., its particular Being is made manifest).

Stanza four: *The palm stands at the edge of space* (there is nothing but Being itself beyond the created order; the cosmos is not set within an infinite chaos). *The wind moves in the trees* (this particular is not static but alive within the compass of time). And as the bird's *feathers dangle* in the Being-created wind and by dangling become even more brilliant).

Scott does not give such a detailed "reading" of the poem. He merely says, "Stevens is a profoundly religious poet. But he exemplifies a kind of

39. Ibid., 36–37.

40. If we substitute for "bronze distance" the phrase "bronze décor," we get a much less cosmic sense of scene. "Décor" suggests the decoration of a room, perhaps even that the bird is the central figure of a painting.

sensibility for which the direction of transcendence is not upward but downward." And further: "the bird stands for Stevens as something like a sacrament of the mystery of Being—'mere Being.'"[41]

So where does Stevens fit in the hierarchy of types of *signals of transcendence*? It may look like he is off the chart, perhaps living in a separate sort of reality. But I agree with Scott and suggest that his view of reality is in the final analysis shot through with *signals of transcendence* at Level 4. They are to be noticed more in the utter particularity of things than the general propositions of philosophy or theology. This thing—any *thing*—is a manifestation of Being. It could not be if Being was not, and every being cries out, "There is Being itself other than my being a being; if there were not, I would not be." I am. Therefore, as an intuitive entailment (there is no logic here), Being is. If we listen as hard as Stevens listens, we too will hear the cry.

"The way up and the way down are the same," said Heraclitus. Stevens would seem to agree.

Václav Havel: Close But No Cigar

Václav Havel, a playwright and vocal dissident in Czechoslovakia under communist rule, became, after the Velvet Revolution in 1989, the first president of the new Czech Republic and served in that capacity for ten years. Before that, over a span of fourteen years, Havel spent five in prison for his plays and political writing, and there he wrote many letters to his wife. These were later published as *Letters to Olga*, and in them Havel describes two special *signals* that he says revealed to him the *transcendent* nature of fundamental reality, what he variously called *Being, mystery of Being, order of existence, hidden sphere*, and *final horizon*. The first experience is mystical or spiritual; the second is a profound case of conscience. We will discuss each of these as they relate to Havel's worldview. The first concerns the glorious and unitive nature of Being.

Being: The Shimmering Tree

Twice in *Letters to Olga* Havel describes and reflects on a sudden, unexpected experience of being drawn out of time into a "moment of supreme

41. Scott, *Visions*, 38.

bliss, of infinite joy, . . . a moment of supreme self-awareness, a supremely elevating state of the soul, a totally harmonic merging of existence with itself and with the entire world."[42] This occurred while he was in Hermanice as he was looking through the prison fence at the crown of a tree whose leaves "shimmered and trembled slightly."[43] Here is his later recollection of this experience:

> As I watched the imperceptible trembling of its leaves against an endless sky, I was overcome by a sensation that is difficult to describe: all at once, I seemed to rise above all the coordinates of my momentary existence in the world into a kind of state outside time in which all the beautiful things I had ever seen and experienced existed in a total "co-present"; I felt a sense of reconciliation, indeed of an almost gentle consent to the inevitable course of things as revealed to me now, and this combined with a carefree determination to face what had to be faced. A profound amazement at the sovereignty of Being became a dizzying sensation of tumbling endlessly into the abyss of its mystery; an unbounded joy at being alive, at having been given the chance to live through all I have lived through, and at the fact that everything has a deep and obvious meaning—this joy formed a strange alliance in me with a vague horror at the inapprehensibility and unattainability of everything I was so close to in that moment, standing at the very "edge of the finite"; I was flooded with a sense of ultimate happiness and harmony with the world and myself, with that moment, with all the moments I could call up, and with everything invisible that lies behind it and which has meaning. I would even say that I was somehow "struck by love," though I don't know precisely for whom or what.[44]

In this experience, Havel passes beyond the first horizon, the experience of the prison yard, the pile of iron on which he sits, the work he is taking a break from, even the tree itself, the slight breeze and the sun. He is on the brink of the second horizon, the very "edge of the finite," and he

42. Havel, *Letters*, 221.

43. A shimmering tree also impressed Havel's mentor T. G. Masaryk. "One winter I was on a train going through a tunnel, and just as we came out I caught sight of a tree with all its leaves: the tunnel had protected it. It was gone before I knew it, but it was like a revelation. In that split second I understood pantheism, the divine in nature. Understood it but never accepted it" (Karel Kapek, *Talks with T. G. Masaryk*, 175). Dillard likewise notes the profound effect of "the tree with lights in it" that she saw one day as she walked along Tinker Creek (See Dillard, *Pilgrim*).

44. Havel, *Letters*, 331.

experiences it as sovereign, endless, not just benign and beautiful, but worthy of love. Einstein is credited with saying that the most important question is "Is the universe friendly?" Havel would perhaps respond, "I don't know about the universe, but Being itself is more than friendly."

Being: the Voice of Conscience

The second experience reveals for Havel the moral nature of *Being*. Here Havel ponders why, when he boards a street car late at night with no conductor to observe him, he always feels guilty when he thinks of not paying the fare. Then he comments about the interior dialogue that ensues:

> Who, then, is in fact conversing with me? Obviously someone I hold in higher regard than the transport commission, than my best friends (this would come out when the voice would take issue with their opinions), and higher, in some regards, than myself, that is, myself as subject of my existenceintheworld and the carrier of my "existential" interests (one of which is the rather natural effort to save a crown). Someone who "knows everything" (and is therefore omniscient), is everywhere (and therefore omnipresent) and remembers everything; someone who, though infinitely understanding, is entirely incorruptible; who is for me, the highest and utterly unequivocal authority in all moral questions and who is thus Law itself; someone eternal, who through himself makes me eternal as well, so that I cannot imagine the arrival of a moment when everything will come to an end, thus terminating my dependence on him as well; someone to whom I relate entirely and for whom, ultimately, I would do everything. At the same time, this "someone" addresses me directly and personally (not merely as an anonymous public passenger, as the transport commission does).[45]

These reflections are close, if not identical, to a fully theistic conception of God. Surely some Being that is omniscient, omnipresent, and good, and who addresses you directly and personally, must himself (itself just doesn't fit these criteria) be personal.

Havel, too, sees this. And yet he draws back from the conclusion:

> But who is it? God? There are many subtle reasons why I'm reluctant to use that word; one factor here is a certain sense of shame (I don't know exactly for what, why and before whom),

45. Ibid., 345–46.

but the main thing, I suppose, is a fear that with this all too specific designation (or rather assertion) that "God is," I would be projecting an experience that is entirely personal and vague (never mind how profound and urgent it may be), too single-mindedly "outward," onto that problemfraught screen called "objective reality," and thus I would go too far beyond it.[46]

So, while what he experiences manifests characteristics that seem to demand a commitment to theism, Havel avoids this conclusion by shifting his attention from Being (as an objective existent) to himself (as a reflector on his conscious experience). What Havel does draw from this experience—to very good advantage, by the way—is that Being has a moral dimension. Being, then, is the "good" ontological foundation for human moral responsibility, both on an individual level as users of the transport system and on a public level as politicians.

Did then Havel somehow become a closet Christian in the final years of Czech communism, or what Havel calls post-communism? Early in his presidency, Havel had to clarify his religious commitment. Some had thought that he had converted to Catholicism. He admits to becoming closer friends with some Catholics and Protestants, but he expressly denies conversion to either expression of Christian faith, saying he has not changed his mind from what he wrote in the prison letters.[47] There Havel explicitly rejects the Christian version of theism; and because his comments expand on those we have just noted, it will be useful to consider them here.

Havel was raised as a Catholic, but he seems never to have made a personal commitment:

Ever since childhood, I have felt that I would not be myself—a human being—if I did not live in a permanent and manifold tension with this "horizon" of mine, the source of meaning and hope and ever since my youth, I've never been certain whether this is an "experience of God" or not. Whatever it is, I'm certainly not a proper Christian and Catholic (as so many of my good friends are) and there are many reasons for this.[48]

46. Ibid., 346. Yet later on Havel does occasionally use the term *God* for Being, but then clarifies that he does not have in mind a fully theistic conception. (See, for example, "Faith in the World," 53).

47. Havel, *Disturbing*, 189–90.

48. Havel, *Letters*, 101.

In short, he gives several reasons. First, this "god of mine" is simply what he is and as such does not merit worship. Second, to do so would not "improve either the world or myself."[49] Third, he has a "constant compulsion to reconsider things—originally, authentically, from the beginning."[50]

Finally, Havel's fourth reason involves self-analysis:

> When it gets right down to it, I am a child of the age of conceptual, rather than mystical, thought and therefore my god as well—if I am compelled to speak of him (which I do very unwillingly)—must appear as something terribly abstract, vague and unattractive (all the more so since my relationship to him is so difficult to pin down). But it appears so only to someone I try to tell about him—the experience itself is quite vivid, intimate and particular, perhaps (thanks to its constantly astonishing diversity) more lively than for someone whose "normal" God is provided with all the appropriate attributes (which oddly enough can alienate more often than drawing one closer).[51]

At this point Havel reverts to being a child of the modern or perhaps postmodern world. The experience is transcendent, not the reality. So Havel comes close to Christian understanding of reality. Close, we might say, but no cigar.

From the standpoint of the apologetic value of *signals of transcendence*, what does Havel tell us? We will take up this question in chapter 10.

Worldview Borderlines

We began in this chapter with C. S. Lewis, who moved from an early fascination with Nordic mythology to modern atheism to deism to a full experience of the God of the Bible. *Signals of transcendence* and a curiosity about where they pointed and what they meant led him to a deep faith in Christ and to becoming a creator of literature that sparkles with such signals. His story is well known, and he remains a beloved figure of both Christian intellect and imagination.

We then saw that the journey of Albert Camus was quite different. His Christian childhood did little to prepare him for the challenges of the

49. Ibid.
50. Ibid.
51. Ibid.

mid-twentieth-century social and intellectual conflict and the challenge of nihilism. He moved from an intense commitment to the possibility of creating meaning by individual human effort alone to an attraction to the beautiful organ music played in a church in Paris. From there, puzzled by what he was hearing from the pulpit, he gradually moved toward Christian faith, though never making this move public.

Again, as with Camus, Wallace Stevens moved slowly through an intellectual and aesthetic journey all his own, finally taking communion and asserting that he was at last "in the fold." His tale is told in his poetry, especially revealing in his final poems that his search for reality—a reality that he had thought he might be creating in his poetry—had ended with a Being not his own, one whose *signals* he finally recognized. He too had come home to Christian faith as mediated by the Catholic Church.

Václav Havel, of course, tells a different story. He grew up in a nominal Catholic family, became immersed in the art world of a basically secular society, a world in high tension with the foreign-controlled atheistic political system of Czech communism. His artistic talent for absurdist drama with communism as the butt of the jokes and his intellectual commitment to dissident political discourse landed him in jail. While there, he had time to ponder the meaning of much more than political and artistic reality. *Signals of transcendence* led him to realize that there was an ultimate reality to which he and all people were responsible. Yet he drew back. Why? He says he was afraid that he would be going too far to become a Christian; this ultimate reality he experienced as the *horizon of being* only appeared to be personal. It did not display for him the fully biblical God. Recent publications have not indicated a change of mind. Till his death in December 2011, as far as I can tell, he remained essentially a deist. And deism is what we will see in several forms in the next chapter.

7

Spots of Time

Deism, Panentheism, Romanticism

> I felt a sense of pain when I beheld
> The silent trees, and saw the intruding sky—
> Then, dearest Maiden, move along these shades
> In gentleness of heart; with gentle hand
> Touch—for there is a spirit in the woods.
>
> —WILLIAM WORDSWORTH, "NUTTING," LL. 53–57.[1]

Many *signals of transcendence* do not appear to point to any clearly defined *transcendent*. They are special moments when consciousness is heightened, when people suddenly seem transported beyond the confines of their immediate environment, when time seems to stop, when they have an exalted feeling of the presence of something they can neither explain in words or identify in nature. In general these are Level 2 or Level 3 *signals*; they form the substance of this chapter.

I remember visiting a class in Western Civilization at the University of Kansas. One of the three professors leading the class asked students to lean back, close their eyes and reflect on times they had been to their aged great aunt's large gabled Victorian mansion. Her son had died in the First World War, and she had left the room exactly as he had left it

---

1. Wordsworth, *Selected Poetry*, 146.

years and years ago. When she on tiptoe showed it to them, what did they feel? Wasn't it spooky? Didn't you hesitate to stay in the room or to touch anything? Or what has it felt like to walk into a dark wood as the light is fading and the branches hang low and the path gets less and less visible? Wasn't this an odd feeling? Didn't you sense something you could not identify? Didn't you want to get out of the woods quickly, and didn't you turn and do so?

As I recall this now, I think of my own reaction to a poem I first heard—when was it?—in childhood? or a bit later? In any case, it haunts me:

> Yesterday upon the stair
> I met a man who wasn't there.
> I met him there again today.
> God, I wish he'd go away.

These professors were trying to induce in their sophomore students a feeling they would normally not have moving around the campus, attending class, living in the dorms, going home on weekends. Why? Because they were introducing the class to early twentieth-century American romantic poems, at least one of which was by Edwin Muir. I have, sadly, forgotten the specific poem. The professors knew the students would find its "world" difficult to understand or accept. They wanted them not only to suspend "disbelief for the moment" and thus affirm "poetic faith"; they wanted them to realize that such a "world" could, in fact, exist.[2]

This approach to teaching was at the time, and still is, frowned on because it calls the bluff of the established principle of teaching literature: to point and identify but never to raise the truth or falsity of what is pointed to or identified. That would be to violate both the aesthetic distance between art and reality and the objectivity of the academic attitude to truth. Such objectivity is, of course, impossible, and the teacher's views—whatever they are—will be transmitted and inculcated without being identified or given the chance to be evaluated by their students. This is the case regardless of how objective teachers consider themselves to be. Beneath it all, objectivity of this sort implies that there is no truth to know, only opinion to be identified.

In any case, these students were asked to see these experiences as *signals* of some sort of *transcendence*. They were challenged again to feel these *signals* along the veins of the hearts and minds and to consider

2. Coleridge, *Biographia Literaria*, XIV, 518.

them as actual encounters with the infinite. What kind of infinite? What kind of *transcendent*? Well, that would depend on what kind of experience. The lower the level, as described in chapter 1, the less specific is the nature of the *transcendent* revealed. We need to consider a few examples. I will start with one of my own experiences.

Some Examples

An Early Encounter with Modern Art

When I was an undergraduate at the University of Nebraska, I delivered films for the audio-visual department. This took me into most of the buildings on campus, one of which was Morrill Hall that harbored two of my most favorite displays on campus—the reconstructed skeletons of mastodons and other long-extinct exotic beasts that roamed the Nebraska prairies in prehistoric times, and also the fascinating collection of paintings of the art department. I could scarcely deliver film to either of these departments without lingering. Ancient petrified bones and weird ultra-modern abstract art equally attracted and held my attention. But one painting really zapped me.

As I made my many treks through the galleries, I had become more and more puzzled by an abstract painting. I do not recall the artist; I doubt that he or she had a high reputation then or now. The painting normally hung without a frame on a gallery wall. Bright splashes of thick oil paint, yellow-blending-into-orange, covered the entire rectangular canvas. I could see no particular order to these inch-wide multi-colored brush strokes. Why was this considered a work of art? Who chose it for display? It pictured no distinct object, either realistic or fantastic, ordered or distorted. It was "about nothing" as far as I could tell. To an undergraduate from a realistic ranch where everything in the world is distinctly something, even if unidentified, this was odd. Of course, I had yet to learn about painting of any kind, let alone a work of a post-impressionist or Dada or abstract artist. I was now learning by exposure and not at all by explanation.

I had seen this painting many times as it hung on various walls in various galleries. Always came the question: Why is this painting here? Many paintings I had learned by experience to recognize and appreciate as art. So it was week after week as I delivered and picked up educational films

Then it happened. One day on a whim, as I was leaving a long hallway where paintings were displayed, I glanced back for one last longing look.

There, fifteen feet away and in the middle of the wide hallway, the puzzling painting, lit by brilliant klieg lights, glowed. The thick oil paint glistened and glittered, luminescent. Suddenly the work of art became its own self. Its surface was its essence. And its essence was Beautiful! That was it! It was a thing of beauty; its beauty was its truth; its truth was its beauty. Or so Keats might say. I had become satisfied that indeed the painting was art. The aesthetic of the art was its *transcendence*.

A rather low level of *transcendence*, yes. Of course. But the painting had *aesthetic* meaning. The meaning was its beauty.

Was the beauty of the painting a *signal*? Did it stealthily reveal an infinite-personal God who is more fully revealed to us in Jesus Christ? That would require a leap beyond both logic and direct experience. Too much to conclude by far. But was this painting a *signal* from such a God? Clearly, it *could* be. One thing it could not be: It could not be only oil on canvas.

So what Level of *transcendence* did the painting *signal*? Level 1? Of course. The painting was no mere natural object; it *signaled* the existence of its immediate creator, an intentional artist. Level 2? Yes, beauty is a category beyond the realm of the merely material. Beauty involves matter so ordered that it can trigger an experience that goes beyond the human recognition of the mere existence of oil on canvas. The beauty of this painting required more than a material foundation. If things are beautiful, they cannot be explained solely in terms of material causes. As Annie Dillard says,

> Beauty itself is the language to which we have no key; it is the mute cipher, the cryptogram, the uncracked, unbroken code.[3]

Well, then, how about Level 3? Does it *signal* the existence of something personal? Yes, to a degree: certainly the painting was produced by a person. Well, not necessarily a divine person. Still, if the painting has exceptional beauty, a beauty, one might say, that appears "out of this world"

3. Dillard, *Pilgrim*, 109.

(that is, when its beauty is inconceivable without a spiritual reality), then it does point in that direction.

This is how we get the argument I have mentioned before:

> There is the music of Johann Sebastian Bach.
> Therefore there must be a God.
> You either see this or you don't.

Okay, then how about Level 4? No, we do not here have a *signal* of the "profound depths of the Thou" or of a fully personal, fully *numinous* and holy God or a God whom we could identify with the biblical God or Allah. Beauty *signals* only so much. There is more to God than *aesthetics*, more to an encounter with God than aesthetic experience. My experience was, however, consistent with Christian or Islamic theism. Deism, pantheism or panentheism could equally well explain the experience. So this particular *signal of transcendence* spans Level 1 through the lower reaches of Level 3 and belongs as an illustration in the present chapter.

Notes from a Spiritual Writer

Robert Benson, author of several books on prayer, writes about the Caribbean island he and his wife travel to for their annual vacation. He is a watcher for *signals of transcendence*:

> One way or another I have spent most of my life watching for certain signs and wonders of Something Unnamed that is at the center of everything. Over the years I have come to see that some sitting still is required if one is to see such things. I think that is why I am drawn to the still, blue, almost eternal hour before cockcrow. And it is why I wait at the railing to watch the sun slip away. . . .
>
> I do not know the name of what it is that I will come to see. Home may be as good a name as any.[4]

Though Benson may well be a theist, he does not draw from this experience anything specifically Christian or even theistic. This particular *signal* points only to a vague sort of deism. It is, in other words, a Level 3 (2) (a) *signal of transcendence*.

---

4. Benson, *Home*, 68–69.

Comments of a Nature Photographer: Mary Randlett, who has illustrated a series of poems by poet Denise Levertov, once wrote this in a letter to the poet:

> To see the movement of water in this lake one must look at something like this rock to get the light right and the level of viewing—suddenly the waters start moving, ripples form, the clouds move in and away across the island, outlined in light like ice. Get down much lower, all movement stops and the whole scene is a liquid white. Playing with light, form and movement in space—I simply get lost, time stops.[5]

Again here is a Level 3 (2) (a) *signal*. Her experience did not point her past a basic Wordsworthian *spot of time*.

William Wordsworth and Spots of Time

Beyond a doubt, Wordsworth in his early work was a nature poet par excellence. But nature to him more than the merely material; it was an icon of a deeper reality. And what was that reality? Wordsworth was never loath to state his religious, aesthetic, and philosophic views, though what he means may be difficult to pin down. After all, he was writing poetry, not philosophy. We will begin with one of his more dramatic descriptions—the now famous section from "Lines Composed a Few Miles above Tintern Abbey":

> And I have felt
> A presence that disturbs me with the joy
> Of elevated thoughts; a sense sublime
> Of something far more deeply interfused,
> Whose dwelling is the light of setting suns,
> And the round ocean and the living air,
> And the blue sky, and in the mind of man;
> A motion and a spirit, that impels
> All thinking things, all objects of all thought,
> And rolls through all things.[6]

These lines reflect the great Romantic attachment to the sublime, the exalted feeling of magnanimity. Perhaps Wordsworth was wrong: perhaps there is no such "motion or spirit"; perhaps to say only this about the

5. Randlett, *Mary Randlett Landscapes*, 33.
6. Wordsworth, *Selected Poetry*, 101.

divine is inadequate or misleading to the point of being sentimental or even idolatrous. I have no doubt that some of what Wordsworth wrote was rather sentimental even for his own time. But he was completely serious. Take, for example, these simple lines from "The Tables Turned," which I remember from my first undergraduate study of his poetry:

> One impulse from a vernal wood
> May teach you more of man,
> Of moral evil and of good,
> Than all the sages can.[7]

I quickly memorized them. But no way then or now can I agree with this sentiment. The poetry sings; the ideas intrigue; but the intellectual effect never took hold for me. Vernal woods themselves do not and cannot do this sort of thing. More than nature itself is necessary to inculcate the moral sense. These lines may be Wordsworth at one of his more memorable moments, but not at his most accurate insights. At the same time, the final line of the four that follow have been remembered by many modern anti-technologues:

> Sweet is the lore which Nature brings;
> Our meddling intellect
> Mis-shapes the beauteous forms of things:—
> We murder to dissect.

If killing to get the scientific truth we seek is what we do, then the last line puts it well. My cancer research scientist friend has deliberately killed thousands of rats. Has indeed murdered to dissect? That may be what we want him to do, but Wordsworth has made it impossible quickly to dismiss the moral implication.

In making these comments, I am probably being obtuse, dancing around the topic that is the center of our concern. What sort of *transcendent* is Wordsworth sensing? That is the question. Who or what is this "motion and spirit, that impels / All thinking things"? To address that question we must examine the form in which his impressions of the divine have come to him. Wordsworth calls them "spots of time."

Somewhere between the far edge of *signals of transcendence* at Level 2 and the near edge of Level 4, we find what Wordsworth called "spots of time." Wordworth's poetry is filled with poetic renderings of moments in his life when through a direct experience of nature he has felt something

7. Ibid., 80.

far more than material reality, something that brings a freshening sense of life.

It will be helpful to separate several important strands in Wordsworth's notion. First is his basic notion of *spots of time*; second, illustrations of those experiences from his poetry; and third, his understanding of the constitution of reality—how the human mind and spirit interact with nature and "nature's God."

Spots of Time Defined

Wordsworth's definition comes in poetic form in *The Prelude*, a long narrative poem, initially intended for his projected "epic," *The Recluse*, a work he never finished. The following presentations of *spots of time* were written first in 1799, expanded in 1805, and revised before appearing in print in 1850:[8]

> There are in our existence spots of time
> Which with distinct pre-eminence retain
> A vivifying virtue, whence, depressed
> By false opinion and contentious thought,
> Or aught of heavier or more deadly weight
> In trivial occupations and the round
> Of ordinary intercourse, our minds
> Are nourished and invisibly repaired—
> A virtue by which pleasure is enhanced,
> That penetrates, enables us to mount
> When high, more high, and lifts us up when fallen.
> This efficacious spirit chiefly lurks
> Among those passages of life in which
> We have had deepest feeling that the mind
> Is lord and master, and that outward sense
> Is but the obedient servant of her will.
> Such moments, worthy of all gratitude,
> Are scattered everywhere, taking their date
> From our first childhood—in our childhood even
> Perhaps are more conspicuous. Life with me,
> As far as memory can look back, is full
> Of this beneficent influence.[9]

8. Several versions of some sections of the poem still exist. Documentation will be to the specific version I am quoting. Though the term "spots of time" appears primarily in *The Prelude*, Book XI (1805) and Book XII (1850), illustrations from his poetry come much earlier.

9. *Prelude*, 1805, XI, 257–78 (478).

The salient features of these "spots of time" are that they are triggered by seemingly ordinary events, come unannounced, take the poet by surprise, and lift up the human spirit. More significantly, they improve the poet's grasp of (1) his own nature, especially its moral development, (2) the nature of external nature and ultimately (3) the nature of the divine. Each of these features becomes more and more obvious as they are recorded in *The Prelude* and many other Wordsworth poems.

Exemplary Spots of Time

The First Part of Wordsworth's "Two Part Prelude of 1799" primarily narrates five significant spots of time dating to his life as a child roaming the "wilds" of the Lake District near his home in Grasmere. The first spot is a summary of spots and begins with his experience as

> a four years' child,
> A naked boy, among thy silent pools
> Made one long bathing of a summer's day,
> Basked in the sun, or plunged into thy streams,
> Alternate, all a summer's day, or coursed
> Over the sandy fields, and dashed the flowers
> Of yellow groundsell—or, when crag and hill,
> The woods, and distant Skiddaw's lofty height,
> Were bronzed with a deep radiance, stood alone
> A naked savage in the thunder-shower?[10]

A second spot occurs as he, still as young boy, wanders among the cliffs, snaring woodcocks, and stealing the snared birds of others:

> . . . when the deed was done
> I heard among the solitary hills
> Low breathings coming after me, and sounds
> Of undistinguishable motion, steps
> Almost as silent as the turf they trod.[11]

The tale of a third spot of time follows immediately. Wordsworth tells of scaling the steep cliffs:

> . . . Oh, when I have hung

10. *Prelude*, 1799, First Part, 17–26 (8).
11. Ibid., First Part, 46–50 (9).

Above the raven's nest, by knots of grass
Or half-inch fissures in the slippery rock
But ill sustained, and almost (as it seemed)
Suspended by the blast which blew amain
Shouldering the naked crag, oh, at that time,
While on the perilous ridge I hung alone,
With what strange utterance did the loud dry wind
Blow through my ears! The sky seemed not a sky
Of earth—and with what motion moved the clouds![12]

Quickly he comments:

The mind of man is fashioned and built up
Even as a strain of music. I believe
That there are spirits which, when they would form
A favoured being, from his very dawn
Of infancy do open out the clouds
As at the touch of lightning, seeking him
With gentle visitation—quiet powers,
Retired, and seldom recognized, yet kind,
And to the very meanest not unknown—
With me, though, rarely in my early days
They communed. Others too there are, who use,
Yet haply aiming at the self-same end,
Severer interventions, ministry
More palpable—and of their school was I.[13]

This explanation is a bit difficult for a twenty-first-century reader to un-
tangle, but, so it seems to me, Wordsworth is saying that every child is
instructed by its natural environment. Nonetheless, some favored few, including him, are gifted with more dramatic episodes, one of which he will
now narrate. It is indeed a fascinating tale. Since I first read Wordsworth
some sixty years ago, it is, except for "Lines Composed a Few Miles above
Tintern Abbey," my favorite passage from Wordsworth. It is too long to
reprint here (160 lines), but I will quote its more powerful passages and
try aptly to summarize the rest.

In one of his frequent walks along a lake, the young Wordsworth
chances on a shepherd's skiff inside a cave and tethered to a willow tree.
The moon is up, the wind is down, the lake is calm. In an "act of stealth
/ And troubled pleasure," he unties the boat and rows out on the lake,

12. Ibid., First Part, 57–66 (9).
13. Ibid., First Part, 67–80 (10).

leaving behind a perfect wake that melts "into one track / Of sparkling light." As the boat moves away from the shore, a rocky crag appears on the near horizon; with each stroke it becomes larger and taller, then behind it etched against the stars,

> a huge cliff,
> As if with voluntary power instinct,
> Upreared its head. I struck, and struck again,
> And, growing still in stature, the huge cliff
> Rose up between me and the stars, and still,
> With measured motion, like a living thing
> Strode after me. With trembling hands I turned
> And through the silent water stole my way
> Back to the cavern of the willow-tree.[14]

The effect of this was immediate:

> There in the mooring-place I left my bark,
> And through the meadows homeward went with grave
> And serious thoughts; and after I had seen
> That spectacle, for many days my brain
> Worked with a dim and undetermined sense
> Of unknown modes of being. In my thoughts
> There was a darkness—call it solitude,
> Or blank desertion. No familiar shapes
> Of hourly objects, images of trees,
> Of sea or sky, no colours of green fields,
> But huge and mighty forms that do not live
> Like living men moved slowly through my mind
> By day, and were the trouble of my dreams.[15]

Throughout Wordsworth's poetry there are countless spots of time. I can identify some thirty in *The Prelude* texts alone. Some of the notable ones involve riding horses, a dead man rising from a quiet lake, a "hunger-bitten girl" in London, a shepherd boy losing his way when looking for a lost sheep, a shepherd in a fog, a tree and acorn, a boy bird-calling, an old soldier and his tale. Many are accompanied by comments on their impact on Wordsworth's moral development or his sense of the divine in nature.

14. Ibid., First Part, 108–16 (11).
15. Ibid., First Part, 117–29 (11).

The Fundamental Constitution of Reality

What in the world, or out of it, makes up reality? What is the really real—a reality so real that nothing could be realer? Is it God? Is it material stuff—matter and energy, say? Or is there no final difference between material stuff and the stuff of divinity?

Wordsworth is constantly dropping hints, or skirting these questions, or even at times plunging deeply into them but without clearly enunciating his conception. So, what were his notions? It's hard to say. Or, perhaps, more to the point, it's hard to believe that—despite his constant allusions to spirit, mind, nature and the divine—Wordsworth himself had a clear set of notions. To be unkind we might suggest that, well, in the final analysis, he just didn't know what he was talking about.

Still, let's see if we can at least get a ghost of an answer by looking at a few of the passages where the subject of the nature of reality bubbles up through the surface of the poetry. Wordsworth, of course, was not writing professional philosophy; he was penning poetry. He wanted his readers to experience his own experience of nature in the raw. With multiple metaphors, shifting and changing perspective, shifting and jiving more like a jazz musician than a classical composer, Wordsworth, as I say in mixed metaphors, wove the fabric of his poetry from threads of many colors.

That we puzzle over the seeming imprecision of his verbal gymnastics is more to be expected than to be surprising. In the definition of spots of time (*Prelude*, XI, 168) he calls the initiator of the uplift to his emotion an "efficacious spirit," a spirit not his own, but one external to himself. As a result of his cliff-hanging spot of time, he declares his belief in "spirits" (*Prelude*, First Part, 69). So, too, spirits are also invoked a few lines later:

> Ye powers of earth, ye genii of the springs,
> And ye that have your voices in the clouds,
> And ye that are familiars [spirits] of the lakes
> And of the standing pools, I may not think
> A vulgar hope was yours when ye employed
> Such ministry—[16]

Elsewhere it is nature as such that is the source of religious emotion:

> From nature does emotion come, and moods
> Of calmness equally are nature's gift—

16. Ibid., First Part, 186–91 (13).

This is her glory.[17]

In childhood, Wordsworth himself performs the task:

> A child, I held unconscious intercourse
> With the eternal beauty, drinking in
> A pure organic pleasure from the lines
> Of curling mist, or from the leveled plain
> Of waters coloured by the steady clouds.[18]

The link between the developing human mind of a baby and external nature is profoundly intimate:

> No outcast he [the growing baby], bewildered and depressed!—
> Along his infant veins are interfused
> The gravitation and the filial bond
> Of nature that connect him with the world.
> Emphatically such a being lives
> An inmate of this *active* universe.
> From nature largely he receives, nor so
> Is satisfied, but largely gives again;
> For feeling has to him imparted strength,
> And—powerful in all sentiments of grief,
> Of exaltation, fear, and joy—his mind,
> Even as an agent of the one great mind,
> Creates, creator and receiver both,
> Working but in alliance with the works
> Which it beholds.[19]

On the other hand, Wordsworth alludes to nature as a

> . . . universal power
> And fitness in the latent qualities
> And essences of things, by which the mind
> Is moved by feelings of delight, to me
> Came strengthened with a superadded soul,
> A virtue not its own.[20]

---

17. Wordsworth, *Prelude*, 1805, XII, 1–3 (488).
18. Wordsworth, *Prelude*, 1799, First Part, 394–98 (18–19).
19. Ibid., Second Part, 291–305 (28–29).
20. Wordsworth, *Prelude*, II (1805), 343–48 (92).

Moreover, nature is personified when Wordsworth says that through his "fits of vulgar joy. . . . The earth / And common face of nature spoke to me / Remememberable things . . ."[21]

Finally, to add to the confusion, note these lines from *The Recluse*, the epic poem of which *The Prelude* was to be a part. Wordsworth is re-counting his move to Dove Cottage in Grasmere and the first few months of his time there wandering through the valleys with his sister Dorothy. His aim is to trace the growth of "a poet's mind," that is, how he came to a deeper consciousness of nature and his own self-determined role in revealing her inner secrets. His invocation of the Muse Uranus is, to put it too mildly, astonishing in its revelation of how he thought his own mind could become deeper and richer than the mind of God himself:

> Urania, I shall need
> Thy guidance, or a greater Muse, if such
> Descend to earth or dwell in highest heaven!
> For I must tread on shadowy ground, must sink
> Deep—and, aloft ascending, breathe in worlds
> To which the heaven of heavens is but a veil.
> All strength—all terror, single or in bands,
> That ever was put forth in personal for—
> Jehovah—with his thunder, and the choir
> Of shouting Angels, and the empyreal thrones—
> I pass them unalarmed. Not Chaos, not
> The darkest pit of lowest Erebus,
> Nor aught of blinder vacancy, scooped out
> By help of dreams—can breed such fear and awe
> As fall upon us often when we look
> Into our Minds, into the Mind of Man—[22]

Wordsworth the would-be epic poet wanted to add to and go further than his hero Milton. *Paradise Lost* chronicled the whole scope of human and divine reality. Milton said, "let me fit audience find, though few."[23]

---

21. Ibid., I (1805), 609, 614–16 (68 and 70).

22. Wordsworth, *Recluse*, ll., 777–93. In *Selected Poetry*, 400.

23. John Milton also appealed to Urania, the "heavenly one," the Greek muse of astronomy, *Paradise Lost*, Book VII, ll. 30–31. He likewise appealed to Chaos, "the primal region out of which God, by means of the Holy Spirit, created the world" (*Paradise Lost*, Book I, Elledge in *Paradise Lost*, 150); Erebus, "place of darkness between earth and Hades in Greek myth; also the first child of Chaos, in Hesiod's *Theogony*"; empyreal thrones, "thrones of highest heaven" (*Paradise Lost*, Book II, l., 430; see Van Doren in Wordsworth, *Selected Poetry of William Wordsworth*, 723).

Prior to his invocation of Urania, the Greek muse of astronomy, Wordsworth quotes this line. Indeed, like *Paradise Lost*, *The Recluse* in its long projected final form was not intended for the ordinary reader, but for an audience like Milton's, a sophisticated, intelligent prober of ultimate reality. Milton had succeeded in his project. But how could Wordsworth think his epic could be so magnificent? Because its subject was even more worthy, more profoundly transcendent than Milton's. Wordsworth scope would be "the Mind of Man" which "can breed" more "fear" and "awe" than Heaven, Hell, Angels, Chaos, and even Jehovah himself!

Are we Wordsworth's fit audience? Well, we and many others like us are his audience. What is our response? Don't we read this today and want to exclaim: More depth of *transcendence* than God himself! You've got to be kidding. It is obvious from the tenor of the text that Wordsworth was far from kidding; he was setting forth a goal he, with the help of his powerful poetic Muse, fully intended to accomplish.

Let us shudder with a *numinous* fear as we contemplate this statement of extreme Romantic imagination. And then let us come back to reality. Wendell Berry comments: "It is hard to tell which is greater here, Wordsworth's spiritual presumptuousness or his poetic impudence. And what are we to make of the proposition that a mind so large can at the same time be so small as to enter itself with awe and fear? . . . It would be hard to overestimate the silliness of this mind."[24]

So what shall we conclude? *Spots of time* are mostly Level 3 *signals* that took Wordsworth into the presence of a divine that was ontologically *immanent* in nature and instructive for life, an awesome presence that represented a standard of morality and acted as a judge of good and evil. He did not think that the *transcendent* was merely whatever the Mind of Man imagined. It was an objective reality that the Mind of Man through the agency of the human Imagination could actually experience. So Wordsworth responded to his spots of time with a goal to act as a prophet of what he thought he had found. What precisely was that reality? Perhaps we should go no further than what we glean from the above quotations and admit we can't really answer that question. After all, poetry is seldom precise philosophy. Moreover, as Wordsworth matured these *spots of time* either became less frequent or less significant. His poetry also became a great deal less interesting and less read by both his contemporaries and ours.[25]

24. Berry, "Poetry and Place," 173–74.

25. Wordsworth and his close friend Samuel Taylor Coleridge both had much

Ralph Waldo Emerson and the Currents of Universal Being

To read Ralph Waldo Emerson (1803–82) from beginning to end can be depressing. For while he was highly sensitive to experience of all kinds—natural and extra-natural—he drew from them two entirely different conclusions, one in his early life lifting him to ecstasy, the other as he grew older pitching him downward to near despair, bolstered by only a faint and unjustified glimmer of hope. We need not dwell long upon his career, either near its beginning nor its end, but we can certainly benefit from seeing how *signals of transcendence* can be betrayed by false interpretation.

Raised and trained to be a Unitarian clergyman, he soon broke even from this unorthodox Christian theism and set himself to be a self-professed prophet of "transcendentalism." Never was a worldview so misnamed. Emerson's transcendentalism is not a view in which one sees through the immanent material world to something beyond it, but one that sees all the spirit as immanent.[26] In the end it localizes the entirety of reality inside the mind of the self-reliant individual. The human heart with its desires and abilities becomes the seat of the divine. Listen to the final lines of a poem he wrote in 1832:

> My heart did never counsel me to sin. . . .
> I never taught it what it teaches me,
> I only follow when I act aright.
> Whence then did this omniscient spirit come?
> From God it came. It is the Deity.[27]

Add to that—and one could add a great deal more in the same vein—this from his famous early essay "Nature" (1836):

to say about the poetic Imagination, distinguishing it from Reason and Fancy, and elaborating on its relation to our knowledge of reality. But to delve into this knotty topic would take us far from our focus on *signals of transcendence*. Readers who would like to pursue this subject might well begin by reading Wordsworth's "Preface to the Second Edition of *Lyrical Ballads*" and Coleridge's *Biographia Literaria*, esp. chapters IV, XIV, and XV.

26. Though Emerson and Thoreau are profoundly linked in the minds of their subsequent readers, there is considerable difference in what each considered ultimate reality and the relation between spirit (or the divine) and matter, the *transcendent* and the *immanent*. For a deeper interpretation of this issue see the essays in Lundin, ed., *There Before Us*, especially those by Packer and Gatta.

27. Emerson, *Selections*, 11.

In the woods, we return to reason and faith. There I feel that nothing can befall me in life,—no disgrace, no calamity (leaving me my eyes), which nature cannot repair. Standing on the bare ground,—my head bathed in the blithe air and uplifted into infinite space,—all mean egotism vanishes. I become a transparent eyeball; I am nothing; I see all; the currents of the Universal Being circulate through me; I am part or parcel of God.[28]

This essay, in fact most of his writing, does not so much recount his encounters with *signals of transcendence* as outline a worldview in which the *immanence* of the *transcendent* plays a highly significant role:

The world proceeds from the same spirit as the body of man. It is a remoter and inferior incarnation of God, a projection of God in the unconscious. . . . It is . . . the present expositor of the divine mind.[29]

This is the worldview that underlies the *signal of transcendence* he gives here:

Day creeps after day, each full of facts, dull, strange, despised things that we cannot enough despise,—call heavy, prosaic, and desart [i.e., off the beaten path]. And presently the aroused intellect finds gold and gems in one of these scorned facts, then finds that the day of facts is a rock of diamonds, that a fact is an Epiphany of God, that on every fact of his life he should rear a temple of wonder, joy, and praise; that in going to eat meat, to buy, or sell, to meet a friend, or thwart an adversary, to communicate a piece of news, or buy a book, he celebrates the arrival of an inconceivably remote purpose and law at last on the shores of Being, and into the ripeness and term of nature. And because nothing chances, but all is locked and wheeled and chained in Law, in these motes and dust he can read the writing of the True Life and of a startling sublimity.[30]

His Divinity School Address (1838) alienated him from any of those whose orthodox Christian faith was more than casual. From this point

28. Ibid., 24. Notice the similarity of this text to Wordsworth's *The Recluse*, ll., 767–93, above. Lest we think that Emerson alone is a vehicle of the divine, in "The American Scholar" he concludes his address to the Harvard Phi Beta Kappa Society with these words: "A nation of men will for the first time exist, because each believes himself inspired by the Divine Soul which also inspires all men" (*Selections*, 80).

29. Ibid., 50.

30. Ibid., Note from June 21, 1838, 90.

on his voice became more and more singular and prophetic. Optimism reigned in his speeches and essays—"The American Scholar" (1837), "The Divinity School Address" (1838), and "Self-reliance" (1841)—then became more restrained in "The Transcendentalist" (1841).[31] In the latter Emerson explains how a transcendentalist begins to experiences full life when he suddenly experiences a powerful *signal of transcendence*:

> When I asked them [the transcendentalists] concerning their private experience, they answered somewhat in this wise: It is not to be denied that there must be some wide difference between my faith and other faith; and mine is a certain brief experience, which surprised me in the highway or in the market, in some place, at some time,—whether in the body or out of the body, God knoweth,[32]—and made me aware that I had played the fool with fools all this time, but that law existed for me and for all; that to me belonged trust, a child's trust and obedience, and the worship of ideas, and I should never be fool more. Well, in the space of an hour probably, I was let down from this height; I was at my old tricks, the selfish member of a selfish society. . . . I wish to exchange this flash-of-lightning faith for continuous daylight, this fever-glow for a benign climate.[33]

But for Emerson the tension within the life of a transcendentalist was becoming more and more obvious, and the ideal became impossible to realize. Day after creeping day did not produce amazing and delightful bolts from the blue. Nature and the world around him did not prove to be the beneficent embodiment of a divine Spirit with the best things in mind for Emerson. On January 28, 1842, his six-year-old son Waldo died and Emerson was devastated:

> Sorrow makes us all children again,—destroys all differences of intellect. The wisest knows nothing.[34]

> Must every experience—those that promised to be dearest and most penetrative,—only kiss my cheek like the wind and pass away?[35]

31. "The Transcendentalist," Whicher says, "paints sympathetically a portrait to which the painter himself is clearly not committed" (*Selections*, 179).

32. An allusion to the experience Paul described in 2 Corinthians 12:1–10: Paul's response was very different.

33. Emerson, *Selections*, 203.

34. Note, January 30, 1842, ibid., 208.

35. Letter to Caroline Sturgis, February 4, 1843, ibid., 208.

I comprehend nothing of this fact but its bitterness.[36]

"The Poet" (1843) retains some optimism for the poet to be "*the true and only doctor* [i.e., teacher]; *he knows and tells. . . . He is a beholder of ideas and an utterer of the necessary and casual.*"[37] The worldview is still transcendentalism, now lifting the poet to status of prophet and maker of religion. But there is less optimism expressed for his success. By 1844, as Stephen E. Whicher puts it, Emerson "contrived to rescue his old hope from his new skepticism" while "he habitually assumed the enigmatic nature of his world and the inherent absurdity of that ever-losing winner, man."[38] Emerson no longer read those day-after-creeping-day facts as bursting with good news. There was now no gospel. And his subsequent essays, "Experience" (1844), "Montaigne; or, The Skeptic" (1845) and "Fate" (1853) make grim and depressing reading. Take these few excerpts from "Experience":

> Fox and woodchuck, hawk and snipe and bittern, when nearly seen, have no more root in the deep world than man, and are just such superficial tenants of the globe. Then the new molecular philosophy shows astronomical interspaces betwixt atom and atom, shows that the world is all outside; it has no inside.[39]

> Life itself is a bubble and a skepticism, and a sleep within a sleep.[40]

> Man lives by pulses; our organic movements are such; and the chemical and ethereal agents are undulatory and alternate; and the mind goes antagonizing on, and never prospers but by fits. We thrive by casualties.[41]

Only in the last few sentences of "Experience" does Emerson offer hope, and it is utterly unjustified by what has gone before.[42] The hope is merely a vestige of a hearty transcendentalism.

36. Note, March 20(?), 1842, ibid., 208.

37. Ibid., 225.

38. Ibid., 253.

39. Ibid., 263.

40. Ibid., 264.

41. Ibid., 265.

42. The final paragraph of "Montaigne; or, The Skeptic" shifts the essay from the skepticism of realism to an ending of hope beyond hope: "Let a man learn to look for the permanent in the mutable and fleeting; let him learn to bear the disappearance of things he was wont to reverence without losing his reverence; let him learn that he is

> We dress our garden, eat our dinners, discuss the household
> with our wives, and these things make no impression, are for-
> gotten next week; but, in the solitude to which every man is
> always returning, he has a sanity and revelations which in his
> passage into new worlds he will carry with him. Never mind the
> ridicule, never mind the defeat; up again, old heart!—it seems
> to say,—there is victory yet for all justice; and the true romance
> which the world exists to realize will be the transformation of
> genius into practical power.[43]

Eventually, Emerson has hope only in a vague Divine Providence, with
the Antislavery Society growing and leading the way: "I hope we have
come to an end of our unbelief, have come to a belief that there is a
Divine Providence in the world which will not save us but through our
own cooperation."[44] Religion has thus been reduced to morality, grace replaced by reliance on community and social cohesion. Gone entirely are
signals of transcendence pointing either up to the divine or down toward
its *immanence* in nature.

My following comment may sound like the conclusion to a ser-
mon, for what I want to suggest is more than casual. Moreover, there
are multiple causes—personal and social, historic and hermeneutic—for
Emerson's movement from Christian faith to optimistic transcendentalism, then pessimism and on to sheer hope in the growing antislavery
sentiment of America. But in line with the thrust of this book, I want to
focus on one specific causal factor. *Signals of transcendence* can be misinterpreted. When they are, they may lead to intellectual and spiritual
disaster. Emerson, so Whicher concludes, in his final years and his final
essays may have regained some measure of acceptance of the ambiguity of the *signals* that issue from human contemplation of nature. But
he never returned either to his earlier optimism or to anything resem-
bling orthodox Christianity with its explanation of both the glory of God
revealed in his creation and the fact of its being "bleared, smeared" by
the results of the fall. He continued to consider the poet—the especially
enlightened among humans, the gifted thinker—the proper and adequate
interpreter of experience.

---

here, not to work but to be worked upon; and that, though abyss open to abyss, and
opinion displace opinion, all are at last contained in the Eternal Cause. . . " (ibid., 301).

43. Ibid., 273–74.

44. Emerson, "The Seventh of March Speech on the Fugitive Slave Law, 7 March
1845," as quoted in Packer, "Signing Off," in Lundin, ed., *There Before Us,* 22.

The intellectual force that lies behind Emerson's intellectual and spiritual journey is the autonomy of human reason. And that has been the bug bear, the bête noire, of modern history. With Emerson it is not science that provides the answer. He knew better what the view of human beings as solely material came to. The growth of hope in technology was a major factor in his own discouragement; it reduced human beings to cogs in a giant machine. But his alternative, that human beings in the vast regions of their intellect and imaginations were the new gods and goddesses, the makers and readers of *signals of transcendence*, was an egotistical idolatry that forever separates human beings from the peace and joy of truth. When the god of experience failed him, the ambiguity of nature's *signals* flooded his soul. Emerson could not resolve the tensions he saw in nature and lived in his experience. This resolution would require the actual ontological existence of a truly personal God—a God who both fully *transcends* his creation and is fully *immanent* as well, a God who in Jesus Christ was incarnated in time and space into his own created world. That option was lost on him.

Loren Eiseley and the Star Thrower

Professionally, Loren Eiseley (1907–77) is best identified as an American anthropologist, with a BA/BS from my own glorious institution, the University of Nebraska, and an MA and PhD from the University of Pennsylvania. He was much better known, however, as a writer on natural science whose work was published in journals such as *The New Yorker, American Scholar*, and *Scientific American*, and collected in several volumes, including *The Immense Journey* (1957), *The Unexpected Universe* (1969), and *The Star Thrower* (1978). And what a writer he was! His essays sing. Why? Because, while he drew a basically accurate scientific picture of the natural world, he saw through its plain material nature to a realm beyond the merely physical. As W. H. Auden said, "Dr. Eiseley's autobiographical passages are, most of them, descriptions of numinous encounters—some joyful, some terrifying."[45] Or as Eiseley himself wrote in "The Slit": "I have done all in my power to avoid errors in fact. I have given the record of what one man thought as he pursued research and pressed his hands against the confining walls of scientific method of his time."[46]

45. Auden, "Considering the Unpredictable," 19.
46. Eiseley, *Immense Journey*, 1–14.

At the same time, Eiseley never equated this *numinous* dimension with a specific notion of the divine. One could label him a deist, but only in a vague sense. In his writing there is little hint of Christian theism from which deism emerged. One could also call him a panentheist, but this too suggests a philosophic specificity that is lacking. One could, and this is normally done, call him a *naturalist*, but this must be taken as one who studied, loved, and wrote penetrating personal essays on his encounter with nature. In this usage, *naturalist* cannot mean one who discounts the possibility of any spiritual dimension at all.

Perhaps the best label for him is *humanist*, meaning in this case one who, while admitting little detail to his conception of what is more than natural, finds his mind exceeding its natural boundaries, enough so to fashion an inner world where miracle and mystery are natural to him.[47] Dip anywhere into his various collections of essays and you will find thrilling encounters, the very descriptions of which send shivers up your spine. Here is one he calls "The Judgment of the Birds":

> . . . I had come over a mountain, that I had slogged through fern and pine needles for half a long day, and that on the edge of a little glade with one long, crooked branch extending across it, I had sat down to rest with my back against a stump. Through accident I was concealed from the glade, although I could see into it perfectly.
>
> The sun was warm there, and the murmurs of the forest life blurred softly away into my sleep. When I awoke, dimly aware of some commotion and outcry in the clearing, the light was slanting down through the pines in such a way that the glade was lit like some vast cathedral. I could see the dust motes of wood pollen in the long shaft of light, and there on the extended branch sat an enormous raven with a red and squirming nestling in his beak.
>
> The sound that woke me was the outraged cries of the nestling's parents, who helplessly flew in circles about the clearing. The sleek black monster was indifferent to them. He gulped, whetted his beak on the dead branch a moment, and sat still. Up to that point the little tragedy had followed the usual pattern. But suddenly, out of all that area of woodland, a soft sound of complaint began to rise. Into the glade fluttered small birds of half a dozen varieties drawn by the anguished outcries of the tiny parents.

47. Ibid.

No one dared to attack the raven. But they cried there in some instinctive common misery, the bereaved and unbereaved. The glade filled with their soft rustling and their cries. They fluttered as though to point their wings at the murderer. There was a dim intangible ethic he had violated, that they knew. He was a bird of death.

And he, the murderer, the black bird at the heart of life, sat on there, glistening in the common light, formidable, unmoving, unperturbed, untouchable.

The sighing died. It was then I saw the judgment. It was the judgment of life against death. I will never see it again so forcefully presented. I will never hear it again in notes so tragically prolonged. For in the midst of protest, they forgot the violence. There, in that clearing, the crystal note of a song sparrow lifted hesitantly in the hush. And finally, after painful fluttering, another took the song, and then another, the song passing from one bird to another, doubtfully at first, as though some evil thing were being slowly forgotten. Till suddenly they took heart and sang from many throats joyously together as birds are known to sing. They sang because life is sweet and sunlight beautiful. They sang under the brooding shadow of the raven. In simple truth they had forgotten the raven, for they were the singers of life, and not of death.[48]

Or consider the following: Eiseley sees a man throwing starfish from the shore back into the sea; he speaks with him for a few moments and reflects on this as an encounter with something more than just extraordinary, though he does not say what. Something, however, is lurking. He writes,

"Tarry thou, till I come again"—an old legend survives among us of the admonition given by Jesus to the Wandering Jew. The words are applicable to all of us. Deep-hidden in the human psyche there is a similar injunction, no longer having to do with the longevity of the body but, rather, a plea to wait upon some transcendent lesson preparing in the mind itself.[49]

Is Eiseley promulgating the New Age notion of the self as the center of reality? No, not at all. Rather, he is puzzling metaphorically over the ability of the human mind to feel that something is missing and yet to come. Does this suggest deism? No, for no creator seems in mind. Panentheism?

48. Eisley, *Star Thrower*, 33–34.
49. Ibid., 175.

Well, maybe. But then consider these lines two pages later in the same essay.

> As the spinning galactic clouds hurl stars and worlds across the night, so life, equally impelled by the centrifugal powers lurking in the germ cell, scatters the splintered radiance of conscious-ness and sends it prowling and contending through the thickets of the world.[50]

However we label his overall take on reality as a whole, we must see it as somehow being *alive* in a way unaccounted for by ordinary materialism. This strikes us in his view of the origin of life. Eiseley has no doubts about life's haphazard chain of causes: neither the snowflake nor human life was intended:

> There is no logical reason for the existence of a snowflake any more than there is for evolution. It is an apparition from that mysterious shadow world beyond nature, that final world which contains—if anything contains—the explanation of men and catfish and green leaves.[51]

Could this "final world" be divine? Interestingly Eiseley is well aware of Rudolf Otto's *The Idea of the Holy*. In "Science and the Sense of the Holy," he writes:

> Ever since man first painted animals in the dark of caves he has been responding to the holy, to the numinous, to the mystery of being and becoming, to what Goethe very aptly called "the weird portentous."[52]

At the same time he takes a truncated view of the *numinous*, the *holy* and the *mysterium tremendum*. He uses the terms, but he never mentions the ancient Hebrew and Christian conceptions of the divine. His *numinous* is more than spooky but less than theistic. "Yet still," he says, "the question haunts us, the numinous, the holy in man's mind."[53] Human beings are more than what we normally think of as material, more than Carl Sagan's star stuff; humanity's humanness is, perhaps we might say, humanly spiri-tual. Even if the cosmos at times seems cosmically spiritual, just exactly how or why is forever hidden from us.

50. Ibid., 177.
51. Eisley, *Immense Journey*, 27.
52. Eisley, *Star Thrower*, 189.
53. Ibid.

Emily Dickinson's Certain Slant of Light

It has taken me several days to write this chapter. And in that time it has become apparent that once one leaves the province of a full-fledged theism, signals of transcendence seem fewer and fewer to come by in English and American literature. I surely should have predicted this. What happens to *signals of transcendence* once worldviews involve less and less transcendence?

Obviously, less and less significance is given to ecstatic moments.

Perhaps my recent experience of rereading a large complement of the brief but marvelous poems of Emily Dickinson is exemplary. I have often admired her poem beginning "There's a certain Slant of light."[54] Its vision I see; its emotions I feel; its conclusion I understand.

> There's a certain Slant of light,
> Winter Afternoons—
> That oppresses, like the Heft
> Of Cathedral Tunes—
>
> Heavenly Hurt, it gives us—
> We can find no scar,
> But internal difference,
> Where the Meanings, are—
>
> None may teach I it—Any—
> 'Tis the Seal Despair—
> An imperial affliction
> Sent us of the Air—
>
> When it comes, the Landscape listens—
> Shadows—hold their breath—
> When it goes, 'tis like the Distance
> On the look of Death —

This is, of course, a remarkable poem, one of hundreds in her corpus. Moreover, if Dickinson has any worldview that includes the transcendent, it is Christian theism. She would never put up with a deistic or transcendentalist world view. God is either a personal God, or he is not a god. Certainly, while she views the self as powerful in imagination, she does not consider it divine in any way. Death has too much dominion for

---

54. Dickinson, *Complete Poems*, 118–19.

her; it fascinates her, puzzles her; she writes poem after poem imagining such matters as the consciousness of dying, the permanence of death, the possibility of life with God, the struggle with belief in such a life and in a God who would give it. But, so it seems, she seldom experiences the presence of God.

The "certain Slant of light" could with some poets spell an angled glimpse into the light of the sun, a signal of God's presence. It might not give a "Heavenly Hurt" but a joy divine; "the Heft / of Cathedral Tunes" might exalt the listener; the "Meaning" might suggest ecstasy not "Despair." "Shadows" might very well hold their breath because the "Slant of light" illumines and suggests a "look of life." But all of that is reversed. The "transcendent" meaning of the "Slant of light" opens the way to despair. Yet, I see what she means. I can feel the same way, for I have "seen" that "Slant of light." I resonate with her. The difference is that most of the ecstasy Dickinson seems to feel ties her to the world of nature; it rarely points beyond the present. Think of that delightful poem beginning "I taste a liquor never brewed": [55]

> I taste a liquor never brewed—
> From Tankards scooped in Pearl—
> Not all the Vats upon the Rhine
> Yield such an Alcohol!
>
> Inebriate of Air—am I—
> And Debauchee of Dew—
> Reeling—thro endless summer days—
> From inns of Molten Blue—
>
> When "Landlords" turn the drunken Bee
> Out of the Foxglove's door—
> When Butterflies—renounce their "drams"—
> I shall but drink the more!
>
> Till Seraphs swing their snowy Hats—
> And Saints—to windows run—
> To see the little Tippler
> Leaning against the—Sun—

Lest we think that the final stanza suggests transcendence, let's look again. The Seraphs are getting their joy from nature alone and from seeing a

55. Ibid., 98–99.

drunken nature lover lose her material bearings. This is not to say that Dickinson could not be a Christian theist and write such a poem; she could. It is rather that one looks long and hard within the works of Dickinson for suggestions that the material world contains signals that bear witness to the presence of a theistic God or any god at all.[56]

Literary scholar Roger Lundin gives us at least one aesthetic explanation for this. Dickinson does not look on nature as a "type" but as a "trope." He writes,

> If nature is a *type*, it is grounded in a reality higher than itself, and every one of its elements point to that ultimate reality. . . . In Rorty's categories, *types* are truths as they are supposedly found [in reality]; *tropes* are truths as they are actually made [by the poet].[57]

Dickinson would like to have nature speak to her, but it did not. Seldom does nature become a trope, though when it does, it usually points to doubt (epistemology) about what reality actually is rather than a confirmation of its character (ontology), to despair rather than hope (emotional implication). Still there are poems of hope:

> For every poem of hers that questions the nature or existence of God, another affirms the goodness of the Divine character and power. . . . Not long before she died, she wrote in a letter that "on subjects of which we know nothing, or should I say *Beings*—. . . we both believe, and disbelieve a hundred times an Hour, which keeps Believing nimble."[58]

God is indeed, as Pascal and many other seekers after God have said, *deus absconditus*. Dickinson writes:[59]

> I know that He exists.
> Somewhere—in Silence—
> He has hid his rare life
> From our gross eyes.

56. See also "The Angle of a Landscape" (ibid., 179) in which she observes the world from her bedroom window. She is fascinated by the scene, but even when among the scenes of nature she spies the church steeple, she finds all of these, steeple included, never "stir at all." There is no genuine theistic transcendence here.

57. Lundin, *Emily Dickinson*, 46, 152, 239.

58. Ibid., 138–39, citing a letter Dickinson wrote to Otis Phillips Lord, April 30, 1882.

59. Dickinson, *Complete Poems*, 160.

Still, there is at least one exception to nature as mere *trope*. Lundin cites "'Heaven' has different Signs":[60]

> "Heaven" has different Signs—to me—
> Sometimes, I think that Noon
> Is but a symbol of the Place—
> And when again, at Dawn,
>
> A mighty look runs round the World
> And settles in the Hills—
> An Awe if it should be like that
> Upon the Ignorance steals—
>
> The Orchard, when the Sun is on—
> The Triumph of the Birds
> When they together Victory make—
> Some Carnivals of Clouds—
>
> The Rapture of a finished Day—
> Returning to the West—
> All these—remind us of the place
> That Men call "Paradise"—
>
> Itself be fairer—we suppose—
> But how Ourself, shall be
> Adorned, for a Superior Grace—
> Not yet, our eyes can see—

But even here none of these natural signals gives us a hint of our personal fate. She sees the place of paradise; she does not see herself in that place. For Dickinson confident belief in God was usually belied by skepticism or even utter disbelief. This century of Darwin, whom she knew of, and of Nietzsche, whose voice was yet to be heard much in America, challenged Christian faith. In its intellectual culture of cold deism and sheer atheism, God's "Hand is amputated now / And God cannot be found—."[61]

Still Lundin hesitates to leave Emily Dickinson either an atheist or an apostate Christian. Her poems toward the end of her life indicate an increasing tendency to affirm the existence of God and his goodness.[62]

---

60. Ibid., 280–81.
61. Ibid., 646.
62. Lundin, *Emily Dickinson*, 166–78.

Still, fully Level 4 signals are mostly absent in her poems. For her God's presence is not that obvious.

Thomas Hardy: Reality as Immanent Will

A much less hopeful spirit animates the mind, poetry and novels of Thomas Hardy. After being raised in an Anglican community and seriously considering conversion to a Baptist form of Christian faith, Hardy moved, as did many of his fellow late Victorians, toward puzzled doubt and disbelief. Still, he cannot completely abandon his hope that there is some great being who is there beyond the visible universe and is, in the final analysis, beneficent. In one of his most anthologized poems, "The Darkling Thrush," dated at the beginning of the new millennium (December 31, 1900), Hardy depicts himself leaning against a "coppice gate." As "the tangled vine-stems scored the sky / Like strings of broken lyres," he sees "the land's sharp features" as "the century's corpse outleant," and then he hears the thrush:

> At once a voice arose among
>   The bleak twigs overhead
> In full-hearted evensong
>   Of joy illimited;
> An aged thrush, frail, gaunt, and small,
>   In blast-beruffled plume
> Had chosen thus to fling his soul
>   Upon the growing gloom.
>
> So little cause for carolings
>   Of such ecstatic sound
> Was written on terrestrial things
>   Afar or nigh around,
> That I could think there trembed through
>   His happy good-night air
> Some blessed Hope, whereof he knew
>   And I was unaware.[63]

By the time this was written, Hardy was no longer viewing the world as a Christian, if he ever did, nor was he a traditional atheist. He now spoke

---

63. Hardy, *Norton Anthology*, 876. See also Hardy's "The Oxen," ibid., 880.

of ultimate reality as an unfeeling "Immanent Will" and "The Spinner of the Years."[64]

The Limited Certainty of Signals

So what can we conclude from this survey of deistic, panentheistic, romantic, and skeptical *signals of transcendence*? Certainly one thing emerges: Apparent *signals of transcendence* do not necessarily lead to the certainty of a fully theistic faith. They require an interpretive grid, a hermeneutic, a way to understand with the intellect what one has first perceived by the senses and/or the intuition. In other words, they do not constitute a complete apologetic. Os Guinness makes much of *signals of transcendence* in his apologetic work *Long Journey Home*. The feeling of thankfulness for being alive, he says, suggests the existence of someone *transcendent* to whom to be thankful. But, he adds, "a signal of transcendence, gratitude for being alive, is not a proof but a pointer. It's an intuition, not a settled conviction. It creates a searcher, not a believer."[65] Such *signals* are "holes torn in life," "spots of time" that cry out for interpretation.

Nonetheless, pursued to their ultimate meaning, they may well be echoes of the most significant voice. As N. T. Wright says, they turn out to be "the voice of Jesus, calling us to follow him into God's new world—the world in which the hints, signposts, and echoes of the present world turn into the reality of the next one."[66]

---

64. See "The Convergence of the Twain" on the loss of the Titanic, lines 18 and 31 (*Norton Anthology*, 879). The Wikipedia entry for Thomas Hardy notes that Hardy considered conversion to the Christian faith and membership in a Baptist church, but declined. According to George Wotton, for Hardy "The Christian god—the external personality—has been replaced by the intelligence of the First Cause . . . the replacement of the old concept of God as all-powerful by a new concept of universal consciousness. The 'tribal god, man-shaped, fiery-faced and tyrannous' is replaced by the 'unconscious will of the Universe' which progressively grows aware of itself and 'ultimately, it is to be hoped, sympathetic'" (*Thomas Hardy*, 36).

65. Guinness, *Long Journey*, 50.

66. Wright, *Simply Christian*, 225.

8

Everything Much, Nothing at All

Nirvana as Negative Cosmic Consciousness

The world is dew—
The world is dew—
And yet,
And yet…

—ISSA[1]

In this chapter we enter a world the West finds strange and incomprehensible, both for what it seems to affirm and deny and for why it should do so. Almost everything in this Eastern conception turns most Western worldviews on their heads. I say *most* because Western nihilism, which has resulted from the failure of Western worldviews to remain intellectually tenable, does have some affinity with Buddhist conceptions, though not to those in line with Hinduism.

We are now acquainted with the intimate relationship that *signals of transcendence* have with the worldviews in which they are embedded or to which they point. This intimate relationship persists as we turn to Buddhism in particular and perhaps some forms of Hinduism as well.

---

1. Guinness, *Dust of Death*, 223. Henderson, *Introduction to Haiku,* 131, translates this from the Japanese as "The Dew Drop World— / a dewdrop world it is, and still, / although it is . . ." (ellipses in the original).

We will begin with the experience of a young man totally unfamiliar with Eastern thought who now believes he has had a Zen Buddhist-like experience in Tokyo.

A Young American in Tokyo

In the early spring of 1956 while I was in the U.S. Army in transit through Japan to Korea, I wandered along the Ginza, a major street in the inner city of Tokyo. The footprints of sky-high office buildings covered each city block. There were no frontage setbacks with green space or even ornamental trees or statues. I wandered and looked and wondered. Suddenly, in front of me was a tiny open space, say, four by six feet. I looked intently.

I had never seen a Japanese rock garden. But I knew that this was one of them. Raked into small curving parallel ridges, rough grayish-brown gravel covered the flat surface. Inserted into them were rocks of varying sizes, seemingly without pattern. I was puzzled. What's this all about? This, by the way, was my frequent response to Japanese art of all kinds, from music to drama to gardens to the wood block paintings I later came to admire. For the most part I still feel lost in the presence of Asian culture. But my curiosity kept my attention focused on the rock garden. Again suddenly, the garden became all I saw. I had lost all connection to anything else including a sense of where I was standing or the passing of time. All I saw was the garden and it looked as small as what my vision could encompass and as large as the cosmos. Clock time and measured space disappeared. But not for long. How long I don't know. But I came away still puzzled about what had happened to me or in me or in the world. Only when I began reading about Zen Buddhism years later did it dawn on me.

Had I had an infinitesimal taste of the infinite? Was this a brief encounter with Nirvana—the consciousness of pure undifferentiated, unnamable, unspeakable reality as some Japanese Buddhists speak of it? Buddhists do not, of course, claim to explain it intellectually. Rather they attempt to recreate the direct experience through the indirection of art—gardens, literature, music, drama, painting. Such gardens as I saw become for a Buddhist brief *signals of transcendence*—but a very different kind of *transcendence* from that conceived of by Western theists.

In an attempt to link the Buddhist "understanding" of this *transcendence* with the Western forms we have considered above, let me coin a phrase: *nirvana as negative cosmic consciousness.* Like Zen Buddhists, I know of no better way to explain this term than by way of indirection, in this case the indirection of the haiku poetry of the seventeenth-century poet, Matsuo Bashô.[2]

Bashô and the Soundless Leaping Frog

Many of the details of the life of Matsuo Bashô (1644–94) can only be considered probable.[3] So it is probable that he was born and raised in a low-ranking Samurai family, entered the service of a young Samurai master, and first served as a page. For our purposes the details of his life are not important; what is important is that he quickly became fascinated by poetry and early spent much of his time composing haikus, the intriguing three-line seventeen-syllable (in Japanese) poems, many of which first appear to be mere images. But the aesthetically greatest haikus are not the simple expressions of childish imagination, no matter how clever. Some of them, when properly grasped, convey the essence of a Zen Buddhist worldview, and do so more fully than can any direct description, no matter how sophisticated. We can see this in Bashô's most well-known haiku.

> The ancient pond
> A frog leaps in
> The sound of water.[4]

This is a deceptively simple poem, often learned and imitated by children in America as well as Japan. It is deceptive because from our Western worldview, it appears, like many of Bashô's poems, to be only a simple picture, an image of sight and sound. The sight: an ancient pond and a frog leaping in. The sound: the sound of water. The scene is spare; the

2. The comments in this section are adapted from my *Naming*, 149–52.

3. Uedo, *Matsuo Basho*, 19–35.

4. This haiku has probably been translated more than any other. I quote it from the translation in which, so far as I remember, I first encountered it (Keene, *Japanese Literature*, 39). For nearly 150 other delightful translations, imitations, and take-offs of this haiku, see Sato, *One Hundred Frogs*.

action is quickly over. What else is there? Not much. Indeed, but enough to encompass the whole of reality as Zen views it.[5]

The *ancient pond* is first of all a pond, not a symbol of anything. But it is ancient; it has been around for a long time; it carries the past in its present. The *frog* is first of all a frog, again not a symbol of anything; it is in the present. So both the frog and the pond together are in the present. The *frog leaping* is first of all a frog leaping, not a symbol of anything; the present moves. Then *the sound of water* is first of all the sound water makes when a frog leaps in; not a "plop" or a "bloop," though that is the way it is sometimes translated. In the Japanese the phrase is not onomatopoetic; it is just a phrase like "the sound of water." And that's important, for "the sound of water" makes no water sound like the sound of water. The physical sound of the frog entering the water is not the sound of the words "the sound of water." The sound of the intersection of past and present is no sound, for sound takes time, vibrations are matter in motion. The interface between past and present is not itself a part of matter in motion.[6]

By reading this poem, revisioning its setting and entering into its spirit, we can be teased out of thought. Our aesthetic experience then becomes a glimpse into what I take to be a major part of the experience of satori or nirvana. So pause again: imbibe, read and reread this haiku. I am not suggesting this because I want to promote a totally Zen view of reality, but because there is an element of reality, as understood by Christians, in it. Like the Zen Buddhist, we too live in the present. Often we miss it. So let us allow ourselves a doorway into recognizing its subtle reality.

Recognizing this haiku as a *signal of transcendence,* however, encourages us not just to look at what first appears but to ask what understanding of reality, what kind of mindset, lies behind the picture. If it is a Western mindset, then, indeed, we do have just what we have first noticed: an image of a frog jumping into an old pond with an accompanying plop. But if we examine the worldview background of Bashô himself, we will find something very different. Bashô was a Zen Buddhist priest with

5. My reading of the poem was suggested by Keene, *Japanese Literature,* 39, but I have modified and elaborated on it considerably. For comments by twelve Japanese critics, see Uedo, *Basho,* 140–42.

6. One form of Buddhism takes this notion so seriously that it conceives of the world as a string of pearls, each being created from nothing at each point along the string.

a Zen mind. We will not be able to see what his haiku is doing until we examine his worldview.

The Zen mind is a Zen moment, a concentration of attention on a chronologically dimensionless present. It is the timeless intersection between past and future. It is and is not, neither one nor the other, yet both at once. Try thinking of the present in any other way. There is consciousness; yet this consciousness is a consciousness of what is always in motion. What one is conscious of at one instant is gone when one thinks about what it is.

Now all of this seems simply descriptive of consciousness. It is always conscious of something, but what it is conscious of is constantly changing. Consciousness itself is not a consciousness of itself; it is always of the other, and the other changes. What Zen does is to exalt this insight into a worldview. Zen proclaims that because consciousness is always conscious of change and never of permanence, change is all that is permanent; in other words nothing is permanent. This then is raised to a philosophic principle. The only permanent "thing" is not a "thing" at all. It is an absence of "thingishness." It is the Void. It is *nirvana as negative cosmic consciousness*.

Here we meet the crucial claim in Zen: human beings are capable of grasping all the reality there is. Nothing could be more opposite to the Christian worldview than that. Christians hold that there is a much more to reality than can be directly perceived by our consciousness or dreamt of in Zen philosophy. God is there as the Creator of both our consciousness and the world of which it is conscious and only partially conscious of at best.

There are several more haiku I have found as doorways into the appreciation of the present. I enjoy Bashô's haikus because they alert me not to the Void but to God's marvelous creation and the glories inherent in each moment. After all, there would be no conscious present if God had not created the world to be what it is and us to be what we are. If there are ancient ponds and frogs leaping, if there are crows on branches, if there are seasons, if there are gulls that cry out, then these haikus can help us see them in their immediate presence to us:[7]

---

7. These haikus, all by Bashô, are given in the translation used by Keene, *Japanese Literature*, 40.

On the withered branch
A crow has alighted—
Nightfall in autumn.

The sea darkens,
The cries of the seagulls
Are faintly white.

Such stillness—
The cries of the cicadas
Sink into the rocks.

Still, if we are to be responsible in the way we interpret *signals of transcendence*, we must also see these haikus as presentations of Zen. As such they give us a glimpse into the mindset of many other people, not just from Japan but from everywhere that Zen Buddhism has influenced people's minds and lives.

At the same time, Zen poets are sometimes ambiguous, not just because Zen itself revels in the seeming contradiction of *negative* consciousness, that is, of being conscious of the Void and/or the Fullness of the Void, but because Zen poets, like people in all cultures and all worldviews, experience the world itself as contradictory or at least paradoxical.

Makoto Ueda, for example, points out that Bashô himself "gradually became nihilistic. He had become a poet in order to transcend worldly involvements," but he became involved with popularity and fame. His first response was to quit writing, but he kept being drawn back; so he gave up contact with people; then again opened the gate to them. Finally, Bashô's solution was based on the principle of "lightness," a dialectical *transcendence* of sabi. Sabi urges a person to detach himself from worldly involvements; "lightness" makes it possible for him after attaining that detachment, to return to the mundane world.[8]

In declining health he wrote:

This autumn
Why am I aging so?
Flying towards the clouds, a bird.[9]

8. Uedo, *Matsuo Basho*, 34.
9. Ibid.

His last haiku was this:

> On a journey, ailing—
> My dreams roam about
> Over a withered moor.[10]

Though Bashô's poetry is heavily imagistic, shunning adjectives, if possible, it is shot through with deep human emotion. Not all human experience of *transcendence* leads to a quiet acceptance of *negative cosmic consciousness*.

Gary Snyder: Modern American Zen

While Zen Buddhism is ultimately a radical reversal of Christianity, it is also, perhaps (I am guessing here), the most attractive form of Eastern religion, even the most attractive form of Buddhism, to people raised in the West, including those raised in a specifically Christian context. Why is this? One major factor is that Zen Buddhism combines two key features of the Christian worldview—a respect for the beauties, even glories, of the natural world and a way to transcend them. It provides a way of acknowledging the multiplicity of human experience and the complexity of the natural world while grasping their unity at a *transcendent* level.[11] The All is One, thus denying the reality of multiplicity. This is advaita vedanta Hinduism. The All is not-One because the All is Not; nonetheless, from the Not emerges from the All. This is Zen Buddhism.

Of course, this understanding of *immanence* and *transcendence* is totally different from the Christian view. Christians understand ultimate being to be the Triune God who is within his singular being the persons of the Father, Son, and Holy Spirit. This *God* is Being himself, a personal being who exhausts every character of possible being. He is. Or as he says of himself, *I AM*. All else than him is creation–multiplicity (the many): angels, the cosmos, and everything in the cosmos. Creation is open to *transcendence* by human beings made in his image. Moreover, in God *transcendence* is *immanent*.

In American Buddhism, especially as we see it in the poetry of Gary Snyder, the respect for nature includes a sense of *transcendence* that at

10. Ibid., 35.

11. The theme of the One and the Many permeates philosophy, East and West. Think, for example, of the ancient philosopher Heraclitus: "We step and do not step into the same rivers" (Fragment 41).

first may look a lot like the Christian concept, but which turns out to be its mirror image. Let us see how this works out in a few of Gary Snyder's poems.

We will begin with his most recent collection, *Mountains and Rivers Without End*, published intentionally as an "epic," though it does not take the traditional narrative form but is a sequence of poems that mark a trek toward an overall American Zen Buddhist's vision of reality. Beginning with a reflective verse description of an ancient Chinese painting, included as the frontispiece of the book and ending with "Finding Space in the Heart," the epic becomes, as Snyder says, "a sort of sûtra—an extended, poetic, philosophic, and mythic narrative of the female Buddha Tarâ."[12] For those who would like to see for themselves the overall vision of Snyder, this may not be the work to start with. There is much that will be obscure to a first reader, but it should probably be the one with which to end.

The final poem, "Finding Space in the Heart," pictures the painting of a picture, that is the constructing of a conscious life. It ends this way:

> *Walking on walking,*
> *under foot earth turns*
>
> *Streams and mountains never stay the same.*
>
> The space goes on.
> But the wet black brush
> tip drawn to a point
> lifts away.[13]

Here, then, is a central theme in Snyder's worldview—change is eternal but reality draws, or is drawn by the painter, to a single point and then the pen is lifted—conscious life is transcended. Who is doing the painting? The consciousness of the human painter. Who is doing the walking on the turning earth whose streams and rivers continue to fill the ever scrolling canvas? The painter, the watcher, the reader. Who is transcending? Ah, who is to say!

12. Snyder, *Mountains*, 158. As for his inspiration Snyder once wrote that "the voice that speaks to me as a poet, what Westerners have called the Muse, is the voice of nature herself, whom the ancient poets called the great goddess, the Magma Mater. I regard that voice as a very real entity" (*Turtle*, 107).

13. Snyder, *Mountains*, 152.

Snyder's poetry is itself a *signal* of Zen *transcendence*. Contemplating the poetry as if it really were a sûtra, the contemplator can begin to experience the world as Snyder does. This is what *signals of transcendence* do. They lift one out of the world as normally experienced into a world beyond this one, in the case of Buddhism, a reality in which the rich and beautiful multiplicity of this world is left behind to be replaced by the "consciousness" of pure "consciousness," that is the consciousness of the Not-Being beyond all being.

Westerners, especially Christians, may think of this as a trick of the mind or a delusion of the evil one or a lapse into irrationality. This is understandable but beside the point. Here is *transcendence* nonetheless. What is at stake is which *transcendence* is real. The God who is *I AM* or the immaterial, non-spiritual *Not One* who is the *Plenum Void*, the full emptiness? Which *signal* is "truly" *transcendent*?

On a poetic level, we may compare the poetry of Gary Snyder with that of Wendell Berry. These two are friends and have been since the beat generation of the fifties. They write poems to and about each other. Snyder's "Berry Territory," set on Berry's farm, reflects on a walk Snyder took together with Wendell and his wife Tanya. It's a description of their looking down a woodchuck hole and deciding someone is home. It's plain, simple, and short but longer than a haiku. Nothing openly suggests anything other than the capture of a moment of time, not much longer than that taken for a frog to leap into a pond:

> *(Walking the woods on an early spring dry*
> *day, the slopes behind the Lanes Landing Farm*
> *on the Kentucky River, with Tanya and Wendell)*
>
> Under dead leaves Tanya finds a tortoise
>   matching the leaves—legs pulled in—
>
> And we look at the woodchuck holes that dive
>   under limestone ledges
>   seabottom strata,
>   who lives there brushes furry back
>   on shell and coral,
>
> Most holes with leaves and twigs around the door,
>   nobody in.
> Wendell, crouched down,
>   sticks his face in a woodchuck hole

> "Hey, smell that, it's a fox!"
> I go on my knees,
> put the opening to my face
> like a mask. No light;
> all smell: sour—warm—
> Splintered bones, scats? feathers?
> Weathering bodies—wild—
>
> Some home.[14]

Now compare that with Berry's *Sabbath* poem we examined in chapter 4. Recall the final lines:

> For as I walk the wooded land
> The morning of God's mercy,
> Beyond the work of mortal hand,
> Seen by more than I see,
>
> The quiet deer look up and wait,
> Held still in quick of grace.
> And I wait, stop footstep and thought.
> We stand here face to face.[15]

Berry could have but didn't write Snyder's poem, but Snyder never could and never would have written Berry's. Nature is nature in both, but Snyder's nature is all there is (and, being utterly transitory, it isn't). Berry's nature is the workmanship of God whose creatures—humans and deer—can commune and do so in the presence of the Presence of the *transcendent* Creator-God.

I love the poetry of Snyder; it is realistic and points beyond itself. I adore the poetry of Berry; it triggers an experience of the really real, the truly true, the goodly good and the beautifully beautiful. You may wish to return to the Berry poems quoted in chapter 4. But here are two more by Snyder. The first is "Old Pond." You may notice its comedic replacement of Bashô's frog with the poet himself.

> Blue mountain white snow gleam
> Through pine bulk and slender needle-sprays;
>   little hemlock half in shade,
>   ragged rocky skyline,
> single clear flat nuthatch call:
> down from the treetrunks

14. Snyder, *Axe*, 12–13.
15. Berry, *Timbered Choir*, 26.

up through time.

At Five Lakes Basin's
Biggest little lake
    after all day scrambling on the peaks,
    a naked bug
    with a white body and brown hair

    dives in the water,

Splash![16]

If Snyder is less the Buddhist here, it is not because of the humor (the humor is pure Zen) but because the naked bug makes a big sound! Now, below is a poetic cosmogony—"No Matter, Never Mind," whose pure Zen title is seemingly belied by its content:

The Father is the Void
The Wife Waves

Their child is Matter.

Matter makes it with his mother
And their child is Life,
    a daughter.

The Daughter is the Great Mother
Who, with her father/brother Matter
    as her lover,

Gives birth to the Mind.[17]

Snyder is indeed the quintessential American Buddhist poet. His presentation of this worldview is itself a *signal* of a creativity that can finally only be explained by the existence of the Creator—the God of Abraham, Isaac, and Jacob, the Father of our Lord Jesus Christ.

16. Snyder, *Axe*, 70.
17. Snyder, *Turtle*, 11.

Andre Comte-Sponville: French Atheist/Buddhist

The malleability of views of reality seems infinite. A little twist here, a slip there, an imaginative addition around the corner and a Western thinker can become an Eastern advocate without totally losing his Western orientation. So it is with Andre Comte-Sponville, a French philosopher, once a professor at the Sorbonne. The title of his recent book trumpets the paradox: *The Little Book of Atheist Spirituality*. Interesting and easily read, this primer on spirituality without God can serve as another example of how religious-type experiences have nearly infinite explanations and surprising interpretations.

Fear of death, for Comte-Sponville, for example, is fear of "nothing." "What frightens us is our own imagination."[18] Our moral motions come from past experience and practice; they are not based on anything *transcendent*. One needs only to believe "in one's parents and mentors, one's friends (provided they are well chosen) and one's conscience."[19] Of course, there is "no way for a lucid atheist to avoid despair," but one can do it cheerfully and with courage.[20] Though raised a Christian who has retained most of Christianity's moral notions, he finds himself closer to Buddhism and Taoism, with "Buddha and Lao-tzu more convincing than Moses or Saint Paul."[21] Comte-Sponville also dismisses the reality of miracles, whether by Jesus or otherwise, thus eliminating the possibility of at least one *signal of transcendence*. Furthermore, he dismisses the existence of God, using the traditional arguments for atheism, just as easily answered (by the way) by the traditional critiques of theists.[22] Nothing new here.

But *being* itself strikes him as an irreducible mystery.[23] Still it is a mystery that does not *signal* a *transcendent* being who creates the universe and sustains it in being. The *transcendent* is just a mystery. So Comte-Sponville ceases to speculate: "Faced with the silence of the universe [on why it exists], silence seems to me a far more appropriate response."[24] He

18. Comte-Sponville, *Little Book*, 7; cf., 148–49.

19. Ibid., 42.

20. Ibid., 51–54. Such cheerful despair is similar to that offered by both Steven Weinberg and Anthony Simon Laden.

21. Ibid., 62.

22. Ibid., 63–123.

23. Comte-Sponville discourses at length on the puzzle of being (ibid., 83–103).

24. Ibid., 103.

has nothing to say; so, as Wittgenstein suggests, he says nothing. None-theless, he does present a brief for "spirituality without God."

For Comte-Sponville "the spirit is not a substance . . . [but] a function."[25] It is the way the brain functions when confronted with the mystery of being—the "infinite, the eternal and the absolute," all of which are mysterious and remain outside the bounds of knowledge: "To be an atheist is not to deny the existence of the absolute; rather it is to deny its transcendence, its spirituality, its personality."[26] This results in an overall metaphysic of "naturalism, immanentism or materialism."[27] The appropriate spiritual response, therefore, is not religion or philosophy but silent contemplation. This contemplation, then, is the doorway to a Western form of atheism that includes a Buddhist acknowledgment of the Void. "Spirituality has more to do with experience than thought . . ." Comte-Sponville says,

> This is something anyone can experience by looking up at the night sky. All you need is a bit of concentration and silence. If the sky is very dark and clear, and you are in the country rather than the city, and you turn out all the lights, look up, and take the time to contemplate in silence. . . . Darkness, which sepa-rates us from what is close at hand, brings us near to what is far away. You cannot see the far side of your own yard, but you can see billions of kilometers away with the naked eye. What is that whitish, opalescent streak? The Milky Way, "our" galaxy, or at least the one to which we belong—some one hundred bil-lion stars, the nearest of which, with the exception of our own sun, is thirty trillion kilometers away. What is that bright dot? Siriu—eight light years (that is, eighty trillion kilometers) away. And what is that barely visible gleam of light over there, near Pegasus's Square? A galaxy known as Andromeda (there are billions of galaxies, each of them comprising billions of stars), some two million light years or twenty billion billion kilometers away! At night, everything changes scale. As long as the sun was shining, it locked us into the prison of light that is the world—our world. Now, provided there are no clouds, darkness reveals to us the light of the sky, which is the universe. I can barely see the ground beneath my feet, and yet, far better than in broad daylight, I can see the unfathomable that contains me.[28]

25. Ibid., 135.
26. Ibid., 136–37.
27. Ibid., 137.
28. Ibid., 145–46 (ellipses in the original).

In some, such contemplation of human finitude can trigger fear: "The silence of infinite spaces dismays me," he quotes Pascal as saying.[29] But Comte-Sponville rejects this response. The fear goes when the sense of self goes. Indeed, Buddhism again: the self is a not-self (a paradox if not an outright contradiction, no matter how you read it).[30] Still, if there is no permanence to the self, there is no logic in being dismal about one's finitude (just about one's permanence and therefore human dignity, as understood in Christianity, I would add). *"Carpe diem*? . . . [T]here is nothing to seize and [only] everything to contemplate" and, we might explain, turn into a timeless moment.[31]

Comte-Sponville quotes a number of accounts of "oceanic feeling" that we have been calling *signals of transcendence*, but in every case he dismisses them. They do not point beyond this world to anything but mystery.

After citing a number of religious-like experiences of others, he cites his own. He speaks of his walking with friends in a forest in the north of France.[32]

> Gradually our laughter faded, and the conversation died down. Nothing remained but our friendship, our mutual trust and shared presence, the mildness of the night air and of everything around us. . . . My mind empty of thought, I was simply register-ing the world around me—the darkness of the underbrush, the incredible luminosity of the sky, the faint sounds of the forest (branches snapping, an occasional animal call, our own muffled steps) only making the silence more palpable. And then, all of a sudden. . . . What? Nothing: everything! No words, no mean-ings, no questions, only—a surprise. Only—this. A seemingly infinite happiness. A seemingly eternal sense of peace. Above me, the starry sky was immense, luminous and unfathomable, and within me, there was nothing but the sky, of which I was a part, and the silence, and the light, like a warm hum, and a

29. Ibid., 148; Pascal, *Pensées*, no. 201 (95).

30. Buddhagosa (fifth-century Buddhist scholar once said of his enlightenment, "I am nowhere a somewhatness for anyone" (quoted by Guinness, *Long Journey*, 80).

31. Comte-Sponville, *Little Book*, 174.

32. Ibid., 154, quotes Rolland Romaine, Richard Jeffreys, Margret Monague, Al-bert Camus before his conversion to Christian faith, from the collection of experi-ences made by Michel Hulin, and notes that Freud wrote to Romaine in 1929: "The worlds you are exploring are utterly foreign to me! Mysticism is as inaccessible to me as music."

sense of joy with neither subject nor object (no object other than everything, no subject other than itself). Yes, in the darkness of that night, I contained only the dazzling presence of the All. Peace. Infinite peace! Simplicity, serenity, delight.

The two latter words may sound incompatible, but at the time they weren't words, they were experience: silence, harmony. It was as if a perfect chord, once played, had been indefinitely prolonged, and that chord was the world. I felt fine. Incredibly fine! So fine that I didn't even need to notice it or hope it that it would last. I can scarcely even say that *I* was walking—the walk was there, and the forest, and the trees and our group of friends. ... The *ego* had vanished: no more separation or representation, only the silent *presentation* of everything. No more value judgments; only reality. No more time; only the present. No more nothingness; only being. No more frustration, hatred, fear, anger, or anxiety; only joy and peace. No more make-believe, illusions, lies; only the truth, which I did not contain but which contained me. It may have lasted only a few seconds.[33]

Comte-Sponville continues his account for many more lines, adding detail after detail of satisfaction and joy in his experience. He concludes:

What was death? Nothing. What was life? Only this palpitation of being within me. What was salvation? Only a word, or else this state itself. Perfection. Plentitude. Bliss. Such joy! Such happiness! Such intensity![34]

Other similar experiences followed, though they became less frequent. But what can we make of this intense experience? Did he experience an objective *transcendent* or did he merely have an *experience* being lifted out of his normal consciousness? It seems to me clear that the latter was the case. For him, the world remained what it was before—a universe of cause and effect, of joy and sorrow, of temporary life and eventual death. Mystery is the "light of being"; mystery is all there is.[35]

Is this atheism? Yes, but with a Buddhist flavor, for Buddhism is, after all, a type of atheism, which Comte-Sponville declares to be self-evident. The experience gained by contemplation is the guarantee of its truth.[36]

33. Ibid., 156–57.
34. Ibid., 157.
35. Ibid., 163.
36. Ibid., 189–92.

Experience, Interpretation, Meaning, Truth, and Reality

If we were to go no further than this in our reflection on *signals of transcendence*, we might justifiably conclude that identifying a *signal of transcendence* gets us nowhere in our pursuit of truth. Everyone seems to interpret what they detect as such a *signal* within their individual worldview. To theists the *signal* displays the presence of the Triune God; to atheists an unusual *signal* is a misfiring of neurons in the brain; to Buddhists a *signal* announces the paradoxical character of a reality that is and is not what it is perceived to be; to romantics and New Agers a *signal* unmasks the physical world as a *mysterious* place subject to the subject that perceives it. Or so it seems.

Is there any way out of the conclusion that such seemingly religious experiences are nothing any of us can rely on as a clue to what reality actually is? Does a God or even a divine impersonal spirit actually exist, or is it a figment of our minds or, worse luck, just the machinations of our brain? It's time we dealt further with this—perhaps the most important—question. We need to find a confident answer. We will address this challenge in chapter 10. But first we must address the most perplexing adoption of *signals of transcendence* of all. We do so now.

9

I Am God

Transcendence as Immanent in the Self

> I could legitimately say that I had created the Statue of Liberty, chocolate chip cookies, the Beatles, terrorism, and the Vietnam War....And if they [people] reacted to world events, then I was creating them to react so I would have someone to interact with, thereby enabling myself to know me better.
>
> —SHIRLEY MACLAINE, *IT'S ALL IN THE PLAYING*[1]

I write this chapter with much reluctance. Still I cannot avoid it. There is no worldview in the Western world today that is more fully based on experience, much of it religious experience. In fact, beginning, middle and end, New Age spirituality grows out of, is justified by and ends in individual religious experience. With the New Age, however, it is the interpretation of that experience that is so highly problematic.

With a very few basic but highly questionable assumptions and religious experiences—many of which appear to be *signals of transcendence*—the New Age practitioner sets off on a journey toward unbridled pride and self-delusion. Or that is the way it looks to anyone who holds a traditional Western understanding of rationality and theological justification. Not only is ordinary logic, the adherence, for example, to the principle of non-contradiction, put aside, but so is a firm grasp of where

1. MacLaine, *It's All*, 174.

one is in both historical time and geographic space. To put it in New Age terms, the participants soon see themselves at one with the cosmos, maybe even as the creators and the sustainers of the cosmos. Lost in the cosmos would be a more accurate way to describe where they have arrived.

For years this mode of grasping the nature of reality has not so much puzzled me—actually, it's very easy to understand—as it has baffled my ability to understand why anyone could be so wrong about so many things. But it is not just anyone who becomes a New Age aficionado. Scientists, actors, anthropologists, sociologists, psychiatrists, medical professionals, even an occasional philosopher, have not only become adherents but have taken leadership roles, introducing and bringing many people into the circle of New Age thinking and practice.[2]

I know these are harsh words, perhaps unwise for the opening words of this chapter. If they are not true, they are *argumentum ad hominum*—character assassination, name calling, mudslinging—laid down before the data. That's why I must lay aside the poison keyboard and strive to give the New Age understanding of religious experience the dignity of being taken seriously. It is, after all, taken seriously by thousands, probably tens of thousands, perhaps hundreds of thousands of people in the world today. So how do New Age adherents understand religious experience?

Signals of Transcendence or Signals of Immanence?

As in previous chapters, I will start by giving examples of religious experiences which appear to parallel those we have been recognizing as potentially *signals of transcendence*.

A Young Medically and Psychoanalytically Trained Experimenter

John Lilly, MD (1915–2001) was a "scientific visionary" and dolphin researcher with a focus on consciousness and neurophysiology.[3]

2. For a long list and more detailed analysis of professionals, intellectuals and celebrities who are New Age believers, see Sire, *Universe*, 166–213.

3. Lilly's web page (www.johnclilly.com): "John Lilly was the twentieth century's foremost scientific pioneer of the inner and outer limits of human experience. He was a relentless adventurer whose 'search for Reality' led him repeatedly to risk life and limb, but whose quests resulted in astonishing insights into what it means to be a human being in an ever more mysterious universe. John passed to the other side on

In the days before LSD became an illegal drug, he experimented on himself. Under the care of an experienced user of LSD, Lilly was guided through his first trip. Here is his account:

> I started out by looking at a marble-top table and saw the pattern of the marble become alive, plastic, moving. I moved into the pattern and became part of it, living and moving in the pattern of the marble. I became the living marble.
>
> I lay down on the bed between two stereo loudspeakers and went with Beethoven's *Ninth Symphony.* The music entered into me and programmed me into a deeply religious experience. The whole experience had first been programmed and stored in my very early youth, when I was a member of the Catholic Church serving Mass and believing, with the intense faith of youth, in everything that I was learning in the church.
>
> I moved with the music into Heaven. I saw God on a tall throne as a giant, wise, ancient Man. He was surrounded by angel choruses, cherubim and seraphim, the saints were moving by his throne in a stately procession. I was there in Heaven, worshiping God, worshiping the angels, worshiping the saints in full and complete transport of religious ecstasy.[4]

This account comes early in Lilly's adult life. Still it becomes immediately clear that Lilly does not understand his journey to Heaven within a Christian worldview. Rather the experience, he says, was a combination of his former life in the Catholic Church and the chemical stimulus of LSD. Actually nothing at all *transcendent* was being signaled. The experience was only an early harbinger of what he would soon see to be an encounter with his higher or inner self.

Not much later, he accidentally gave himself an antibiotic shot with a dirty needle. The effect was to send him into another odd experience:

> I became a focused center of consciousness and traveled into other spaces and met other beings, entities, or consciousnesses. . . . *I am a single point of consciousness, of feeling, of knowledge. I know that I am. That is all. It is a very peaceful, awesome, and reverential space that I am in. I have no body, I have no need for a body. There is no body. I am just I. Complete with love, warmth, and radiance.*

September 30, 2001. We can only imagine what limits he is trancending [*sic*] now."

4. Lilly, *Center*, 10.

Lilly says that he met beings who were *"far greater than I. . . . Their magnificent deep powerful love overwhelms me. . . .* I stayed in this state for many hours in earth time. . . Then I came back to my body in the hospital."[5]

In one's growth toward a full understanding of one's self, Lilly says, one needs a guide, but the ultimate goal is for the self itself to *transcend* its ordinary self as caught in the material world. At this point Lilly is well on the way to experiencing himself (or, rather, experiencing his *self*) as "the center of the cyclone," the realization that he is, in the final analysis, the center of the universe. As he says, he "is one of the boys in the engine room pumping creation from the void into the known universe; from the unknown to the known I am pumping."[6] The remainder of his autobiography charts the forms of consciousness that constitute the inner world of fully aware human beings, and, for that matter, the forms of reality that constitute the universe. The principle that governs reality is simple:

> In the province of the mind, what is believed to be true is true or becomes true, within limits to be found experientially and experimentally. These limits are further beliefs to be transcended. In the province of the mind, there are no limits.[7]

In other words the self, whether it knows it or not, is the kingpin of reality, the maker of the only universe that matters, the kingdom of the inner mind.

An Actress and Dancer Turned Spiritual Advisor

"So this book is about a quest for my self," says Shirley MacLaine in the opening chapter of *Out on a Limb*.[8] She might have said this for all of her many autobiographies.[9] In *Out on a Limb* she puts most of what she is learning about her "self" in the mouth of others whom she has taken as her guides. Some of these guides remain identified merely by their first

---

5. Ibid., 25–27.

6. Ibid., 210.

7. Ibid., 5.

8. MacLaine, *Out*, 5.

9. MacLaine's earlier autobiography, *Don't*, 237–38 and 252–63, with its description of early "religious" experiences and her subsequent comments makes this clear. See also *Dancing, It's All in the Playing, Going Within, Camino,* and *Sage-ing While Age-ing.*

names—David, for example, or John who comes via the voice channeled by Kevin Ryerson. They explain to her who she really is.

"*You* are everything," says David. "Everything you want to know is inside of you. You are the universe."[10] Then John supposedly clarifies who David is, "... [Y]ou were and are a twin soul of the entity you call David."[11] And later he says, "*You* are God. *You* know you are Divine."[12]

As spiritual pilgrims MacLaine and David traveled in the ancient world of Incan Peru. High in the Andes and relaxing in one of the sulfur baths, David explained how the universe, the yin and the yang, the positive and the negative, the substance of the quarks, are all displayed in a single atom. Perhaps the whole universe is contained in a drop of water, MacLaine mused. David explained: "Our bodies are made out of atoms; our souls are made of this Source of energy."[13] MacLaine was thrilled by his words of spiritual science. Gradually she began to feel a "kind of tunnel" open in her mind; she felt herself flowing into space while her body remained in the sulfur bath. Ascending out over the river and the mountains, she saw her soul connected to her body by a silver cord. Gradually she descended and entered her body.[14] Eventually, she sums up what she has learned from her experiences in Peru:

> My soul knew it was going to be all right, no matter what happened to the body. My soul—my own, subconscious, individualized piece of the universal energy—believed it was a part of everything, even of the crashing, tumultuous storm outside. My soul knew it would survive, that it was eternal, that it was ongoing and unlimited in its understanding that this, too, was part of the adventure we call life.[15]

Her growing stack of autobiographies lays bare both her troubling relationships with her friends and lovers and the ecstasies she derives from a multitude of spiritual experiences. Through these ecstatic experiences and from what she has learned from spiritual guides and channelers, she claims to have already lived thousands of lives: a harem dancer, "a

10. MacLaine, *Out*, 87.

11. Ibid., 203.

12. Ibid., 209.

13. Ibid., 325.

14. Ibid., 327–29.

15. Ibid., *Out*, 348. How she can be conscious of what her subconscious knows without her subconscious becoming conscious MacLaine does not explain.

Spanish infant wearing diamond earrings, and in a church, . . . a monk meditating in a cave, . . . an infant lifted by an eagle and deposited with a primitive family in Africa, where I became frustrated because they were not as advanced as I, . . . a ballet dancer in Russia . . . [and] an Inca youth in Peru." She was also "involved with voodoo" and, as a "princess of the elephants" in India, once saved a village from destruction and taught her people a higher level of morality.[16] Through her own and the seemingly transcendent experiences of others, she basks in the joy of discovering her identity as divine. She is the author of her own experiences and therefore the author of her own reality, the only reality that matters.

For her, as for Lilly, "*All and everything that one can imagine exists.*"[17] Ultimately she sums up her findings, using catch phrases from a multitude of sources which to her say the same thing: "*The Kingdom of Heaven is within you. Know thyself and that will set you free; to thine own self be true; to know self is to know all; know that you are God; know that you are the universe.*"[18]

Lest we think she takes for herself an identity no one else has, claiming to be the one and only God, she is quick to say that each of us can learn who we are. We too are divine, but like her before she began her pilgrimage, we just don't know it.

But enough of this elucidation of MacLaine's New Age worldview. What should interest us is the similarity of her spiritual experiences to those we have described in earlier chapters. The following one—one of very many in her books—is typical. Under the tutelage of Chris Griscom, "a very experienced acupuncturist in psychictherapy,"[19] MacLaine meets

16. MacLaine, *Dancing*, 353–59, 366.

17. Lilly, *Center*, 51.

18. MacLaine, *Dancing*, 350. This mélange of sayings combines phrases from many sources: *The Kingdom of Heaven is within you* is probably a misquotation of Luke 17:21 where Jesus says (as translated in the King James Version), "The Kingdom of God is *within* you" (this verse is more accurately translated as "The Kingdom of God is *among* you [plural]," or "*in the midst* of you [plural], emphasizing the communal nature of God's reign among his people), *Know thyself* (the Delphic Oracle quoted by Socrates), *that will set you free* (the words of Jesus in John 8:32 attached to a very different notion from "know thyself"), *to thine own self be true* (the words of Polonius, the old fool in Shakespeare's *Hamlet*), *know that you are God* (reflective of Psalm 46:10 in which Yahweh is quoted as saying, "Be still and know that *I* am God [and you are not!]," an exactly opposite notion).

19. Ibid., 297.

and speaks with her Higher Self (H.S.) and deepens her own spiritual experiences.

> I found new levels of meaning in the simplest act. If a bird sang outside my window, I longed to know the hidden message of its song. When the sun drenched hot on my skin, I wondered if intelligence lived behind the sun's gaseous rays. I drove alone for hours into the desert night until the moon sank below the granite mountains.
>
> And when I lay out under the stars, I felt connected to everything above me.
>
> It was a wondrous time for me.
>
> Sometimes I found myself crying. Other times I was overcome with joy. I was expressing myself *to* myself.
>
> I meditated on the smallest speck I could see until I felt it become infinitely huge. Then I meditated on a mountain until it became a speck. The more I found the center of myself, the further out I could go in understanding.
>
> I went into the hills and found a big tree. I encircled it with my arms and asked H.S. to tell me the tree's secret to peace.
>
> H.S. said, "It is standing still."
>
> I began to lose my sense of time. An instant was an hour. Sometimes I would forget where I was. Other times I didn't recognize landmarks and drove past a familiar turnoff. New York and Hollywood were another planet.[20]

MacLaine's quest for her "self," with which *Out on a Limb* begins, seems to reach an answer at the end of *Dancing in the Light*:

> The total understanding and realization of my self might require eons for me to accomplish. But when that awareness is achieved, I will be aligned completely with that unseen Divine Force that we call God.
>
> For me to deny that Divine Force now would be tantamount to denying that I exist.
>
> I *know* that I exist, therefore I AM.
>
> I *know* that the God-source exists. Therefore IT IS.
>
> Since I am part of that force, then *I AM* that *I AM*.[21]

The arrogance these words display is astounding. Both MacLaine and Lilly seem to live in a world apart. What are those of us schooled in the Western notion of a reality—whether (1) created by God as in theism

20. Ibid., 369–70.
21. Ibid., 404.

or (2) standing alone as in naturalism—to make of such an explosion of egotism? One answer is to discount the intelligence of the authors. Walker Percy does this in style:

> Doctor John Lilly, after claiming all manner of mystical and philosophical knowledge for the dolphin and after spending years trying to communicate with dolphins, changed his profession: to the study of the effect of mind-altering drugs on the individual human consciousness. He jumped from a tank of dolphins into the tank of himself.[22]

When Percy imagines how a successful two-person space-ship crew might be constituted, his first of four suggestions is this:

> A pair of good-humored and well-qualified astronauts, a man and a woman, who have no religious scruples and no marital or emotional attachments, a Burt Reynolds and a Shirley MacLaine type, each highly skilled technically, each sexually experienced and happily and actively and somewhat casually heterosexual, and who, though not well known to each other, find each other attractive—but who, let us admit it, are a little dumb and know next to nothing of Western civilization, literature, or history, beyond last year's winner of the Super Bowl and the comparative ratings of Snyder, Carson, and Letterman during the last rating sweeps.[23]

But calling a person's intelligence into question is hardly an explanation. What we need to explain is why such a radical departure from traditional Western thought (from the Middle Ages to the present time) could even happen—apart, that is, from a few misguided and gullible people who never make a significant impact on culture at large. Perhaps a survey of the flow of intellectual history will help.

A Radical Paradigm Shift: Transcendence Becomes Immanent

What has happened here to the notions of *immanence* and *transcendence*? Are MacLaine and Lilly responding to *signals of transcendence* and being taken out of the present world into a separate spiritual reality, or is our understanding of the ordinary visible world flawed and MacLaine and

22. Percy, *Lost*, 169.
23. Ibid., 215.

Lilly revealing to us the *immanence* of the divine. In other words, is the ordinary material world itself not ordinary at all but at its own intrinsic root the same as the divine?

It seems to me that the latter is the case. A radical paradigm shift in the Western world that has taken centuries to be realized is now attempting to *become* the dominant paradigm.[24] In the Christian worldview that characterized the West from the Middle Ages to the Renaissance, the really real is the *transcendent* God of theism—"immortal, invisible, God only wise," who created the universe out of nothing by his "word of power." There are also created spiritual beings called angels, some of whom rebelled and now constitute the essence of evil. Human beings could learn about the material universe from the application of human reason and about the really real through God's revelation in Scripture.

In the late seventeenth century this view began to decay; in deism the really real gradually became merely an impersonal Force rather than a personal God with character; all knowledge became the result of the application of human reason.

In the nineteenth century God not only lost his personality and a personal interest in his creation, he was effectively denied his existence by intellectuals who decided that God was not needed as an explanation of anything. The universe itself is all there has been, is now, and will be.

These early naturalists were optimistic about the autonomy of human reason and its ability to justify notions of morality and to provide a confident foundation for human flourishing. But when the implications of what Nietzsche called the "death of God" sank in, confidence in reason as a foundation for meaning in life began to disappear. Nihilism, another name for pessimistic naturalism, seeped into the background of twentieth-century Europe and North America.

The main attempt to overcome the incipient despair of nihilism came first in the form of existentialism—the view that even though there is no foundation for ethics, each person can affirm his or her own ethic and, as Sartre would say, in doing so affirm this ethic for all others. Existentialism is fundamentally an incoherent worldview, but it has had a staying power. Primarily its resultant impact on Western thinking is to assert the value of the subjective character of human life. The world may not fit our desires as human beings, but we can bravely rebel against its

24. The intellectual history that follows is fleshed out in more detail in my *Universe*. Several highly relevant studies focusing on the nature of the self include Percy, *Lost*; Barrett, *Death*; and Taylor, *Sources*.

absurdity—pain, suffering, war, violence, disease—and craft a personal world of value.

With existentialism, a great paradigm shift was almost complete. The objective existence of a *transcendent* or *spiritual* realm and the firm foundation it provided for both ethics (a firm set of moral values grounded in the character of a personal and good God) and intelligence (the ability to use reason, both in the scientific methods and in theology based on revelation) was being replaced by the ability of the mind to construct its own subjective reality. The early naturalistic stages of existentialism did not abandon the concept of an objective reality that truly existed—an objective reality that was able to be understood by the various scientific methods. It just drew a solid line between the objective world of material reality and the subjective world of meaning and values. Facts and values became separate realities.

Then, too, as the nineteenth century drew to a close, a new worldview that had been dominant in the East for many centuries was introduced into the growing pluralism of Western thought. Eastern pantheism, though it had its intellectual introduction in the works of Emerson and Whitman, began to become a serious worldview contender. If Western theistic and naturalistic optimism had reached a dead end in nihilism with the notion that there is no way forward for the mind as conceived as only materialistic, then perhaps a worldview with none of the heritage of the West would provide both an optimistic foundation for life and a way out of the despair of nihilism. Serious consideration of various Eastern religions marked the world of many intellectuals and spiritual searchers from the middle of the twentieth century till today. But its foundational notion was at first seen to be utterly different from either Christian theism, the dominant form of theism in the West, and from naturalism into which much of the West had moved. How so?

First and foremost, the East affirmed that the entire cosmos—everything that is, was or will be—is actually divine spirit. "Atman is Brahman," is the claim of the advaita vedanta system of Hinduism. That is, *the individual soul of every one or every thing is divine.* There is no God the creator, no Trinity, no being who transcends the material universe. In fact, there is no material universe as such; matter itself is only an illusion, one that must be overcome by seeking a unity of one's own *soul* with the *Soul* of which it is merely a spark. Hinduism in actual practice takes a myriad of forms and not all would agree with what I have written above.

Still the notion that every one and every thing is finally *divine* lies at the base of all of them. We have seen in the previous chapter the way in which Zen Buddhism sees the plenum-void (the ultimate empty-fullness) as the unifying reality. Moreover, both Hinduism and Buddhism reject material science as a method for achieving a full grasp of reality.

So into this history of the growing pluralism of Western worldviews came the New Age movement whose central thesis is simple: The individual self is the center of reality: *The self is the really real. Immanence* replaces *Transcendence.* There is only one kind of reality—not the dualism of God and his creation, not the one reality of pure materialism with the possible dualism of mind and matter, not even the simple monism of the One that is the All as in Eastern pantheism. Rather the whole of the cosmos is now seen as the projection of the self; every apparent individual self is a manifestation of the One. With Eastern thought providing the notion that everything is divine and Western thought emphasizing the dignity of each individual, the New Age marries East and West and declares the individual self is divine on its own.

The paradigm shift is now complete. In the New Age paradigm, everyone is the master of the cosmos, which turns out to be whatever any individual sees it to be. So called religious experience is not really religious; it is people getting their imaginations working. Pain and suffering are illusions; morality is whatever anyone wants it to be. Going inside is the way to know this, and one can go inside with help at first from a guide like Shirley MacLaine or others similar to her. When one gets the hang of it, one can simply go it alone, realizing one's divinity and basking as one wills in one's own reality: Specks of dust can become mountains, mountains specks of dust.

The only problem comes when going inside no longer works, when cancer erodes the body, the brain and the imagination; or when one finds oneself in a refugee camp at the mercy of the inadequate food and water; or when all sorts of material reality refuses to accede to imagination. This is, of course, no problem so long as it is true that the next incarnation of whatever remains of one's self at death is re-embodied in another form. Many in the Eastern world accept this and, if only for a while, "live with it."

But paradigm shifts as radical as the one I have just charted are never universal. The New Age paradigm (or more broadly, worldview) only adds one more new and different worldview to the mix, one radically different from the theism that characterized Europe and the New World in the Renaissance. Now theism (Christian and otherwise), deism, naturalism, nihilism, existentialism, pantheism all lie, as it were, side by side on the map of Western conceptions of reality.

The religious or transcendent-like experiences accompanying each of them do not point unambiguously to the truth of any of these worldviews. These experiences must be interpreted, and the interpretations vary with (1) the power of one of the more dominant worldviews which seems most likely to provide the explanation and (2) the openness of each person to imagine any other explanation than the one obvious to most of the community in which each person is embedded.

The Self as a Little Less than God

If it seems impossible to believe that anyone really conceives of themselves as God the I Am Who Is the Final Reality, I agree. It surely must be impossible to go all the way. Those who do, if there really are any, are probably living in a psych ward. What many Westerners who are attracted to the notion that they are God actually do believe is that they are, or can be, in control of their lives; that the universe is indeed the projection of their highly powerful and imaginative selves; that, if they can't do what they might reasonably be expected to do if they were a god who projected his or (often) her own reality, they just need to do more meditating or change meditation techniques or get a new spiritual guide till they get back on track. In other words, they may well conceive their godhood as growing toward perfection in both its moral character and its ability to conceive a perfect world. Gods too can grow up.

Moreover, many people sympathetic to New Age modes of thinking stop well short of concluding that they are God itself/himself/herself. Their religious experiences lead them to believe that the material world is not all there is, but that the spiritual or non-material world is the shadow of the spiritual world, the less "real" of reality's dual nature. The individual sees himself or herself as a god who can control their own experience and their own sense of morality but easily acknowledges that all other humans have the same capacity as they do but just may not know it. Others are caught in the shadow world, the material world of illusion, or they are confused and believe God is beyond them. Either of these could come into the light if they just performed the right techniques—meditation or crystals or acupuncture or some other exotic technique such as shamanism.

But let us be clear. These New Age religious experiences that we have been calling *signals of transcendence* are not merely *signs* pointing to *transcendence*. They are the final *transcendent* itself; that is, they are merely *immanent*. Or to put it, I hope, more clearly: these experiences are only that—experiences. They have pointed to a *transcendent* reality that is not there.

A Yaqui Guide to Immanence

Carlos Castaneda has narrated some of the most fascinating religious or spiritual experiences (or more likely invented stories of these experiences). He began his graduate studies in anthropology by locating a man he called Don Juan, a Yaqui Indian shaman.[25] Through him Castaneda learned the techniques of Yaqui shamanism and experienced numerous encounters with a nonordinary reality. By the use of peyote and under the guidance of Don Juan, Castaneda watched a dog become transparent; then he became a transparent dog himself, even forgetting he was a man.[26] From a paste made from the *Datura* plant, "devil's weed," he learned to fly. When he tried to get Don Juan to tell him whether he flew in the ordinary world and would have seen himself fly there had he also been on the ground watching, Don Juan just laughed at him. He flew in the way people do when they take the "devil's weed."[27] When he experienced the "little smoke," he moved his head through a pole and found himself entering a wall as if it were a sponge, became terrorized when he could not extract himself, and then, without knowing how, he appeared back in the room again. Did this really happen, he wondered. Don Juan told him that all there is to reality is what you feel.[28] In some of his drug trips he encountered dangerous spirits and had to learn how to respond to them.

Castaneda narrates and comments on many such Yaqui-like "religious" experiences.[29] What he finally offers as a rational explanation is

25. De Mille confirms the fictional character of Castaneda's books; see *Castaneda's Journey*.

26. Castaneda, *Teachings*, 24–26. Later he became a crow (ibid., 119–29).

27. Ibid., 88–94.

28. Ibid., 96–102.

29. See Castaneda's *A Separate Reality*; *Journey to Ixtlan: Tales of Power*; *The Eagle's Gift*; *The Fire Within*; and *Falling Bodies Take to Light*, among others.

that the Yaqui way of knowing is not able to be rendered in a Western language such as English or Spanish because there is no way of describing in such a language the nature of the reality that Yaqui shamans (if not the typical Yaqui) understand through their experience. That is, this nonordinary realm is declared to be "real" but not accessible to people in their ordinary states of mind and by the language they use to describe it.

Conceptual relativism is a more sophisticated way of describing this situation. Castaneda himself adopts such a theory.[30] The theory is that language is so tied to knowledge that the same reality can be described in languages so different from each other that translation between them is impossible. That is, there is a radical disjunction between objective reality (reality as it really is) and perceived reality (the way we understand that reality by virtue of our symbol systems). Reality is what it is; the symbols we use to describe it are arbitrary. One person sees an arrow flying toward its prey; another person sees a demon about to slay its victim. But each person sees only sees one thing. Neither description actually describes reality as it is; both can have pragmatic value. If you see either an arrow or a demon, you defend yourself accordingly.

It is hard to see how, if *conceptual relativism* correctly explains the situation, there can be any *signal of transcendence* at all. First, one is not experiencing a *signal*; one is just experiencing reality itself. Second, the glory of the mountain scene is merely the experience of that glory; it neither points beyond to any *transcendent*, nor is it itself *transcendent*.

Moreover, the theory of *conceptual relativism* is internally incoherent. It is only an explanation within the ordinary language of the Western world. There may be another theory in another language that is just as valid. If so, both theories are arbitrary. They say nothing about what reality really is; in fact, nothing can be said about reality itself. The reality portrayed by every language, including that of science, is merely a linguistic construct. If using that language gets you what you want, that's enough to satisfy. No description, no account of an experience, can say anything about what reality really is because every statement is arbitrary. *Conceptual relativism* is an example of what Helmut Thielicke called *ciphered nihilism*.[31] That is, it appears to convey knowledge but does not because it cannot.

30. Castaneda, *Teachings*, 173–79.
31. Thielicke, *Nihilsm*, 63–65.

A New Age Vision of the Cosmos

For the New Age in general, the cosmos, while unified in the self, is manifested in two more dimensions: the visible universe, accessible through ordinary consciousness, and the invisible universe (or Mind at Large), accessible through altered states of consciousness. In this view reality should not be construed to consist of both a *transcendent* realm (the realm of God as creator) and an *immanent* realm (the cosmos as created with both material and spiritual beings). Rather the cosmos is one in reality; there is only a visible (material) and invisible (non-material) aspect.

The *five ordinary senses* (sight, touch, hearing, taste, and smell) give access to the visible material aspect of reality. *Cosmic consciousness* brings into direct experience the invisible (non-material) aspect. All of us live our lives conscious of the visible world. It is the world of ordinary reality. There is, however, a realm accessible only by means of *cosmic consciousness*. What is that world like? Marilyn Ferguson summarizes some of its characteristics:

> Loss of ego boundaries and sudden identification with all of life (a melting into the universe); lights; altered color perception; thrills; electrical sensations; sense of expanding like a bubble or bounding upward; banishment of fear, particularly fear of death; roaring sound; wind; feeling of being separated from physical self; bliss; sharp awareness of patterns; a sense of liberation; a blending of the senses (synesthesia), as when colors are heard and sights produce auditory sensations; an oceanic feeling; a belief that one has awakened; that the experience is the only reality and that ordinary consciousness is but its poor shadow; and a sense of transcending time and space.[32]

Some of these characteristics of the experience of cosmic consciousness sound religious, others not. But do they *signal* the presence of a transcendent realm or are they merely features of the subjective consciousness of those who experience them? That is, are they *signals* of something and if so what? Or are they the *thing* itself, that is, only the working of a brain super-loaded with stimuli produced by meditation or stress or some other purely natural cause? If they point, is what they point to reality or illusion?

New Agers usually conclude that at least some of these experiences indicate the existence of a reality that is more than material, but they

32. Ferguson, *Brain*, 60.

refuse to recognize them as pointers to the existence of a *transcendent* theistic God, Christian or otherwise. The cosmos is merely what it appears to be in these experiences.

Perhaps this explains what my Starbucks friend, let's call her Patty, means when she tells me that she is God and so am I. That is, each of us lives in the only world we know, the world of ourselves. Every experience is an inner experience; we are in control of those experiences and can blot out whatever we don't want to *see*. What we do not *see* simply does not exist in any way that can make a difference to us. We need not call on anyone else to decide for us what is good to do; we arbitrate our own sense of morality. Of course, there are others like us and not like us. That's okay. The radical individualism of the American character combines with the Eastern notion that we are all divine or sparks of the divine. Nothing especially metaphysical is being consciously claimed; very little of this view is obviously ontological. Experience is itself the mode of being. New Agers do not recognize that there can be no experience to be experienced if there is (1) no being to have the experience or (2) if there is nothing to experience. In other words an ontology of experience itself as such is impossible. But those who speak as Patty does do not seem to be concerned with incoherence.

In any case, with the New Age no one gets past the immanent; one only sees more (spiritual or non-material stuff) of what is naturally there. The cosmos is, in the final analysis, precisely as it is in naturalism, all there is, was, and will be. The only difference is that it has an invisible realm that is itself not to be equated with mere sticks and stones.

In what limited sense, then, is the individual self the center of the universe? The self is the center of the only reality over which it has control—the inner life of each person. Everyone does in fact have a private sense of reality. Every worldview says this. But the New Agers tend to say that somehow all their actions are based on what they perceive and this is enough, especially when what they perceive sometimes takes them to strange seemingly nonmaterial places, filling them with delightful awe and wonder. The New Age operates on the epistemology of ecstasy. For many of them it is satisfying enough for them to discount any account of a real encounter with a *genuine transcendent*, or even something *pointing* them to the existence of a *transcendent* God or *leading* them to directly experience this *transcendent* God himself/herself/itself.

This sidetracking of the *signal* aspect of creation and the human experience of creation poses a significant challenge to any Christian apologetic that relies heavily on Christian experience and only lightly on rational coherence, biblical revelation, and traditional Christian theology. We turn, therefore, to Christian apologetics.

10

Echoes and Arguments

Signals in Apologetics

True mystics are not necessarily those who have visions, but rather those who have vision. They see the extraordinary, the mystical, in everyday events. If we desire such vision, we will have to give our brains a bath! Our minds must be cleansed of prejudgments about what God looks like. We will have to take a brush and scrub away all those grade school pictures of God and erase all the statements made by saints about their experience of the Divine Mystery. Only then can we begin to see the true picture.

—EDWARD HAYS, *IN PURSUIT OF THE GREAT WHITE RABBIT*[1]

W e must now step back. We have been focusing on one aspect of Christian life—*signals of transcendence*. We must look now at a broader picture. We need to see how these *signals* fit into the whole of our experience as God's people. Part of that picture is how we attain and how we hold confidence in our commitment to God. Here apologetics takes a central role.

Apologetics is both the defense of the Christian faith in the light of multiple alternative challenges and the rational and emotional justification of the faith that sustains our Christian commitment. We come to believe in Christ because he becomes for us the be all and end all of our

1. Hays, *In Pursuit*, quoted in Shawchuck and Job, *Guide to Prayer*, 376.

grasp of life itself. He becomes life's substance, its meaning, its import, its focus and its *telos*—what it has been created to be and to become.[2] Then we live in that faith upheld by our own personal apologetic for Christ. This can grow into a profound and credible case for Christian faith to those whose lives we share.

We may look, then, on apologetics this way:

> Christian apologetics lays before the watching world such a winsome embodiment of the Christian faith that for any and all who are willing to observe there will be an intellectually and emotionally credible witness to its fundamental truth.[3]

Given this very general definition of apologetics, where do *signals of transcendence* fit? These *signals* are recognized by people of both Christian and non-Christian faiths and those with no religious faith at all; they are interpreted in a variety of ways, from a full dismissal by atheists to an acceptance of the *signals* as reality itself by New Agers. Since the same *signal* can seem to point in different directions, how much epistemic value do *signals* have?

Put in popular and much more personal language: How reliable are *signals of transcendence* as a revelation—affirmation and/or justification—of any particular understanding of reality? Can I trust that what I draw from them is true or, perhaps, closer to the truth than what I have previously thought?

A second question arises from the New Age construal of their religious experiences. For example, as we saw, Shirley MacLaine has concluded that both she and, for that matter, everyone else is the God who created all of their own reality. John Lilly has experienced being at the "center of the cyclone," that is, the core of ultimate reality. Their experiences are certainly at Level 4 as defined in chapter 1. Aren't they *numinous* experiences? Are they as likely to be interpreted correctly in a New Age way as Rudolf Otto interprets them in a fully theistic way? Or is the New Age interpretation so different from theism that they are nothing short of blasphemous?

---

2. As the Apostle Paul said, "For me, living is Christ and dying is gain" (Phil 1:21).
3. Sire, *Little Primer*, 26; also see Moser, *Evidence*, 185–230.

The Human Condition

First, let us reflect on our situation. Many, if not most, people experience moments of heightened awareness. As I write this, a fire truck goes screaming by on a main thoroughfare I can see from my window. I was immediately reminded of the danger my family faces as the temperature has plummeted and the furnace is constantly running. I am also reminded that two houses have nearly burned to the ground in our suburb in the past few nights.

More to the point, I write this in the immediate wake of Christmas, a time rich in religious signals, and New Year, a time of looking back and forward—the old year of joys and sorrows done, the coming new year of—ah! God alone knows what. How shall I interpret the heightened awareness of the birth of Christ in ages past and its long influence on civilization and on my life? What shall I take from the two Lessons and Carols I attended a few days apart? Was God saying to me what he said to Julian of Norwich? "All shall be well and all shall be well and all manner of thing shall be well"? Or was my heightened awareness not so much a sense of the presence of God as a purely emotional reaction triggered by beautiful organ solos played by my longtime friend? Or was, perhaps, the experience merely aesthetic?

What about some sixty years ago when I saw the three thunderheads, felt the electricity of the moment, and shivered in awe as I thought of the presence of the holy Trinity? Was this really a *signal of transcendence* or a young boy's misinterpreted fear of lightning?

No, there must be something genuine about such experiences, something not really explained by nature doing its thing, animals surviving to procreate another day by taking shelter from electric storms. Even atheists like David Hume, Steven Weinberg, or Albert Camus recognize the force of these moments of surprise or awe or wonder.[4] Okay. But to conclude that there actually exists something that is more than, or other than, material is not to identify what that is. And signals that point to something extra-material have, as we have seen, been interpreted in many contradictory ways—in terms of panentheism (Wordsworth), pantheistic union of the self and the divine (Emerson), nihilistic denial of the self (Buddhism), all of them ways far removed from any particular version of theism—Jewish, Christian, or Islamic.

4. Evans, *Natural Signs*, 23–24, 73, 104–6.

To me, however, the New Age construal of heightened awareness that leads to seeing oneself (one's *self*) as the divine center of reality is the most troublesome. My first reaction is shock! Surely, whatever else we are, we are not in control of all that is! That's preposterous! Madness! The height of egocentric arrogance! Unthinkable!

Except for one thing: One's being God is not unthinkable. It's been thought many times by many people. No longer is such self aggrandizement confined to the cultural fringe; its presence is felt in every profession, in every academic discipline, and in every city and village in the Western world. I am not engaging here in fear mongering. I am by no means afraid of this view of reality and its ubiquity in modern society. There is nothing more to fear about the presence of the New Age thinking than of atheism or any other alternative to profound and serious Christian faith. It is no more a black beast seeking to destroy Christianity than any other non-Christian worldview. Rather, I am amazed at the ease with which New Age proponents speak about their "religious experiences" and are so sure that they understand what they mean. They really do believe that they are in control of their own reality and that theirs is all the reality that, in the final analysis, there is. One may only be king, queen, and vassal of pointland. But pointland is All.

So, to the two questions with which we began: What epistemic value does religious experience have? And is there a way to discern which of two contradictory interpretations of Level 4 signals is correct—theistic or New Age? If *signals of transcendence* can help us justify our Christian faith, it is important for us to know this.

We will attempt to answer these questions by looking at how Christian apologists and philosophers have understood and used *signals of transcendence*. We begin with four modern apologists—a sociologist (Os Guinness), a pastor (Tim Keller), a biological scientist (Francis Collins), and a biblical scholar (N. T. Wright). Then we turn to four philosophers—William James, William Alston, Keith Yandell, and C. Stephen Evans.

Four Modern Apologists

Os Guinness: Signals that Trigger a Quest

Os Guinness, whose DPhil in sociology from Oxford University focused on the work of Peter Berger, uses *signals of transcendence* to mark the beginning of the quest for meaning undertaken by intellectuals such as Malcolm Muggeridge, Michel Foucault, Leon Tolstoy, Fyodor Dostoevsky, G. K. Chesterton, and C. S. Lewis.

Muggeridge, as a young English spy in Africa during World War II, had reached a despair so deep he decided to commit suicide. He took off his clothes and waded into the Indian Ocean off a beach in Mozambique. Soon he could see only the lights of a distant town:

> But all of a sudden he began to tremble, and then, without thinking or deciding, he began to swim back to shore, his eyes fixed on the glow from Peter's Café and the Costa da Sol: "They were lights of the world; they were the lights of my home, my habitat, where I belonged. I must reach them. There followed an overwhelming joy such as I had never experienced before; an ecstasy."[5]

It was many years before Muggeridge would finally turn to Christ as his Lord and Savior, but this experience signaled both the nadir of his despair and the beginning of his hope for meaning. In contrast Michel Foucault's experience in Death Valley took him away from transcendent hope to full-bore sexual license. Not all *signals* lead to life. Still, there is what Dante Gabriel Rossetti called an atheist's worst moment: "The worst moment for an atheist is when he is genuinely thankful, but has nobody to thank."[6]

Guinness calls these experiences "holes torn in life." They begin the serious quest; they are not the end. Gratitude is "not a proof but a pointer. It's an intuition, not a settled conviction. It creates a searcher, not a believer. . . . It's possible that a signal of transcendence may lead nowhere. There may in the end be too great a gap between the heart that desires and the reality that disappoints."[7]

Guinness relies on *signals* to shock the potential seeker into seeking but not to provide answers. "The search for answers is essentially conceptual."[8] In the remaining two-thirds of *The Long Journey Home* he traces the intellectual steps along the way—the accumulation and coherence of various types of evidence, the overcoming of obstacles such as the problem of evil and pain, the character and teaching of Jesus, the

5. Guinness, *Long Journey*, 25.

6. Quoted in ibid., 50.

7. Ibid., 50–51.

8. Ibid., 68.

facing of responsibility, and the stepping out in faith. The journey toward meaning may be long and arduous but the goal is worth every step.

> To be sure, the commitment of faith is more than reason—it is, after all, a whole person who makes the commitment,and whole people are more than walking minds. And yet faith is never less than rational. It is more than reason because we are whole people; it is never less than reason because . . . it is neither against reason nor lacking in reason. It is thoroughly rational yet also wholly personal.[9]

And he quotes G. K. Chesterton:

> If I am asked, as a purely intellectual question, why I believe in Christianity, I can only answer . . . I believe in it quite rationally upon the evidence. But the evidence in my case . . . is not really this or that alleged demonstration; it is an enormous accumulation of small but unanimous facts.[10]

Tim Keller and the Reasons for God

Tim Keller, founder and pastor of Resurrection Presbyterian Church in New York City, has written perhaps the best work of Christian apologetics so far in this century. It is based on and directed to today's New Yorkers, not by any means the most likely people to be interested in traditional Christianity. In the first half of *The Reason for God*, Keller addresses the doubts expressed by people with whom he has had multiple conversations, many of whom have turned from disappointment, discouragement, and despair to hope and confident faith in Christ. The doubts are many: Can there really be only one religion? How could a good God allow suffering? Isn't Christianity a straitjacket? The church has caused vast injustice, hasn't it? You mean a good God would send someone to hell? Hasn't science disproved religion? Surely, you can't take the Bible literally, can you? Then Keller presents a positive case for the Christian faith beginning with *signals of transcendence* which he calls "the clues of God." They include the mystery of the big bang and the puzzle: why is there something rather than nothing, the fine tuning of the universe, the regularity of nature, the phenomenon of beauty, and *sehnsucht* or the

9. Ibid., 174.
10. Ibid., 150.

longing for something more. He also explains why our innate sense of morality and justice can only be explained by the existence of a personal God whose righteousness underlies our sense of morality and explains our longing for justice.

He completes his case for Christian faith with an exposition of the Christian worldview and its power not only to explain what we experience but to answer our deepest needs. He traces the flow of God's dealing with his creation and elaborates on the character of God as Trinity, the human predicament of sin, God's response of grace, the "true" story of the cross, and the death and resurrection of Jesus. He does not, however, return or expand on the "clues of God" as he completes his case. Interestingly, he does not mention the profoundly deep *numinous* experiences and the accompanying *mysterium tremendum* so emphasized by Rudolf Otto. Like Os Guinness, his apologetic focuses on the rationality of Christian faith and the coherence of the Christian worldview.

N. T. Wright and Echoes of a Voice

With many thanks to biblical scholar N. T. Wright, this book is called *Echoes of a Voice*.[11] It's a wonderful phrase that captures the origin of the teleology—the beginning of the end of the role of *signals of transcendence*.

Part One of Wright's three-part apologetic focuses on four *signals*: "the longing for justice, the quest for spirituality, the hunger for relationships, and the delight in beauty."[12] Each *signal*, each voice, joins the more direct revelation of God to become "the voice of Jesus, calling us to follow him into God's new world—the world in which the hints, signposts, and echoes of the present world turn into the reality of the next one."[13]

We have discussed all of these voices in this and earlier chapters. So there is no need to elaborate here. Suffice it to say, Wright in Part One understands each of these *signals* to point to a realm beyond the material world. Without that transcendent world these phenomena would be empty of meaning; with it the present world bristles with significance. Wright clearly describes the overlap between earth and heaven as they merge not only in the life and works of Jesus and such Christian rites as baptism and the Eucharist, but in our ordinary human encounters with

11. N. T. Wright, *Simply Christian*, 3.
12. Ibid., x.
13. Ibid., 225.

the world. Part Two focuses on central themes of the Christian faith: God, Israel, Jesus, the kingdom of God, the Holy Spirit and life in the Spirit. Part Three elaborates on how Christians are to reflect the image of God.

Alone among the four apologists, Wright gives the most epistemic weight to *signals of transcendence*. Perhaps this is because he sees more of the *numinous* in the daily world of his own experience:

> We are called to live at the overlap both of heaven and earth—the earth that has yet to be fully redeemed as one day it will be—and of God's future and this world's present. We are caught on a small island near the point where these tectonic plates—heaven and earth, future and present—are scrunching themselves together. Be ready for earthquakes![14]

We will return to this important whole-life import of *signals of transcendence* in the concluding section of this chapter.

Francis Collins and the Language of God

Francis Collins, the head of the Human Genome Project, writes *The Language of God* as a work of Christian apologetics. He does so primarily by showing how most modern science is closely interwoven with the Christian worldview. Scientists like Steven Weinberg and Richard Dawkins may declare that science makes religion passé, shows its falsehood, and makes those who believe in God primitive nincompoops. But Collins quickly dissents and details the ways modern science actually contributes to the credibility of Christian faith. The centerpiece of his argument is the amazing structure of the DNA code. There is no need here to summarize his argument. It does indeed prove a challenge to the cavalier atheism of some modern pundits. That argument can stand on its own.

Rather I want us to notice that before Collins clarifies the mysteries of the human genome, he talks of his own spiritual journey:

> In my early teens I had had occasional moments of the experience of longing for something outside myself, often associated with the beauty of nature or a particularly profound musical experience. Nevertheless, my sense of the spiritual was very undeveloped and easily challenged by the one or two aggressive atheists one finds in almost every college dormitory.[15]

14. Ibid., 161.
15. Collins, *Language,* 15.

Gradually he became agnostic and then "shifted from agnosticism to atheism.¹⁶" What is of most interest to us is his description of the *signals of transcendence* that he experienced along his way to faith:

> As a boy of ten, I recall being transported by the experience of looking through a telescope that an amateur astronomer had placed on a high field at our farm, when I sensed the vastness of the universe and saw the craters on the moon and the magical diaphanous light of the Pleiades. At fifteen, I recall a Christmas Eve where the descant on a particularly beautiful Christmas carol, rising sweet and true above the more familiar tune, left me with a sense of unexpected awe and a longing for something I could not name. Much later, as an atheist graduate student, I surprised myself by experiencing this same sense of awe and longing, this time mixed with a particularly deep sense of grief, at the playing of the second movement of Beethoven's Third Symphony (the *Eroica*). As the world grieved the death of Israeli athletes killed by terrorists at the Olympics in 1972, the Berlin Philharmonic played the powerful strains of this C-minor lament in the Olympic Stadium, mixing together nobility and tragedy, life and death. For a few moments I was lifted out of my materialist worldview into an indescribable spiritual dimension, an experience I found quite astonishing.¹⁷

His own discoveries have also astonished him. "Moreover recently, for a scientist who occasionally is given the remarkable privilege of discovering something not previously known by man, there is a special kind of joy associated with such flashes of insight."¹⁸ He delightfully quotes Annie Dillard as he concludes his account of *signals* and science: "What is the difference between a cathedral and a physics lab? Are they not both saying: Hello?" Here Christian scientist and Christian romantic meet and rejoice.¹⁹ We notice again that, as with Guinness and Keller, these signals are very much at the beginning of Collins's movement to faith—anomalies within his materialistic worldview, anomalies that lie fallow until they combine with other experiences. "My most awkward moment came when an older woman, suffering daily from severe untreatable angina, asked me what I believed." He really had no idea. In his embarrassment

16. Ibid., 16.
17. Ibid., 35–36.
18. Ibid., 36.
19. Ibid., 39, quoting Dillard, *Teaching*, 89.

before this Christian woman and his reflection, he realized that at age twenty-six he had never "really considered the evidence for and against belief." This "haunted me for several days," he says, and he recognized his "willful blindness"; all his arguments "seemed very thin," and he was terrified.[20] In short, Collins set out to find out what was the case for God. Helped primarily by C. S. Lewis, he finally came to faith.

Signals of transcendence played a role in Collins's spiritual journey, but they did not on their own take him far. Again, we may ask, Is this because Collins does not record a full-fledged encounter with the *numinous*?

Four Philosophers

William James and the Experience, Perhaps, of Reality

There are many difficulties involved in rightly determining what specific aspects of reality various *signals of transcendence* point to. One way is to avoid any attempt to find a general one-fit-all interpretation by shifting attention from what the experience indicates about reality to what it means to the person with the experience itself. William James (1842–1910) does this in his now classic work *Varieties of Religious Experiences*. Rather than identifying the levels of *transcendence* that are signaled, as I have done in chapter 1, James focuses on the four characteristics of the experiences (which he calls *mystical*) themselves:

> 1. *Ineffability*. "[N]o adequate report of its contents can be given in words. . . . [I]ts quality must be directly experienced; it cannot be imparted or transferred to others."
>
> 2. *Noetic quality*. They seem to be states of knowledge and carry with them their own justification.
>
> 3. *Transiency*. "Mystical states cannot be sustained for long."
>
> 4. *Passivity*. The feeling that a superior power has taken over one's will.[21]

Then he ranks these experiences according to the strength of their sense of religiosity. This is similar to what I have labeled as Levels, depth or

20. Ibid., 20.
21. William James, *Varieties*, 292–93.

height of the *transcendence* experienced. In his exposition and illustration of each level, James moves from the simple sense of the "deepened significance" of an idea to the full-throated mystical sense of the presence of, or unity with, the divine.

> 1. A "deepened sense of the significance of a maxim or formula which occasionally sweeps over one."[22]

> 2. The "sudden feeling . . . of having 'been here before,' . . . a sense of mystery and of the metaphysical duality of things, and the feeling of an enlargement of perception."[23]

> 3. "[D]eeper plunges into mystical consciousness," e.g., the feeling that everything has meaning, "hallowed moments."[24]

> 4. "Cosmic consciousness," a sense of the presence of the whole cosmos, intellectual enlightenment, "moral exaltation, an indescribable feeling of elevation, elation, and joyousness, . . . a sense of immortality, a consciousness of eternal life, not a conviction that he shall have this, but the consciousness that he has it already."[25]

> 5. The sense that "the usual barriers between the individual and the Absolute" have been overcome. "In mystic states we both become one with the Absolute and we become aware of our oneness."[26]

When he has surveyed and given numerous illustrations of this range of *signals*, James concludes:

> It [the mystic range of consciousness] *is on the whole pantheistic and optimistic, or at least the opposite of pessimistic. It is anti-naturalistic, and harmonizes best with twice-bornness and so-called other-worldly states of mind.*[27]

22. Ibid., 294.
23. Ibid., 295.
24. Ibid., 296.
25. Ibid., 306, quoting Bucke.
26. Ibid., 321.
27. Ibid., 323.

Two observations immediately come to mind. Though in several earlier lectures James cited many religious experiences from Christian theists, in his "Lectures on Mysticism" (XVI and XVII) he has selected religious experiences from mostly non-theistic sources.[28] Moreover, he has totally ignored biblical accounts of religious experiences such as those of Moses and Isaiah. When he refers to the Apostle Paul, as he does briefly twice, he suggests that Paul's "blinding heavenly vision" was a *photism*, that is a "hallucinatory or pseudo-hallucinatory luminous" phenomenon.[29] Later James says, "In Paul's language, I live, yet not I, but Christ liveth in me" (Phil 1:21) and interprets this as meaning "Only when I become as nothing can God enter in and no difference between his life and mine remain outstanding." But the context of this verse in Paul's letter belies completely the meaning James extracts from the verse. Paul is reflecting on the value of his living longer and serving Christ longer, not on his becoming experientially one with Christ. To be fair, James does cite his source of this interpretation, a French manuscript by Wilfred Monod. But contrary to both Monod and James, the Apostle Paul is about the last person to confuse his life with the being of God.[30]

When James does discuss the experiences of a few medieval mystics, he fails to see that, despite their talk of unity with the divine, none of them is essentially pantheistic.[31] Rather, James says, "This overcoming of all the usual barriers between the individual and the Absolute is the great mystic achievement. In mystic states we both become one with the Absolute and we become aware of our oneness.... In Hinduism, in Neo-platonism, in Sufism, in Christian mysticism, in Whitmanism, we find the same recurring note."[32] He draws from this the conclusion that these religious experiences do indeed demonstrate the universal presence of a consciousness of the non-material. That seems fair enough. But he avoids noting two distinctive differences: (1) Christians rarely, if ever, interpret their experience as having become one (in essence or being) with God

28. Ibid., 201. Throughout Lectures VI and VII and especially Lectures IX–XV, James cites numerous conversion experiences of Christian theists that fit the category of mystical he treats in "Mysticism" (Lectures XVI and XVI).

29. Ibid. James seems to have in mind here Paul's experience on the road to Damascus (Acts 9:3–9). James makes no note of the association of the light with the voice of Jesus, Paul's subsequent blindness, and his relief from this days later. What is really quite astounding, I think, is that James notes only the presence of light and none of the broader context in which it is interpreted in Acts.

30. Ibid., 320–21.

31. Ibid., 311–18.

32. Ibid., 321.

and (2) their relationship is with God as a Person (or as the only fully personal *Person*) with their own personhood.

What he cannot do, nor does he even try to, is answer the question we have been asking: What or Who is the object of our experience? What we want to know is this: When we think we are experiencing a realm beyond the physical, or a realm of the spirit, are we ever in the very presence of the Trinity or one or more persons of the Trinity—the Father, the Son and the Holy Spirit?

James's question is not about what or who we encounter in religious experience. His question is only psychological: "Do mystical states establish the truth of those theological affections in which the saintly life has its root?"[33] Theology, *traditionally* construed as untangling and interpreting biblical revelation in straightforward propositions about the truth of reality, has been reduced to theological *affections*, emotional sensations that undergird an especially good life. To wit: good feelings lead to good actions.

If this seems to strip religious experience of any right to be considered a *signal of any transcendence*, be assured it does. James, however, does not seem to think so. Again, he asks,

> Does it [the mystic range of consciousness] furnish any *warrant for the truth* of the twice-bornness and supernaturality and pantheism which it favors? . . .
>
> In brief my answer is this,—and I will divide it into three parts:—
>
> (1) Mystical states, when well developed, usually are, and have the right to be, absolutely authoritative over the individuals to whom they come.
>
> (2) No authority emanates from them which should make it a duty for those who stand outside of them to accept their revelations uncritically.
>
> (3) They break down the authority of the non-mystical or rationalistic consciousness, based upon the understanding and the senses alone. They show it to be only one kind of consciousness. They open out the possibility of other orders of truth, in which, so far as anything in us vitally responds to them, we may freely continue to have faith.[34]

33. Ibid., 319.
34. Ibid., 323–24. See Alston, *Perceiving*, 279–82, for a critique of James's criteria.

The very way in which James couches the first answer to his question belies the possibility of its being an answer to the question he (and we, too) ask. The religious experiences, he says, have "absolute authority" for those who have them. That does not tell us that the experiences themselves have any metaphysical bearing. Their "authority" is completely subjective. The experience, I suppose one might say, is "true," but only as an experience. It's a tautology: *The experiencer has had an experience. Period.*

This interpretation is confirmed by his second comment: Nothing requires anyone else to think that what another person experiences is actually as the experiencer has interpreted it. Anyone other than the experiencer has the right to be critical; in fact, the critic has a right to deny that there is any such divine reality to be experienced. The atheist or naturalist, in other words, has no obligation to be swayed toward religious belief. Oddly enough, James follows his list of three principles by admitting that many mystical experiences are not, after all, pantheistic. He notes the distinctive Christian theistic character of much of what the medieval Spanish mystics say they experience, though he does not seem to have incorporated this into his earlier ruminations.[35]

Finally religious experiences challenge the naturalist's notion that he or she has an exclusive corner on the truth. James adds, ". . . [T]he existence of mystical states absolutely overthrows the pretension of non-mystical states to be the sole and ultimate dictators of what we may believe."[36] Is it something about the strength of the experiences or about their universality that raises the challenge? James has given no other reason for this conclusion. In other words, if James is correct, then religious experience should give very little justification for the truth of the *born-againness* and *pantheism* or *Christian* and *Islamic theism* to which the experiences seem to point.

In Lecture XVIII, "Philosophy," James reveals a bias that shows that it would be impossible for him to conclude that a theistic mystical experience might actually support a theistic metaphysic, that is a view of reality in which a personal God pays attention to individuals in time and space and reacts to them by answering prayers or judging them or saving them through the sacrifice of his Son.

35. James, *Varieties*, 313–19.
36. Ibid., 327.

For James, the only philosophy that is worth pursuing is *pragmatism*, one of the few distinctly American contributions to philosophy. In its minimal form *pragmatism* is an empirical philosophy: "the true is what works well, even though the qualification 'on the whole' may always have to be added."[37]

Suffice it to say here that the philosophy of pragmatism addresses our key questions by a wave of the hand: they have no determined answers; they are not worth addressing in the form that calls for an answer in line with truth considered as a statement of the way things actually are. James's works of philosophy, however, are well worth the time to read and ponder. But we are asking other questions—questions about *signals of transcendence* that are designed to help us discover what actually is the case. After all the Christian religion claims to be all about reality—the reality of God, of us, of the universe. We want to know all there is that can be known. It may sound arrogant to think such truth is available to us, but nothing short of this should be our goal: "You shall know the truth, and the truth will make you free" (John 8:32). Yes, Jesus said that, and William James did not pay much attention to what Jesus said.

For James the abstract character theology attributes to God—being *one* and *living, personal, omnipotent*, etc.—has no impact on the experience people have. For him they bore no experiential weight. Some of them show the vestiges of paganism and were not worthy of belief by any intelligent person today (for James at the beginning of the twentieth century, let alone for us at the beginning of the twenty-first). Darwin, for example, had squashed the argument for God from design; Hume had done the same for the notion of cause and effect.[38] James leaves us with religion, but it has become a meager sort of moral salvation. James's own view of religion, for example, consists of two elements:

1. An uneasiness; and

2. Its solution.

1. The uneasiness, reduced to its simplest terms, is a sense that there is *something wrong about us* as we naturally stand.

37. Ibid., 348. James's major presentation of this view is found in *Pragmatism*.
38. James, *Varieties*, 334, 371, and James, *Pragmatism*, 56.

2. The solution is a sense that *we are saved from wrongness* by making proper connection with the higher powers.[39]

As for God, James cites Professor James H. Leuba, who says, ". . . so long as men can *use* their God, they care very little who he is, or even whether he is at all":

> The truth of the matter can be put this way in this way: *God is not known, he is not understood; he is used*—sometimes as a meat-purveyor, sometimes as moral support, sometimes as friend, sometimes as an object of love. If he proves himself useful, the religious consciousness asks for no more than that. Does God really exist? How does he exist? What is he? are so many irrelevant questions. Not God, but life, more life, a larger, richer, more satisfying life is, in the last analysis, the end of religion. The love of life, at any and every level of development, is the religious impulse.[40]

James's massive study of religious experience helps us see the complex character of justifying religious belief through religious experience. But it gives us no clue to answering our question: Does religious experience ever act as a justification for specific religious belief? James's conclusion:

> It must always remain an open question whether mystical states may not possibly be such superior points of view, windows through which the mind looks out upon a more extensive and inclusive world.[41]

He does not deny that mystical states are superior points of view, only that the question is open "whether" they "may not possibly be" so. Given his reduction of mystical states to mere subjective experience, he can offer no more help in answering our serious question: What is the epistemic value of what we have been calling signals of *transcendence*?

William Alston and Perceiving God

Christian philosopher William P. Alston's contribution to the analysis of Christian religious experience has been both wide and deep. In his massive study, *Perceiving God: The Epistemology of Religious Experience*,

39. James, *Varieties*, 383.
40. James H. Leuba, "Contents," 571–72, quoted in ibid., 382.
41. James, *Varieties*, 327.

Alston asks this question: Is religious experience a reliable source of justified belief about God? By God he means the orthodox Christian God of
the Bible and the creeds. His complex answer is a qualified yes. Boiled
down to its essence, he concludes that if the experience has arisen sponta-
neously or within the context of standard personal or corporate worship
and if there are no other explanations that are more likely, it is rational for
the experiencer to believe he or she has encountered God.[42]

So far, so good. Alston has focused his attention solely on Christian
religious experiences. If Alston is either correct or on the right track,
we have reason to accept the value of these Christian religious experiences both for the personal assurance that they give that we are truly
encountering God and for the presentation and defense of Christian faith
in evangelism and apologetics. But there is a problem, one that Alston
acknowledges. What about the religious experiences that lead to or are
embedded in non-Christian religious practices and systems of belief?
Within the framework of his main argument, he gives scanty help, for
many of these non-Christian experiences share much of the prime facie
value he accords to Christian experiences. He concludes:

> Thus it can hardly be denied that the fact of religious diversity
> reduces the rationality of engaging in CMP [Christian Mystical
> Practice] (for one who is aware of the diversity) below what it
> would be if this problem did not exist.[43]

Still, he says,

> ... [A]though this diversity reduces somewhat the maximal de-
> gree of epistemic justification derivable from CMP, it leaves the
> practitioner sufficiently prima facie justified in M-beliefs that it
> is rational for her to hold those beliefs, in the absence of specific
> overriders.[44]

---

42. What Alston actually says is this: "Let's take it, then, that CMP [Christian
Mystical Practice, i.e., intense Christian religious experience] is a functioning, socially
established, perceptual doxastic practice with distinctive experiential inputs, distinctive input-output functions, a distinctive conceptual scheme, and a rich, internally
justified overrider system. As such, it possesses a prima facie title to being rationally
engaged in, and its outputs are thereby prima facie justified, *provided we have no sufficient reason to regard it as unreliable or otherwise disqualified for rational acceptance*"
(Alston, *Perceiving*, 225; italics his).

43. Ibid., 275.

44. Ibid., 279.

Outside the framework of his major argument, however, Alston does suggest a way for Christians to be fully satisfied with the value, strength, and rational validity of their Christian beliefs. The healthy confidence Christians have concerning the truth of their faith has never rested solely on either personal or corporate Christian experience. There is the "growth in sanctity, in sincerity, peace, joy, fortitude, love, and other 'fruits of the spirit'":

> Given the "payoffs" of the Christian life of the sort just mentioned, one may quite reasonably continue to hold that CMP does serve as a genuine cognitive access to Ultimate Reality, and as a trustworthy guide to that Reality's relations to ourselves, even if one can't see how to solve the problem of religious pluralism, even if one can't show from a neutral standpoint that Christianity is right and the others are wrong on those points on which they disagree.[45]

And he adds that

> mystical perception makes its own contribution to the total system of Christian belief. (1) It is the only source of particular beliefs about what God is doing vis-à-vis one at the moment and about God's will for one's own life. (2) It gives the human bearer of revelation access to the divine communicator. (3) It is an important source of our assurance that the source of general revelation, the chief actor in the drama of salvation, and the creator of the universe, really does exist.[46]

Alston does, then, lend heavy support for our taking *signals of transcendence* as serious pointers to God. And, like other apologists who rely on these *signals*, he does not rest his case for Christianity on *signals* alone. In fact, the final section of *Perceiving God* lays out the pattern a full apologetics takes. It is similar to the one I outline below. But for Alston, "The final test of the Christian scheme comes from our trying it out in one's life."[47]

---

45. Ibid., 276.
46. Ibid., 302.
47. Ibid., 304.

Keith Yandell and the Epistemology of Religious Experience.

Christian Philosopher Keith Yandell takes us a good deal further toward our goal. In *The Epistemology of Religious Experience* Yandell first presents a detailed and complex argument for the evidential value of religious experiences, especially those involving the *numinous* as defined by Rudolf Otto. In fact he equates an experience of the *numinous* with an experience of God as understood by traditional Christian faith. Yandell's approach differs significantly from that of Alston, and, frankly, his argument is too complex for me to summarize. But the conclusions he reaches are similar to those of Alston.

> If a person has *numinous* experiences under conditions that satisfy all of the conditions specified in the principle of *numinous* experience—if the numinous experiences occur that are not prevented from being evidence by their failing any relevant tests to check the experiences—then there is experimental evidence that God exists.[48]

Yandell, then, like Alston supports our thinking that religious experiences, especially those we have been calling *signals of transcendence,* point not only to the existence of a vague transcendent order but more specifically to the existence of the God of the Bible. Yandell in fact helps us to discern why these *signals* do not point to the existence of merely vaguer forms of the divine or to Eastern religious conceptions. But we will deal with this later in this chapter. We should first consider the recent work of one more Christian philosopher who supports the general conclusions of both Alston and Yandell.

C. Stephen Evans and Natural Signs of the Divine

What C. Stephen Evans calls a *natural sign* is not quite what we have been calling a *signal of transcendence.* He does not consider, for example, extreme mystical experiences or Otto's experiences of the *numinous.*[49] For

48. Yandell, *Epistemology,* 274 (my paraphrase).

49. Evans, *Natural Signs,* 188–89; on the other hand in *Why Believe?,* 29–49, Evans begins his argument for the existence of God with *signals of transcendence*: he calls them "clues to God's reality" and examines such clues as "the overriding mystery of the sheer existence of the universe" (cosmic wonder) (33), the "mystery of purposive order" (35), the "mystery of the moral order" (39–49), and "the mystery of persons" (50–60).

Evans these experiences are not so much *signs* that point to the existence of God as they are direct perceptions of *God*. Evans's main concern is to show how *natural signs* can become basic assumptions in philosophic arguments for the existence of God. He says:

> The nature of a sign, as I shall develop the notion, is to be a "pointer," something that directs our attention to some reality or fact and makes knowledge of that reality or fact possible.[50]

Here Evans's argument takes an interesting turn. He suggests that, if the theistic God wants to reveal himself to his creation, he would make knowledge of himself available to most people. He calls this the "Wide Accessibility Principle." On the other hand, in order for God to give his creation freedom to make its own decisions regarding his existence, he will need to make knowledge of his presence easily resistible. He calls this the "Easy Resistibility Principle."[51]

This is what Evans claims God has done:

> [T]hese signs, like signs in general, do not point in a conclusive or compelling fashion. Signs have to be perceived, and once perceived must be "read." Some signs are harder to read than others, or, one might say, easier to interpret in alternative ways, even if not all of the possible interpretations are equally plausible. The natural signs that point to God's reality are signs that can be interpreted in more than one way and thus are sometimes misread and sometimes not even perceived as signs. They point to God but do not do so in a coercive manner.[52]

This comment squares well with what we have seen of the many types of *signals of transcendence* in previous chapters. There are a host of ways they can be and have been interpreted or, as Evans says, "read."

Evans devotes most of his discourse to showing how various natural signs form the background for the major premises of various traditional arguments for the existence of God. For example, the sense of cosmic wonder (e.g., surprise and puzzlement at the awesomeness of the stars or the mystery of contemplating the possibility that one might never have existed) stands behind cosmological arguments for God. The beneficial order of the universe (its beauty and fitness) stands behind the argument from design. The universal human sense of obligation, our sense of being

50. Ibid., 2.

51. Ibid., 13–14.

52. Ibid., 2.

accountable for our actions, our intuitive perception of the dignity of human beings—these stand behind moral arguments for God. He mentions others as well. A sense of deep gratitude for life as a gift "seems to require an intentional object"; that points to an intentional, personal giver and may also be a "theistic natural sign."[53]

Still we can ask just how much evidence do natural signs provide. Evans is cautious. He is well aware that experiences must be interpreted and that our interpretations may be wrong. Natural signs are not themselves knock-down arguments for the existence of God as Jesus and the Bible reveal him. And Evans does not consider as natural signs the more dramatic religious experiences, like those of Isaiah in the temple and Moses at the burning bush. So while "we might come to know that naturalism—the doctrine that the natural physical world is the whole of reality—is false," what we learn about the realm of the divine will be limited.[54] As a result, Evans suggests a two-stage apologetics": Stage one is "an argument for the existence of God with at least some of the properties of the God of Abrahamic faiths."[55] Stage two is an argument that such a God has in fact revealed himself in Scripture. Natural signs, then, would stand behind the rational arguments of stage one. Traditional evidential arguments based on the Bible would constitute stage two.

In the long run, Evans provides reason for both confidence and caution in moving from natural sign (or *signal* limited to those of Level 1 through 3) to reality. Since Evans does not treat *numinous* experiences, as Alston and Yandell do, the epistemic value afforded by these signs is limited, but not so limited that they should be dismissed. In fact, leaving *numinous* experiences for a separate epistemic analysis, seeing them not as signs, but potentially as direct experiences of God, may act as a preface to taking these *numinous* experiences as important to a justification of belief in God. We will pick up this notion again below.

Signs, Signals, and Direct Experiences of God

C. Stephen Evans, as we have seen, distinguishes between natural signs and direct experiences of God. He deals little with the latter because he is interested in the relationship between God and elements of the world

53. Ibid., 149.
54. Ibid., 186.
55. Ibid., 5.

experienced as ordinary, material objects, human emotions, and psychological desires and drives. Direct experiences of God, if they occur, do not point to God; they put one in the presence of God. No argument is required for a direct experience of God to have epistemic value.

Perhaps this is the truth behind William James's statement that "mystical states, when well developed, usually are, and have a right to be, absolutely authoritative over the individuals to whom they come."[56] James's mistake, however, was to reduce the "mystical state" to a wholly psychological phenomenon.

The experience itself is the reality. What if the mystical state is in fact the state of experiencing the *numinous*, that is, the state of being in the presence of God? The *numinous*, as Otto describes it, is filled with a rich theistic conception of a holy God. As such the *numinous* is experienced in a form that includes both psychological and epistemological certitude. Its rejection as an experience of God is a denial of God himself. In Calvin's terms, the *sensus divinitatis* has detected or mediated presence of the divine. Nothing more than that is needed for the justification of religious belief in the existence of God. As Plantinga says, "The purpose of the *sensus divinitatis* is to enable us to have true beliefs about God; when it functions properly, it ordinarily *does* produce true beliefs about God."[57]

Evans treats natural signs as easily resistible. The *numinous* is resistible, but not so easily.

Evans does not draw this conclusion, but I wonder if to experience the *numinous* and then to resist is to "sin against the Holy Spirit," to commit the only unforgivable sin. Is it not to be in the presence of God and to say, in effect, "Hell, no," to mean it, and to experience as a consequence severe spiritual blindness? Keep this in mind as we draw the argument of this book together at the end of this chapter.

Transcendence, Yes. But What Transcendence?

We turn now to the second puzzling question: Why should we interpret Level 4 *signals of transcendence* as Christians do and not as do adherents of Eastern religions or the New Age?

---

56. James, *Varieties*, 323.

57. Plantinga, *Warranted*, 179; the entire volume is relevant to this issue, but see especially chapters 6 and 7.

In the opening chapters of this book, I described the ways *signals of transcendence* have been interpreted within the framework of worldviews. To theists the *signals* point to the existence of God and reveal various aspects of his personal character—goodness, compassion, power, intelligence, etc. To deists these *signals* point to an impersonal God, a Force or Energy that generates the cosmos. To the Romantics the *signals* point to the warm moral character of a mostly impersonal Spirit who promotes moral behavior and a sense of deep belonging to the cosmos.

To atheists the experience referred to as a *signal* is not a signal at all; it is only thought to be one. At best they are experiences that produce feelings of human flourishing but are really pseudo-religious firings of the brain's neurons, producing a survival-promoting sense of peace and calm that seems out of this world but is not. All of these worldviews—even that of atheism—are Western. They either assume a dualism of creator and creation or a monism of matter only.

Historically, the flow of modern worldviews begins with *theism* that involves a rich and complex notion of God who personally and intentionally has created and now sustains the material universe. In *deism* God loses his personhood; in *naturalism* God loses his existence; in *nihilism* human beings lose their minds, their morality, and their significance. Responses to nihilism begin with a return to naturalism's initial optimism about human beings at least to the extent that they can create value without a foundation in anything transcendent. This response is called *existentialism*. Another response is to look outside the flow of Western history to the East, rejecting the most fundamental distinctions the West had made between God and the cosmos. All seeming material reality is really spiritual. Everything is God. This is *pantheism*. The amazing thing about this latter move toward seeing everything as divine is that nothing is really transcendent anymore. There can be no signals of transcendence, no natural theology from which one learns about the character of God from nature. Either nature itself is God or it is illusion. If it is God, then it follows that there is no transcendent. If it is illusion, it does not signal the transcendent; rather, it blocks the way toward experiencing reality.

What follows from this historical flow of worldviews is that apparent *signals of transcendence*, if they signal Buddhist or Hindu "transcendence," are illusory; they cannot and therefore do not exist. Whatever these experiences are, they do not point to anything beyond themselves. That means, as well, that experiences of the *numinous* (which requires a

radical distinction between the human self and God) cannot be understood in Eastern terms.

Listen to Keith Yandell on this topic: Yandell distinguishes between
the claims of monotheistic religions, notably Christianity, and those involving Eastern pantheism. His categories of pantheism are both more
complete and more narrowly defined than those discussed in chapter 8
above, but we need not concern ourselves with these details. Yandell finds
no way that the various religious experiences we have been calling *signals
of transcendence* can be considered evidence for any form pantheism
takes. His argument is highly sophisticated, and I hope I am not doing it
an injustice by adapting and applying it to the worldview of pantheism I
have described in this book. But here is that adaptation.

> All forms of pantheism involve an ultimate reality (sometimes
> called God) that is either (1) ineffable (that is, on the face of
> it, incapable of being understood) or (2) has no attributes (the
> Void of Zen Buddhism, the One of advaita vedanta Hinduism),
> or (3) is described in contradictory propositions; therefore, no
> experience, religious or secular, can give any evidence for its
> existence.[58]

This does not, of course, mean that these pantheistic worldviews are
incorrect, only that in the final analysis no argument can be given for
their truth. Take Zen Buddhism as an example. If I am correct, Yandell's
argument is not a criticism that a Zen Buddhist would find problematic.
Buddhist masters and texts neither put forth rational arguments nor offer
experience as a proof. What they do is present techniques (e.g., long ses-
sions of meditation) that lead the meditators toward the sense that they
have been enlightened, after which the Zen master often will say that this
has not happened. Only the master really knows when a novice has been
enlightened, and, as near as I can tell, there is nothing the master will say
(whether he could or not) to explain why the enlightenment has or has
not occurred. The final judgment, whether by the novice or the master,
seems to be based solely on intuition. In any case, the encounter with the
Void leaves no mark on the intellect, though the meditation which empties the self of any knowledge of the self itself might, ironically of course,
lead the novice to a more self-satisfied life.

A similar explanation can be given for other forms of traditional
pantheism. The New Age worldview poses a different problem. New Age

58. Yandell, *Epistemology*, 279–321.

proponents major in religious experiences and find them pointing to all sorts of identifiable gods or ultimate realities—primarily, of course, the reality of their own godhood or unity with the ultimate spiritual powers of the universe. With the New Age, the best way of evaluating the relationship between religious-type experience and ultimate reality is to assess its rationality.

The New Age Exception

Religious or spiritual experiences described by New Agers pose an interesting exception. We have seen that the interpretations of *signals of transcendence* by deists and romantics are not contrary to their interpretation by theists. That is because they are *signals* at Level 2 or 3; the power and awesome grandeur that deists and romantics feel toward transcendent reality is also felt by theists. The guilt and uncomfortable experience that romantics feel is consonant with the theistic concept of God; it only lacks its fully personal dimension. Another way to say this is that theists experience *signals* at Levels 1, 2 and 3 as well as Level 4; in fact, they experience them much more than they do those at Level 4. Signals at Level 4 are very special indeed, and not all theists claim to have had them. There is, then, no problem in concluding that most if not all Level 1–3 *signals* are appropriately interpreted within the framework of a fully theistic worldview.

Level 4 experiences of the *numinous*, as we have seen from Yandell's comments, are strictly theistic in content. If we have had a Level 4 experience, we have more reason to conclude that we have truly been in touch with God or that we have been in the direct Presence of God.

But what about Level 4 experiences that are interpreted as distinctly contrary to theism? To conclude that you are divine, one with the divine, God or the I AM is to belie the very heart of Christian, Jewish, and Islamic faiths. If New Agers have interpreted Level 4 *signals* accurately, then theism itself is false. Some New Agers such as Shirley MacLaine and John Lilly seem as certain of their interpretations as do the Jewish Prophet Isaiah and the Christian Apostle Paul. New Agers and theists cannot both be right about what constitutes fundamental reality.

. The objective reality of the experiences, their two different interpretations, cannot be evaluated by experience. They cannot be judged on the basis of the apparent intensity of the experience, nor by the depth of subjective certainty of each interpreter. The accuracy of the interpretation must be evaluated from a position outside the realm of pure experience and what its meaning seems to be to each interpreter. How can we get beyond experience, especially our own experience, to a place to make a justifiable interpretation?

It looks like reason will have to have a say. Which interpretation is more rationally likely to be correct? For this approach we must turn to the basic principles of rationality—intellectual coherence, consideration of relevant factors such as background beliefs, cultural situation, physical and mental health of those who have the experience, presence or absence of material evidence in time and space (is there an actual place—say the Andes or ancient Israel—where these experiences occurred, or were they described to occur, say, on a spaceship)? Are the experiences connected in any way to known historical events? Think too of what happens to the notions of good and evil. As in advaita vedanta Hinduism and Zen Buddhism, the distinction between them disappears.

The first reaction of most current residents in the U.S. to the experiences recounted by both Shirley MacLaine and John Lilly is to laugh. When they have stopped laughing, they act puzzled. How could someone be so silly as to think that they had created chocolate cookies and the Statue of Liberty? One Christian historian who had spoken with a major New Ager said to me, "She can't think." Some New Agers, however, can think. Their understanding of spiritual experiences tends not to be so silly as MacLaine's appears to be. But if we check out such authors as Marilyn Ferguson, Fritjov Capra (physicist), and Ken Wilber (New Age philosopher), we will find less outlandish and more *reasonable* claims. These, of course, can be and have been subjected to analysis. The general conclusion of those who have researched New Age views has been highly critical.[59]

Of course, given the current secular character of the West, something like this might be said about Moses having a conversation with a voice out of a bush (silly enough) that was on fire and didn't burn up (impossible). Is there a difference between the credibility of these stories? A full answer would take an immense study of biblical texts, their interpretation, archaeological evidence for Moses and the Exodus (very little by the way), the place in the overall worldview of Jewish (first) and Christian (later) culture, a deep theological and philosophical study of

59. Herrick, *Making*; Groothuis, *Unmasking* and *Confronting*; and Sire, *Universe*.

the place of Moses' experience, and so forth. Of course, we cannot do any of that in this book. But we can know that it has been done many, many times, and our libraries are filled with the results.

One more matter is especially important. Alston provides a clue. He is speaking here of an element in some religious experience that raises doubts about its meaning: "If one takes a given perceptual justification to be overridden because the subject's experiences are reinforcing pride rather than humility, one is working within system in which humility is an important part of what God wants to exhibit; and religious traditions will differ on this."[60]

The New Age worldview, among all the worldviews examined in this book, is the only one to major in the exaltation of the self. Zen Buddhism eliminates the self itself. Hinduism sees the self as one with the All, but removes from it any individuality. In all theisms—Judaism, Christianity and Islam—the difference between the self and God is radical. Pride is the fundamental sin of human beings. Could God be God if he were any of us—MacLaine or Lilly or you or me? Are any of us anywhere close to "being" God? Granted, MacLaine herself was surprised to learn she was the I AM. It took lots of odd experiences to lead her to think so. But what is the likelihood that she discovered the truth? It is not odd that people laugh at the claim that they are God. Laughter or tears—either is appropriate.

Apologetics on Stage

To rest our entire case for Christianity on experience alone is surely a mistake. What then is required? How might we envision the scope and character of a full apologetic?

Evans suggests that stage one apologetics focuses on natural signs (Level 1-3 *signals of transcendence*) and the various rational arguments that are based on these experiences. Stage two apologetics then turns to the evidence provided by Scripture. Alston, too, adds depth to his treatment of religious experience by incorporating other traditional arguments for the existence of God. Here is my view. I suggest a different way to use *stage* as a metaphor for the structure of apologetics.

Picture a theater stage on which one sees a complete apologetic. Picture yourself in the audience. What do you see? I trust you will see

60. Alston, *Perceiving*, 191.

a coherent presentation of all the relevant evidence and reasons for the truth of the Christian faith and an answer to all the criticism that might be launched against it.

Main stage—For Christian Apologetics, the Direct Positive Evidence for the Truth of Christian Faith

MAIN STAGE FRONT AND CENTER

In my estimation the best of that positive evidence can be given in one word—Jesus. Jesus is by far the best evidence for the existence of the God of Abraham, Isaac, and Jacob as more fully revealed in what Christians call the Trinity. This requires exposing one's mind and heart to reading the four Gospels in particular, and the New and Old Testaments in general. When questions of historical reliability or meaning arise, they should be addressed by consulting the works of the major biblical and theological scholars.

MAIN STAGE FRONT RIGHT

Here are situated classical and modern intellectual positive arguments for the existence of God and in general the rational credibility of Christian faith, including *signals of transcendence*, not necessarily labeled as such but woven into the dialogue. Accounts of individual Christians and their personal experience will be interlaced with the presentation of abstract arguments so that a sense of the life of the believer is seen to square with the arguments the believer gives.

MAIN STAGE FRONT LEFT

Here stand responses (defeaters) to critiques of the classical and modern positive arguments for the existence of God, and in general the rational credibility of Christian faith. Direct intellectual challenges to alternative proposals—atheism, deism, pantheism, New Age—will also be displayed with personal accounts of the failure of these proposals to deliver on their promises.

Main Stage Back Right

Many people are not ready for stage one. They don't want to start with the Bible because they think it is ancient history—backward looking and untrustworthy. These people need an introduction to what the Bible, especially the Gospels, really is.

Main Stage Back Center

Others have intellectual doubts, thinking, for example, that the presences of suffering and of evil preclude the possibility that there is a God good enough to believe in. Or they think that all religions are the same or that there is no way to tell which if any of them are worth looking into. Answers to these doubts and objections are here.

Main Stage Back Left

Others think that science has solved the problem of the origin of the universe and that evolution has removed any need for God as an explanation of how human beings happened to arrive on earth. Answers to these concerns are here.

So much for what you see. Now what happens when the play begins? The action can start anywhere on stage. If it begins front and center, one sees the argument for Christian faith by seeing Jesus—his life, his teachings, with an emphasis on his death and resurrection and the inherent meaning of all of these. But the action may not begin there. It may begin anywhere else—left/right, back/front. In a good and effective play little action may take place where it begins. Rather, the action may move all over the stage in no predetermined order, just in the order determined by the characters on stage and the response of the audience. Still the play will always include action front and center. And it will not end until the central message of the Christian faith has had a credible presentation. Recall the definition of *apologetics* at the head of this chapter.

> Christian apologetics lays before the watching world such a winsome embodiment of the Christian faith that for any and all who are willing to observe there will be an intellectually and emotionally credible witness to its fundamental truth.

Religious experience, apt accounts of encounters with *signals of transcendence* are indeed vital to a full apologetic, but by no means the end all and be all of a justification for Christian faith. Still they must not be omitted from the master story of God, human beings, and the universe on the ground that they can be misinterpreted. Every argument can be misunderstood. This is a part of the human condition. But every experience and every solid argument has a place in the lived out Christian faith.

Summary Conclusions

If we survey the scope of this book, what conclusions should we draw? How about these eight?

First, *signals of transcendence* exist. Therefore, there is a *transcendent* realm. At the minimum it is characterized by mind that is not exhausted by brain; at the maximum it is as rich and full in being as theism claims, richer and fuller, for the finite mind cannot totally encompass divine reality. In the final analysis, these *signals* point to and, at the highest level, mediate the presence of the God of the Bible.[61] In the final analysis they are "the voice of Jesus, calling us to follow him into God's new world—a world in which the hints, signposts, and echoes of the present world turn into the *reality* of the next one."[62]

Second, naturalism is false. This should not need to be said, but the grip that naturalism holds on the intellectual world of the twentieth and twenty-first centuries is so strong, repetition of this fact is always worth singling out for notice.

Third, *signals of transcendence* do not automatically transmit their meaning. They must be interpreted, and, in doing this, we may make mistakes.

Fourth, except for experiences at Level 4, the epistemic value of these *signals* is not absolute, neither for the one who has had the experiences as William James would say, nor for those who learn of others' Level 4 experiences. Even signals at Level 4 must be carefully weighed to be assured they really are experiences of the *numinous* and not just

61. As Evans says, "Natural signs for God [Level 1–3 *signals of transcendence*] may point to mystery that prepares individuals for an encounter with a greater mystery," to which I would add: These encounters may well be accompanied by a Level 4 *signal of transcendence* or an even deeper engagement with God (Evans, *Natural Signs*, 192).

62. Wright, *Simply*, 225.

astounding experiences that lead to pride as they do with those who claim on the basis of these experiences to be God or a god or the center of reality themselves.

Fifth, *numinous* experiences do not reveal all of who God is. God may be more or other than what we think he is; we may not be fully correct about his attributes.

Sixth, if we are to achieve a more solid set of reasons for our faith, we must not rest our case solely on *signals of transcendence* or religious experience in general.

Seventh, it is not necessary to have had a Level 4 experience for belief in God to be justified. There are other reasons and other evidence for accepting the Christian faith as a true guide both to an intellectual comprehension of reality and to a way of life that leads not only to human flourishing but to the advancement of the kingdom of God among human beings and the cosmos.

Eighth, Christians should always be aware that the separation between the material and spiritual world is amazingly thin. We should expect, but not demand, that we will frequently experience *signals of transcendence*, especially at Levels 1–3. In fact, we should be living with a constant subconsciousness that a world that *transcends* our work-a-day world is always present. In that mode we may expect to perceive more of these signals as they appear, leading us to an inner and sometimes outer response of awe and worship of the Trinity who comes to us as Father or Son or Holy Spirit or even, at the same time, three thunderheads on the western horizon.

The Last Word

Let us leave the last word to William Alston:

> The experience of God greatly enlivens one's religious life, it makes an enormous difference to the quality and intensity of one's devotional life, it greatly stimulates one's aspirations to virtue and holiness, and most important, it makes possible the loving communion with God for which we were created. All this is undoubtedly far more important than the epistemic contribution of mystical perception.[63]

---

63. Alston, *Perceiving*, 303.

Bibliography

Abdalati, Hammudah. *Islam in Focus*. Indianapolis: American Trust Publications, 1975.

Adams, Marilyn McCord. "Love of Learning, Reality of God." In *God and the Philosophers: The Reconciliation of Faith and Reason,* edited by Thomas V. Morris, 137–61. New York: Oxford University Press, 1994.

Alston, William P. *Perceiving God: The Epistemology of Religious Experience*. Ithaca, NY: Cornell University Press, 1991.

Anderson, Ray S. *On Being Human: Essays in Theological Anthropology*. Grand Rapids: Eerdmans, 1982.

Aquinas, Thomas, "Whether the Existence of God Is Self-Evident: Reply to Objection 1," in *Summa Theologica,* 2nd and rev. ed. 2003. Translated by the Fathers of the English Dominican Province. http//www.newadvent.org/summa/00201.htm.

Auden, J. H. "Considering the Unpredictable." In Loren Eiseley, *The Star Thrower*. New York: Harcourt Brace Jovanovich, 1978.

Augustine, Saint. *Confessions*. Translated by Henry Chadwick. New York: Oxford University Press, 1992.

Beckett, Samuel. *The Letters of Samuel Beckett,* Volume I: 1929–1940. Edited by Martha Dow Fehsenfeld and Lois More Overbeck. Cambridge: Cambridge University Press, 2008.

Barrett, Warren. *Death of the Soul: From Descartes to the Computer*. Garden City, NY: Anchor, 1986.

Benson, Robert. *Home by Another Way: Notes from the Caribbean*. Colorado Springs: Waterbrook, 2006.

Berger, Peter. *A Rumor of Angels: Modern Society and the Rediscovery of the Supernatural*. Garden City, NY: Anchor, 1970.

Berry, Wendell. "To the Holy Spirit." In *New Collected Poems*. Berkeley, CA: Counterpoint, 2012.

———. "Poetry and Place." In *Standing by Words*. San Francisco: North Point, 1983.

———. *A Timbered Choir: The Sabbath Poems 1979-97*. Washington, DC: Counterpoint, 1998.

Blackburn, Simon. "Religion and Respect." In *Philosophers Without Gods: Meditations on Atheism and the Secular Life,* edited by Louise M. Antony, 179–93. New York: Oxford University Press, 2007.

Bloesch, Donald G. *God the Almighty: Power, Wisdom, Holiness, Love*. Downers Grove, IL: InterVarsity, 1995.

Bonhoeffer, Dietrich. *The Cost of Discipleship*. New York: Macmillan, 1948.

———. *Letters and Papers from Prison*. London: SCM Press, 1967.

Bonzo, J. Matthew, and Michael R. Stevens. *Wendell Berry and the Cultivation of Life: A Reader's Guide*. Grand Rapids: Brazos, 2008.

Bozzi, Louisa. "No Stone Unturned: A Bug-hunter's Life and Death." In *Times Literary Supplement* (September 11, 1992).

Brooks, David. "The Neural Buddhists." *The New York Times* (May 13, 2008).

Buber, Martin. *I and Thou*. Translated by Roger Gregor Smith. New York: Charles Scribner's Sons, 1958.

Cailliet, Émile. *Pascal: The Emergence of Genius*, 2nd ed. New York: Harper Torchbooks, 1961.

Calvin, John. *Institutes of the Christian Religion*. Translated by Henry Beveridge. London: Clarke, 1957.

"Camus cult hits France." *Financial Times Weekend* (April 30 / May 1, 1994).

Carnell, Corbin Scott. *Bright Shadow of Reality: C. S. Lewis and the Feeling Intellect*. Grand Rapids: Eerdmans, 1974.

Castenada, Carlos. *The Eagle's Gift*. New York: Pocket Books, 1982.

———. *Falling Bodies Take to Light*. New York: Simon and Schuster, 1987.

———. *The Fire Within*. New York: Simon and Schuster, 1984.

———. *Journey to Ixtlan: The Lessons of Don Juan*. New York: Simon and Schuster, 1972.

———. *A Separate Reality: Further Conversations with Don Juan*. New York: Simon and Schuster, 1971.

———. *Tales of Power*. New York: Simon and Schuster, 1974.

———. *Teachings of Don Juan: A Yaqui Way of Knowledge*. Berkeley: University of California Press, 1968.

Childress, Kyle. "Good Work: Learning About Ministry from Wendell Berry." *The Christian Century* (March 8, 2005) 28–33. http://www.religion-online.org/showarticle.asp?title=3157.

Cirurgao, Maria J. "Last Farewell and First Fruits: The Story of a Modern Poet." http://www.catholiceducation.org/articles/printarticle.html?=268.

Coetsee, J. M. "The Making of Samuel Beckett." *The New York Review of Books* (April 30, 2009). www.nybooks.com/articles/archives/2009/apr/30/the-making-of-samuel-beckett.

Collins, Francis, *The Language of God: A Scientist Presents Evidence for Belief in God*. New York: Free Press, 2006.

Coleridge, Samuel Taylor. *Biographia Literaria*, XIV. In *The Portable Coleridge*, edited by I. A. Richards. New York: Viking, 1950.

Comte-Sponeville, Andre. *The Little Book of Atheist Spirituality*. Translated by Nancy Huston. New York: Viking, 2007.

Cook, Robert G. "Remarks Offered at the FBI National Academy Seminar, Division of Continuing Education, University of Virginia," November 22, 1999; revised in July, 2001, 7–8.

Craig, William Lane. "Evidence for Christianity." http://www.bethinking.org/resource.php?ID=100).

Crane, Stephen. *Black Riders and Other Lines*. Kindle: Copeland & Day, 1905.

Critchley, Simon. *Things Merely Are: Philosophy in the Poetry of Wallace Stevens*. London: Routledge, 2005.

Cruickshank, John. *Albert Camus and the Literature of Revolt*. New York: Oxford University Press, 1960.

Dawkins, Richard. "Forever Voyaging." *Times Online*. August 4, 2000, 3S.

De Mille, Richard. *Castaneda's Journey: The Power and the Allegory*. San Bernardino, CA: Capra, 1976.

Dickinson, Emily. *The Complete Poems of Emily Dickinson*. Edited by Thomas H. Johnson. Boston: Little, Brown and Company, 1960.

———. *Letters of Emily Dickinson*, vol. 3. Edited by Thomas H. Johnson. Cambridge, MA: The Belknap Press of Harvard University Press, 1958, 1986.

Dillard, Annie. *Holy the Firm*. New York: Harper and Row, 1997.

———. *Pilgrim at Tinker Creek*. New York: Bantam, 1975.

———. *Teaching a Stone to Talk*. New York: Harper-Perennial, 1992.

Eiseley, Loren. *The Immense Journey*. New York: Harcourt Brace Jovanovich, 1978.

———. *The Star Thrower*. New York: Harcourt Brace Jovanovich, 1978.

Elledge, Scott, editor of John Milton, *Paradise Lost*. New York: Norton, 1975.

Emerson, Ralph Waldo. *"The Later Lectures of Ralph Waldo Emerson 1843–1871*. Edited by Ronald A. Bosco and Joey Myerson. Athens, GA: University of Georgia Press, 2001.

———. *Selections from Ralph Waldo Emerson*. Edited by Stephen H. Whicher. Boston: Houghton Mifflin Company, 1957.

———. "The Seventh of March Speech on the Fugitive Slave Law, 7 March 1845." In Barbara Packer, "Signing Off," from *There Before Us: Religion, Literature, and Culture from Emerson to Wendell Berry*, edited by Roger Lundin, 22. Grand Rapids: Eerdmans, 2007.

Evans, C. Stephen. *Natural Signs and Knowledge of God: A New Look at Theistic Arguments*. Oxford: Oxford University Press, 2010.

———. *Why Believe? Reason and Mystery as Pointers to God*, rev. ed. Grand Rapids: Eerdmans, 1996.

Ferguson, Marilyn. *The Brain Revolution: The Frontiers of Mind Research*. New York: Taplinger, 1973.

Freud, Sigmund. *The Future of an Illusion*. Translated by James Strachey. New York: Norton, 1961.

Giberson, Karl W. *The Wonder of the Universe: Hints of God in Our Fine-Tuned World*. Downers Grove, IL: InterVarsity, 2012.

Groothuis, Douglas. *Confronting the New Age*. Downers Grove, IL: InterVarsity, 1988.

———. *On Pascal*. Stamford, CT: Wadsworth, 2003.

———. *Unmasking the New Age*. Downers Grove, IL: InterVarsity, 1986.

Guinness, Os. *The Dust of Death*. Downers Grove, IL: InterVarsity, 1973.

———. *Long Journey Home: A Guide to Your Search for the Meaning of Life*. Colorado Springs: Waterbrook, 2001.

Hall, Dorothy Judd. "Wallace Stevens's Spiritual Voyage: A Buddhist-Christian Path to Conversation." In *Seeing into the Life of Things: Essays on Religion and Literature*, edited by John L. Mahoney, 277–304. New York: Fordham University Press, 1998.

Hammond, T. H. *In Understanding Be Men*. Downers Grove, IL: InterVarsity, 1968.

Hansen, Ron. "Faith and Fiction." In *A Stay Against Confusion: Essays on Faith and Fiction*. New York: Harper Perennial, 2001.

Hardy, Thomas. "The Darkling Thrush." In *The Norton Anthology of Poetry*, edited by Arthur M. Eastman, et al., 875–76. New York: Norton, 1970.

Havel, Václav. *Disturbing the Peace: A Conversation with Karel Hvízdala*. Translated by Paul Wilson. New York: Knopf, 1990.

————. "Faith in the World," *Civilization* (April/May 1998).

————. *Letters to Olga: June 1979-September 1982*. Translated by Paul Wilson. New York: Henry Holt, 1989.

Hays, Edward. *In Pursuit of the Great White Rabbit*. Leavenworth, KS: Forest of Peach, 1990.

Henderson, Harold G. *An Introduction to Haiku and Poems from Basho to Shiki*. New York: Doubleday Anchor, 1958.

Herrick, James A. *The Making of the New Spirituality: The Eclipse of the Western Religious Tradition*. Downers Grove, IL: InterVarsity, 2003.

Hoekema, Anthony. *Created in God's Image*. Grand Rapids: Eerdmans, 1986.

Hofstadter, Douglas. "Reductionism and Religion." *Behavioral and Brain Sciences* 3 (1980).

Hopkins, Gerard Manley. *The Poems of Gerard Manley Hopkins*, 4th ed. Edited by W. H. Gardner and N. H. MacKenzie. London: Oxford University Press, 1967.

"How Our Brains are Wired for Belief," a transcript of the May 2008 Pew Foundation Forum on Religion and Public Life, hosted by Michael Cromartie. http://pewforumorg/events/EventID=185).

Hutchinson, John A. "Transcendence." In *A Handbook of Christian Theology: Definition Essays on Concepts and Movements of Thought in Contemporary Theology*. Cleveland: Meridian, 1958.

Isam'il Ragi al Faruqi. "Islam." In *The Great Asian Religions*, edited by Wing-tsit Chan, et al. Indianapolis: Macmillan, 1969.

James, William. *Pragmatism* and four essays from *The Meaning of Truth*. New York: Median, 1995.

————. *The Varieties of Religious Experience: A Study in Human Nature*. New York: New American Library, 1958.

Jeffrey, David Lyle, and Gregory Maillet. *Christianity and Literature: Philosophical Foundations and Critical Practice*. Downers Grove, IL: IVP Academic.

Jenkins, Philip. *The Next Christendom: The Coming of Global Christianity*. New York: Oxford University Press, 2007.

Joyce, James. *Portrait of the Artist as a Young Man*. New York: Viking, 1956.

Kapek, Karel. *Talks with T. G. Masaryk*. Translated by Dora Round. New Haven, CT: Catbird, 1995.

Keene, Donald. *Japanese Literature: An Introduction for Western Readers*. Tokyo: Charles E. Tuttle, 1955.

Keener, Craig. *The Bible Background Commentary*. Downers Grove, IL: InterVarsity, 1993.

Keller, Timothy, J. *Reason for God*. New York: Dutton, 2008.

Kidner, Derek. *Genesis: An Introduction and Commentary*. Tyndale Old Testament Commentaries. Chicago: Inter-Varsity, 1967.

King, Don W. "Sacramentalism in the Poetry of Philip Larkin." *The Christian Scholar's Review*, XXXIX, No. 1 (Fall 2009) 60–61.

Kreeft, Peter, and Ronald K. Tacelli. *Handbook of Christian Apologetics*. Downers Grove, IL: InterVarsity, 1994.

Küng, Hans. *Does God Exist: An Answer for Today*. Translated by Edwin Quinn. Garden City, NY: Doubleday, 1978.

Laden, Anthony Simon. "Transcendence Without God: On Atheism and Invisibility." In *Philosophers Without Gods: Meditations on Atheism and Secular Life,* edited by Louise M. Antony, 121–32. New York: Oxford University Press, 2007.

Larkin, Philip. *Collected Poems.* Edited by Anthony Thwaite. London: Faber and Faber, 1988.

Leibniz, Gottfried. "Of the Origin of Things." *The Philosophical Works of Leibniz.* Translated by George Martin Duncan. New Haven, CT: Tuttle, Morehouse & Taylor, 1890.

Leuba, James. "The Contents of Religious Consciousness." *The Monist* (July, 1901).

Levertov, Denise. "The Avowal." In *Selected Poems,* edited by Paul A. Lacey. New York: New Directions, 2002.

Lewis, C. S. *Spirits in Bondage.* XV. Kindle.

———. *Surprised by Joy.* London: Geoffrey Bles, 1955.

Lewis, H. D. "Revelation and Art." In *Morals and Revelation.* London: Allen and Unwin, 1951.

Lilly, John C. M. *The Center of the Cyclone: An Autobiography of Inner Space.* New York: Julian, 1972.

Lundin, Roger. *Emily Dickinson and the Art of Belief.* Grand Rapids: Eerdmans, 1998.

Lundin, Roger, ed. *There Before Us: Religion, Literature, and Culture from Emerson to Wendell Berry.* Grand Rapids: Eerdmans, 2007.

Macaulay, Ranald, and Jerram Barrs. *Being Human: The Nature of Spiritual Experience.* Downers Grove, IL: InterVarsity, 1978.

MacLaine, Shirley. *Dancing in the Light.* New York: Bantam, 1985.

———. *"Don't Fall Off the Mountain."* New York: Bantam, 1970.

———. *Going Within.* New York: Bantam, 1989.

———. *Camino: A Journey of the Spirit.* New York: Pocket Books, 2000.

———. *It's All in the Playing.* New York: Bantam, 1987.

———. *Out on a Limb.* New York: Bantam, 1983.

———. *Sage-ing While Age-ing.* New York: Atria, 2007.

Mackie, J. L. "Conclusions and Implications." In *The Portable Atheist: Essential Readings for the Nonbeliever,* edited by Christopher Hitchens, 246–66. Philadelphia: De Capo, 2007.

Mascall, Eric Lionel. *The Openness of Being 1970—1971.* http://www.giffordlectures.org/Browse.asp?PubID=TPTOOB&Volume=0&Issue=0&ArticleID=4/.

Morris, Simon Conway. *Life's Solutions: Inevitable Humans in a Lonely Universe.* Cambridge: Cambridge University Press, 2003.

Moser, Paul K. *The Evidence for God: Religious Knowledge Reexamined.* Cambridge: Cambridge University Press, 2010.

Mumma, Howard. *Albert Camus and the Minister.* Brewster, MA: Paraclete, 2000.

Neuhaus, Richard John. *American Babylon: Notes of a Christian Exile.* New York: Basic, 2009.

Newman, John Henry Cardinal. *Idea of a University.* Edited by Frank M. Turner. New Haven, CT: Yale University Press, 1996.

Nicholi, Armand. *The Question of God.* New York: Free Press, 2003.

Niebuhr, Reinhold. *The Nature and Destiny of Man: Volume 1, Human Nature.* New York: Charles Scribner's, 1964.

Niebuhr, Reinhold. "The Self." In *A Handbook of Christian Theology: Definition Essays on Concepts and Movements of Thought in Contemporary Theology*. Cleveland: World, 1965.

Nietzsche. "On Truth and Lie in an Extra-moral Sense." In *The Portable Nietzsche*. Translated by Walter Kaufmann. New York: Viking, 1954.

The Norton Anthology of Poetry. Edited by Arthur M. Eastman, et al. New York: W. W. Norton, 1970.

Ornstein, Robert E. *The Psychology of Consciousness*. San Francisco: W. H. Freeman, 1972.

Otto, Rudolf. *The Idea of the Holy*. Translated by John W. Harvey. Harmondsworth: Penguin, 1959.

Packer, Barbara. "Signing Off: Religious Indifference in America." In *There Before Us: Religion, Literature, and Culture from Emerson to Wendell Berry*, edited by Roger Lundin, 1–22. Grand Rapids: Eerdmans, 2007.

Pascal, Blaise. *Pensées*, Translated by A. J. Krailsheimer. Hammondsworth: Penguin, 1966.

Percy, Walker. *Lost in the Cosmos: The Last Self-Help Book*. New York: Washington Square, 1983.

Plantinga, Alvin. "A Christian Life Partly Lived." In *Philosophers Who Believe: The Spiritual Journeys of 11 Leading Thinkers*, edited by Kelly James Clark, 45–82. Downers Grove, IL: InterVarsity, 1993.

———. *Warranted Christian Belief*. New York: Oxford University Press, 2000.

Rahner, Karl. *Spirit in the World*. Translated by William Dytch, SJ New York: Continuum, 1994.

Randlett, Mary. "The Art of Mary Randlett." In *Mary Randlett Landscapes*. Seattle: University of Washington Press, 2007.

Sato, Hiroaki. *One Hundred Frogs*. New York: Inklings/Weatherhill, 1995.

Schönborn, Cristoph, Cardinal. "Reasonable Science, Reasonable Faith." *First Things* (April 2007). www.firstthings.com/article/2007/05/reasonable-science-reasonable-faith-44.

Scott, Jr., Nathan A. "Wallace Stevens' Route." In *Visions of Presence in Modern American Poetry*. Baltimore; John Hopkins University Press, 1993.

Shapiro, Stuart. "Faith and Reason, the Perpetual War: Ruminations of a Fool." In *Philosophers Without Gods: Meditations on Atheism and the Secular Life*, edited by Louise M. Antony, 3–16. New York: Oxford University Press, 2007.

Shawchuck, Norman, and Rueben P. Job, *A Guide to Prayer for All Who Seek God*. Nashville: Upper Room, 2003.

Sherlock, Charles. *The Doctrine of Humanity: Contours of Christian Theology*. Downers Grove, IL: InterVarsity, 1996.

Sire, James, and Carl Peraino. *Deepest Differences: A Christian-Atheist Dialogue*. Downers Grove: InterVarsity, 2009.

Sire, James W. *A Little Primer on Humble Apologetics*. Downers Grove, IL: InterVarsity, 2006.

———. *Naming the Elephant: Worldview as a Concept*. Downers Grove, IL: InterVarsity, 2004.

———. *Rim of the Sandhills: Why I Am Still a Christian*. Ebooks (Kindle and Barnes and Noble), 2012.

———. *The Universe Next Door: A Basic Worldview Catalog*, 5th ed. Downers Grove, IL: InterVarsity, 2009.

———. *Why Should Anyone Believe Anything at All?* Downers Grove, IL: InterVarsity, 1994.

Smith, Christian, and Patricia Snell. *Souls in Transition: The Religious and Spiritual Lives of Emerging Adults*. New York: Oxford University Press, 2009.

Snyder, Gary. *Axe Handles*. San Francisco: North Point, 1983.

———. *Mountains* and *Rivers Without End*. Washington, DC: Counterpoint.

———. *Turtle Island*. New York: New Directions, 1974.

Sommerville, John C. *The Decline of the Secular University*. New York: Oxford University Press, 2006.

Stevens, Wallace. *Collected Poetry and Prose*. New York: The Library of America, 1997.

———. *Opus Posthumous*. Edited by Milton J. Bates. New York: Knopf, 1989.

Targ, Russell, and Harold Puthoff. *Mind-Reach: Scientists Look at Psychic Ability*. No city: Delcourte Press/Elenor Freide, 1977.

Taylor, Charles. *A Secular Age*. Cambridge, MA: Harvard University Press, 2007.

———. *Sources of the Self: The Making of Modern Identity*. Cambridge, MA: Harvard University Press, 1989.

Thielicke, Helmut. *Nihilism: Its Origin and Nature—with a Christian Answer*. London: Routledge & Kegan Paul, 1962.

Uedo, Makoto. *Basho and His Interpreters: Selected Hokku with Commentary*. Stanford, CA: Stanford University Press,1992.

———. *Matsuo Basho*. Tokyo: Kodansha International Ltd., 1982.

"Wallace Stevens' Alleged Deathbed Conversion." http://www.english.upenn.edu/~afilreis/Stevens/conversion.html.

"Wallace Stevens." Poets of Cambridge. http://www.harvardsquarelibrary.org/poets/stevens/php.

Waltke, Bruce K., and James M. Houston. *The Psalms as Christian Worship*. Grand Rapids: Eerdmans, 2010.

Wathen, Brian. *Newsletter [from Russia]*, September, 2006.

Weinberg, Steven. *The First Three Minutes: A Modern View of the Origin of the Universe*. New York: Basic, 1977.

———. "What About God?" In *The Portable Atheist: Essential Readings for the Nonbeliever*, edited by Christopher Hitchens, 366–79. Philadelphia: De Capo, 2007.

———. "Without God." In *The New York Review of Books*, 55:14 (2008). www.nybooks.com/articles/archives/2008/sep/25/without-god/.

———. "The Missions of Astronomy." *The New York Review of Books*," 56:16 (2009) 22.

Wiker, Benjamin, and Jonathan Witt. *A Meaningful World: How the Arts and Sciences Reveal the Genius of Nature*. Downers Grove, IL: InterVarsity, 2006.

Woolf, Virginia. "Modern Fiction." In *The Common Reader: First Series*, 150–58. New York: Harcourt Brace Jovanovich, 1925.

———. "A Sketch of the Past." In *Moments of Being*, 2nd ed. Edited by Jeanne Schulkind. New York: Harcourt Brace Company, 1985.

———. *The Years*. New York: Harcourt & Brace, 1937.

Wordsworth, William. "Preface to the Second Edition of *Lyrical Ballads*." In *Selected Poetry*, edited by Mark Van Doren, 649–69. New York: Modern Library, 2002.

————. *The Prelude: The Four Texts (1798, 1799, 1805, 1850)*. Edited by Jonathan Wordsworth. London: Penguin, 1995.

————. *Selected Poetry of William Wordsworth*. Edited by Mark Van Doren. New York: Modern Library, 2002.

Wotton, George. *Thomas Hardy: Towards A Materialist Criticism*. Lanham, MD: Rowan & Littlefield, 1985.

Wright, N. T. *Simply Christian: Why Christianity Makes Sense*. San Francisco: HarperSanFrancisco, 2006.

Yandell, Keith. *The Epistemology of Religious Experience*. Cambridge: Cambridge University Press, 1993.

Index

Index